THE DESERT VCs

THE DESERT VCs
EXTRAORDINARY VALOUR IN THE NORTH AFRICAN CAMPAIGN IN WWII

Brian Best

FRONTLINE
BOOKS

THE DESERT VCs
Extraordinary Valour in the North African Campaign in WWII

This edition published in 2018 by Frontline Books,
an imprint of Pen & Sword Books Ltd,
47 Church Street, Barnsley, S. Yorkshire, S70 2AS

ISBN: 978-1-52672-106-8

For more information on our books, please visit
www.frontline-books.com,
email info@frontline-books.com
or write to us at the above address.

Printed and bound by TJ International Ltd, Padstow, Cornwall
Typeset in 10.5/13.5 point Palatino

Contents

Introduction

This book includes the VCs who were also awarded the Africa Star. It covers the campaigns in Egypt, Libya, Tunisia, Syria, Ethiopia, Eritrea, Somaliland, Greece, Crete, Corfu, Algeria and Malta. Also it includes the waters of the Mediterranean Sea, under which five VCs were awarded. The main theatre of operations, however, was the deserts of North Africa reflected in the colours of the medal ribbon that were symbolised by the yellow of the desert with a broad red central stripe (Army), a dark blue stripe on the left (Navy) and light blue stripe on the right (RAF). This account is not an in-depth study of the campaigns but one that looks at the action and lives of the forty-four Victoria Cross recipients.

If you had to choose a spot to fight a war then the desert region of North Africa would fit the bill: vast and empty with few centres of population to consider. Apart from the coast, there were few metalled roads to confine one's movements; plenty of open space for flanking movements. The geography of the region consisted of a level inland desert plateau stepping down in steep escarpments to a 30-mile wide narrow coastal plain. Parts of this coastal strip were surprisingly lush and fertile but mainly the terrain was unremittingly dreary; a large ocean of dun-coloured sand and gravel occasionally broken by a rocky outcrop or an eroded hill. For much of the time it was subject to the *khamsin*, the hot dry wind blowing from the Sahara Desert. It was such a stressful phenomenon that the Arabs would say: 'After five days of it, murder can be excused.'

Alan Moorhead further described this in his book, *Mediterranean Front*:

> The *khamsin* sandstorm blows more or less throughout the year, is in experience the most hellish wind on earth. It picks up the surface dust as fine as baking powder and blows it thickly into the air across hundreds of square miles of desert ... It came up through the

engine, through the chinks of the car body and round the corners of the closed windows. Soon everything in the car was powdered with grit and sand. It crept up your nose and down your throat, itching unbearably and making it difficult to breathe. It got in your eyes, matted your hair, and from behind your goggles your eyes kept weeping and smarting ... You sweated, returning again and again to your water-bottle for a swig of warm sandy water, and lay back gasping. I have known soldiers to wear their gas masks in a *khamsin* and others to give way to a fit of vomiting. Sometimes a *khamsin* may blow for days, making you feel that you will never see light and air and feel coolness again ... I hate the desert because of them.

Moorhead was a war correspondent and could take precautions to mitigate the discomforts he and his colleagues had to endure. Not so the soldiers who were thrust into this thoroughly alien environment of sand, thirst, canned food, brackish water, flies, and blinding hot sun followed by freezing nights.

The desert was the ideal place to fight a war – unless you were a participant. No civilian populations were being destroyed. It was straight clean warfare, a battle of courage and wits; almost a chess match between the opposing sides. The essential grimness of total war could not be experienced here and a good reason was the absence of the SS and Gestapo. Women and children were barely involved; their immediate fate did not depend on the battle and relatively few died in the Middle East. There were no movements of refugees typified by the mass of civilians blocking the roads of Europe. It was a war that largely ignored the civilian population.

This open mechanical warfare tended to destroy machines not men. The huge numbers of prisoners taken were nearly all unwounded because there was practically no trench warfare in the desert and once the protective armour was gone there was little the infantry could do in many cases except surrender.

The desert warfare has been compared to that of naval warfare where the ebb and flow of conflict resembles battles between fleets of warships where there is little or no restriction on movement. Territory changed hands many times but few places were thought to be worth fighting for, with the exception of the strategically placed Tobruk and its harbour.

It was a huge arena that was largely self-contained and an intensely apolitical world. Without being misty eyed, it was also noted for its sense of chivalry, as personified by Rommel's reaction to the abortive attempt on his life or the examples of field doctors who performed operations on the enemy because they were fellow humans.

Despite the misery and discomfort that afflicted the interlopers from Europe, the desert was capable of breathtaking grandeur. In Len Deighton's novel *City of Gold,* he vividly describes the desert's featureless beauty:

> Eventually the euphoria that comes with the clarity of the air and magical nights of star-filled skies is replaced by a feeling of lassitude, a weariness brought about by the absence of any visual stimulus. These featureless vistas – without buildings, trees, roads or grass – eventually dulled the mind and made a man retreat unto himself.

It was a region that gave birth to the piratical groups such as the Long Range Desert Group and the Special Air Service, who were able to freely roam behind enemy lines without being detected. Alan Moorhead described it as 'piracy on the high sands'. There were other regions that were arid, including Somaliland, Eritrea, Ethiopia and Syria, but none had the sheer vastness of the North African desert.

Although the majority of the VCs in this book fought on the mainland of Africa between 10 June 1940 and 12 May 1943, there are fourteen others who are entitled to wear the Africa Star. They were awarded the Victoria Cross in countries bordering the Eastern Mediterranean. Five of these were submariners who operated out of Malta and Alexandria, which came within the scope of the Africa Star. Of these, four wore the clasp 'North Africa 1942–43'. The odd one out was Malcolm Wanklyn, whose Africa Star is without a clasp.

New Zealand soldiers who were captured or killed in Greece or Crete in 1941 qualified for the Africa Star. This was because they entered or were based in Egypt on or after 10 June 1940 before being sent to Greece. During these doomed campaigns, three VCs were awarded, including the first of a unique double award to a combat soldier.

The East African or Abyssinian Campaign fought in some of the most remote parts of the world saw four Victoria Crosses awarded, including two to Indian soldiers.

The Australian contingent was stationed in Palestine for training purposes. Once France capitulated and became a *de facto* client and puppet of the Germans, it governed itself from the spa town of Vichy. Once the Germans briefly showed an interest in Iraqi affairs and needed the airfields in Syria, Winston Churchill ordered an occupation of French Lebanon and Syria. The nearest troops were the Australians, who advanced north out of Palestine to fight Britain's recent ally in a swift but fierce campaign. In the two-month campaign, two Victoria Crosses were awarded to Australian servicemen.

Background

North Africa had not figured in Europe's land grab in the way that other countries had. Of minor strategic importance, with little monetary worth and with few centres of population, the southern area of the Mediterranean was regarded as a dry desert region populated by nomads. This changed as the Ottoman Empire began its slow decline in the nineteenth century.

First came the French, who had played a smaller role in Africa than the British but after the defeat of Napoleon cast their eyes south to Algeria as a means to establish a foothold on the continent. In 1830, they occupied Algiers and set about conquering the enormous hinterland, something that would engage their military for 130 years.

What really put North Africa on the map as far as the Europeans were concerned was the opening of the Suez Canal on 17 November 1869. To the accompaniment of Verdi's especially composed *Aida* at the Cairo Opera House and a spectacular firework display, the French-built canal was opened. The 120-mile-long canal was at the time a wonder of the world, cutting sailing time to the Orient from months to weeks.

The Canal was a Franco–Egyptian enterprise but, due to the latter's dire external debts, the British government stepped in and purchased the shares owned by Egypt for £400,000. Although the French owned the majority of shares, the Convention of Constantinople of 1888 opened the waterway to vessels of all nations. In 1882, riots and military intervention prompted Britain to send its army and navy to take control of the country, much to France's dismay. By the beginning of the First World War the whole of North Africa from Morocco to Egypt was colonised by European nations.

A further treaty between Egypt and Britain in 1936 reduced the presence of the British Army but allowed it to maintain a defensive force along the Suez Canal Zone. This gave the British the assurance they needed to protect their vital route to India. With Britain satisfied with the protection of its sea route to the Jewel in the Crown, France continued to expand further to the east and west with the partitioning of Tunisia and Morocco and the sub-Saharan countries to the south.

With the Ottoman Empire beset with uprisings in the Balkans it was vulnerable to Italy's invasion of Libya in 1911. Although it was accorded nominal independence, Libya was colonised by Italy. An estimated 100,000 Italians had been encouraged to settle in the country and been given land taken from the indigenous population during the colonial war in the 1920s. Under Mussolini's instruction, a railway network and a major coastal highway from Tripoli to the Egyptian border was built.

In 1939, laws were passed permitting Muslims to join the National Fascist Party and reforms were made allowing the creation of Libyan military units within the Italian army. By the beginning of the war in North Africa, the Libyan population largely supported the Italians, with some exception in the eastern province of Cyrenaica. Many Allied escapees were often given away, captured or killed by the native population, who saw the Axis as the winning side. Only the Senussi in Cyrenaica gave assistance to the British.

There was a period of peace between the colonial nations, briefly interrupted by a stand-off in 1898 between France and Britain at Fashoda in southern Sudan. France blinked first and the crisis passed. Italy laid claim to Abyssinia (Ethiopia) and Italian Somaliland south of the Horn of Africa. In response, Britain took control of another desert area to the west of Italy's new colony and opposite Aden at the mouth of the Red Sea, which it named British Somaliland. From here it supplied the Aden military enclave with its meat and became known as 'Aden's butcher's shop'.

This period of relative calm could not last and it just needed just one acquisitive individual to provoke a reaction; that man was the Italian Fascist leader, Benito Mussolini.

In 1935, whether to divert public opinion from Italy's dire economic situation or as an expansionist programme to make Italy a main player in the Red Sea area, Mussolini ordered his troops to invade Abyssinia. Supported by a large air force, Italian troops soon overwhelmed the poorly armed native army and Mussolini was able to declare that Abyssinia was now part of the Italian Empire.

Although Britain and France had participated in the 'scramble for Africa' in the nineteenth century, they declared that the international mood was now against further colonialist expansion. The League of Nations imposed sanctions for Italy's use of chemical weapons on the defenceless Abyssinians and for the slaughter of thousands of civilians; an estimated 7 per cent of the population had been killed.

This condemnation pushed Mussolini into an alliance with Adolf Hitler and, on 25 October 1936, the Rome–Berlin Axis was signed. Another reason was the staggering cost of invading Abyssinia. The Italian leader had earmarked the cost of the invasion for modernising his army, which he thought would be ready for a major war by 1942.

Britain wanted Italy on its side just as it had been in the First World War but, with Germany looking the likely victor, Italy sided with Hitler.

The German takeover of its European neighbours in 1938–39 encouraged Mussolini to follow suit. On 7 April 1939, Italy invaded Albania and when Hitler forced the French to surrender, Mussolini threw his lot in with Germany and invaded France on 10–25 June 1940. Italy's gains were tiny compared with Germany's but it gave Mussolini a seat at the victor's table. On 10 July, Mussolini declared war on Britain.

It was now abundantly clear that the forces of fascism were in control of Continental Europe and looking for other territories to conquer.

Chapter 1

The East African Campaign

The East Africa, or Abyssinian Campaign as it is sometimes called, was fought from June 1940 to November 1941 between the forces of the British Middle East Command and the Italian Africa Orientale Italiana (AOI).

Archibald Wavell had been appointed General Officer, Commander-in-Chief Middle East, in July 1939. His immediate task was to protect the Suez Canal and the oilfields in the region. Although not at war with Italy, the anticipation was that within a year Britain would face both Italy and Germany.

In August 1939, Wavell gave approval to the British Military Intelligence's (MIR) covert operation to incite rebellion against Italy's occupation of Abyssinia. Code-named Mission 101, it was run by Colonel Daniel Sandford, the brother of the Zeebrugge VC, Lieutenant Richard Sandford. As advisor to Haile Selassie, he intended to use the emperor as a catalyst for the uprising and Mission 101 focused on the rebellious western province of Gojjam.

In July 1940, encouraged by Wavell, a small special forces unit named Gideon Force was formed under the command of Orde Wingate. Operating on an extended supply line, fifty officers, twenty NCOs, 800 Sudanese and 800 partially trained Abyssinian regulars were split into small groups. Mounting a series of guerrilla attacks on the Italian army, they managed to drive the Italians from Gojjam in six weeks.

An intelligence advantage was gained when the Government Code and Cypher School at Bletchley Park had one of its first successes. In November 1940, it managed to break the high-grade cipher of the Italian army in East Africa. A month later the cipher for the air force, the Regia Aeronautica, was also broken.

1

The British began skirmishing across the Sudanese border, which provoked the Italians to invade and occupy Kassala in the north and Gallabat 120 miles to the south-west. They did not follow through, which gave the weak British force time to augment with the arrival of 5th Indian Division from India. After Wavell's initial success in Libya, the 4th Indian Division was released to the Sudan and Italy found itself in retreat and fighting to save its recently conquered Abyssinia. On 5 May 1941, Emperor Haile Selassie re-entered the capital, Addis Ababa, exactly five years to the day after it was occupied by Italy, so ending Mussolini's aspirations of an Italian African Empire.

Finally, on 1 June 1941, Gideon Force was disbanded. Orde Wingate returned to Wavell's staff in Cairo while several of the officers and NCOs joined the Long Range Desert Group (LRDG).

When General Wavell was sacked by Winston Churchill and sent to India, he immediately became involved in Japan's occupation of Burma. With Gideon Force in mind, he summoned Orde Wingate to India with instructions to form another long-range special force that became better known as the Chindits.

Although not completely prepared for war, the Italian East African forces decided to attack the thinly spread British armies in British Somaliland, Sudan and Kenya. It was during this early period that the first VC was awarded for the African campaigns.

Eric Wilson VC

Eric Charles Twelves Wilson was born on 2 October 1912 at Sandown, Isle of Wight, to The Rev. Cyril C.C. Wilson and his wife, Evelyn (nèe Twelves). He was educated at Marlborough and decided on a military life despite being shy and short-sighted. Nevertheless, he passed his exams and entered RMA Sandhurst in 1931.

In 1933, he was commissioned into the East Surrey Regiment but, attracted to Africa by stories told by his missionary grandfather, he volunteered for secondment to the King's African Rifles. He served in Tanganyika until he secured another secondment in 1939 to the Camel Corps in British Somaliland. With only raw native recruits to work with, Wilson managed to train them into a competent machine gun company. In a later televised interview he quaintly and politically incorrectly called them 'creatures'.

Mussolini's declaration of war on 10 June 1940 two weeks after the fall of France found him without an enemy to attack. With some 350,000 soldiers in Abyssinia and Eritrea, he decided to invade neighbouring British Somaliland, which was defended by a British-officered force of 1,500 that would offer little opposition. Eric Wilson left an account in the Imperial War Museum Sound Archives in which he explained:

> The divisional plan for the defence of British Somaliland relied quite a lot on the French: the French in Djibouti (adjoining British Somaliland) had more forces that we had and more prospects of reinforcements. But shortly before the Italians started their advance from Abyssinia the French in Djibouti packed it in, so then the Italians realised they only had the British to deal with. They desperately needed a propaganda victory and they massed immense forces, by our local standards, and they attacked.

With little terrain suitable for defence, the defenders pulled back towards Berbera on the coast. Most of the country was flat except for the rugged Golis Hills and the Tug Argan Pass. It was decided this was the only defendable place at which to make a stand.

The Somaliland Camel Corps was given the task of delaying the Italian advance at the Tug Argan Pass. With seventy-five men and twelve Vickers machine guns, Captain Wilson positioned his force where it could strike the Italians in the flanks. Although suffering from an attack of malaria, he placed himself in the most forward machine gun post on Observation Hill overlooking the enemy's main advance. The Italians approached along the *tug*, a dry river bed, which gave them good cover. That evening Wilson heard the non-stop revving of engines that heralded a large gathering of the enemy.

The Italian attack opened on the morning of 11 August with an artillery bombardment as two battalions of Blackshirts and three brigades of colonial troops approached Wilson's positions. One of Wilson's crew was wounded when the *sanger* [fortified position] was hit and the machinegun dislodged from its tripod. To Wilson's surprise the gun was undamaged and he had it firing again within minutes. A second enemy shell killed his trusty sergeant, Omaar Kujoog, and badly wounded Wilson in the shoulder and left eye as well as breaking his spectacles. There were greater numbers of the enemy than expected, but Wilson's machine guns kept them at a distance. An Italian mountain artillery battery began firing over open sights but was silenced by a Somali gun and a sudden tropical downpour.

During the night Wilson was able to cobble together bits from the damaged machine guns to keep his company operational. The next day was extremely hot and the water-cooled Vickers became overheated. Fortunately, the Italians were more cautious in their approach and began to creep around the sides of the Tug Argan gap.

On 13 August, the Italians overran the artillery position on nearby Mill Hill and an order to withdraw was sent by runner to Wilson's position but never arrived. Lacking radio communication, Wilson wondered why the British did not return his messages or send reinforcements. He later recalled that he had sent a runner on the first night of the battle to HQ to report on the extent of the casualties:

> You know, I've said this before but I think the British army abandoned me there… and they must have known, from the hell of a noise, that the enemy were knocking me around a bit. But they never even sent a message back.

The Italians were now able to bring heavy fire on Wilson's position. Holding out until the 15th, it was 5 pm when his position was finally overrun. Wilson lay unconscious in the dugout with his dying pet dog and dead soldiers. The Italians just looked in and left him for dead. Wilson and his crew had succeeded in delaying the Italian advance by three days, enabling the rest of the force to escape by sea from Berbera.

During the night, natives came to the battlefield to find their menfolk and tend the wounded. Recovering consciousness, Wilson was found and taken to the shelter of a dried river bed, where he met a white NCO. It did not take long before both were taken into captivity by an Italian patrol.

When news of the action reached London, Wilson was believed to have been killed. A posthumous VC citation appeared in *The London Gazette* dated 11 October 1940. His citation concluded with the sentence:

> The enemy finally over-ran the post at 5 p.m. on 15 August when Captain Wilson, fighting to the last, was killed.

After medical treatment, he was held in a prisoner of war camp at Adi Ugri in Eritrea. It was here that Wilson learned from a fellow prisoner that he had been awarded the Victoria Cross. With other prisoners, he had almost completed an escape tunnel when he was liberated in early 1941, when the Italians surrendered at the conclusion of the East African Campaign.

When he had recovered sufficiently from malaria, he served during 1941–42 as adjutant with the Long Range Desert Group operating around the flanks of Rommel's Afrika Korps in the Western Desert. He then returned to England and on 28 July 1942 was presented with his Cross at Buckingham Palace.

He was promoted to second in command of a battalion of the King's African Rifles and posted to the Far East. As part of the 11th East Africa Division he took part in the advance into Burma down the malarial Kabaw Valley to establish a bridgehead over the Chindwin River. He contracted scrub typhus at Bomapur and spent two months in hospital before being medically downgraded. He returned to East Africa to become the CO of the Infantry Training Centre at Jinja, Uganda. In 1946, he was seconded to the Northern Rhodesia Regiment before retiring as lieutenant colonel in 1949.

He then took up the post of Administration Officer, HM Overseas Civil Service in Tanganyika until 1961. Upon independence he returned to London and joined the Goodenough Trust for Overseas Students, where his fluency in Bantu languages stood him in good stead. He was the honorary secretary of the Anglo–Somali Society until 1990. He was twice married; first to Anne Pleydell-Bouverie, with whom he had two sons. In 1953, he married Angela Gordon and had a son, Hamish.

In a televised interview, Hamish Wilson related that he had joined the Liberation Movement in Somalia to oust Siad Barre. In 1991, he was involved in a battle in the same area in which his father performed his VC exploit.

Eric Wilson died on 23 December 2008 at the age of ninety-six and was laid to rest at St Peter and St Paul's Churchyard, Stowell, near Sherborne, Dorset. His VC group was sold in 2005 and is now in the Ashcroft Trust Collection.

When British Somaliland was taken by Mussolini's army, Churchill was highly critical of General Archibald Wavell, citing few casualties and calling for a court of enquiry. Wavell demurred saying it had been a textbook withdrawal in the face of superior forces. He added, much to Churchill's fury, that: 'A bloody butcher's bill is not the sign of a good tactician.' This, along with Wavell's initial reluctance to deplete his forces to support Greece and the failure of Operation *Battleaxe* to relieve Tobruk, spelt the end of Wavell's desert command. He was then appointed Commander-in-Chief India in time for Japan's entry into the war.

During this largely forgotten campaign in Abyssinia, two further VCs were awarded.

Premindra Singh Bhagat VC

Brought up in a privileged Indian background – his father was an executive engineer in the United Provinces (Agra and Oudh) – Premindra Singh Bhagat was born on 14 October 1918 at Bhagalkot in the hill station of Mussoorie. Known as Prem, he was educated at the Royal Indian Military College, which was the first step to entering the Indian Military Academy that had opened in 1932. Obtaining above average grades, he was commissioned on 15 July 1939 in the Bombay Sappers and Miners and sent to its base at Poona.

He joined the 21 Field Company as part of the 5th Indian Division sent to the Sudan to reinforce the British forces under Lieutenant General Sir William Platt. He disembarked at Port Sudan in early September 1940 and for the next three months was involved in a series of skirmishing operations aimed at keeping the Italians off balance.

Second Lieutenant Bhagat was with the 3/18 Royal Garhwal Rifles when on 6 November they took the border town of Gallabat, described as a 'dirty, smelly little town'. This was the first British offensive action taken in Africa since the outbreak of war with Italy. The victorious force was commanded by Brigadier William (Bill) Slim of 10 Brigade, soon to go on to greater things in Burma.

It is worth describing the Gallabat battle as it illustrates the misconception that all fighting was in a desert. In the history of the 5th Indian Division, Anthony Brett-James describes the battle:

> Rain was falling. The slimy surface of the ground made progress slow and awkward. Later, when the cover of the hills was behind the infantry and, in front, the more level ground that led away towards Gallabat fort, visibility and movement were much reduced by the tall elephant grass…
>
> Slim's plan provided for our bombardment to open with the bombing of Gallabat and Metemma by the Royal Air Force. The planes were late. The minutes ticked past. …It was later discovered that the night's fall of rain had been heavy elsewhere and had turned our advanced landing ground into a muddy expanse. And the bombers had been unable to take off from the treacherous black cotton soil until it had dried a little.

Finally, eight obsolete Wellesley and Vincent bombers appeared over Gallabat and Metemma. They were soon followed by ten Gloster Gladiators, which were opposed by a similar number of Fiat C.R.42s.

To the dismay of the onlookers, five Gladiators were shot down and the Italians were in the ascendency. The commander of the fort summoned bombers to come to his assistance and the Italians had an unhindered command of the battlefield.

The British sent in the tanks of the 6th Royal Tank Regiment and soon the fort was taken, mostly because the native Abyssinian troops had no stomach for fighting on behalf of their Italian masters. The tanks had been sent down the Nile from the Western Desert but could not cope with the change from open sand to rock, bush and hills, as Brett-James continues:

> Mechanical breakdowns, broken tracks, rough boulders that could not be seen in the long grass and mines caused severe losses of 12 cruiser and light tanks; three were out of action from mines and six more from damaged track pins.
>
> Soon after half-past seven, the green success signal flared into the sky.

Brigadier Slim had successfully captured Gallabat but was sanguine about taking Metemma and decided to consolidate his position around Gallabat. The ground was so hard and rocky that even the defence-minded Italians failed to dig trenches for their infantry. Slim decided not to occupy Gallabat but to constantly send out patrols and deny the fort to the enemy.

On the 7 November, the Bombay Sappers and Miners destroyed all the buildings around the town that could aid the Italians. Prem Bhagat's first act of gallantry was noted in the regimental history:

> Next day the enemy, closely following up, had to be delayed at a culvert bottleneck. Two derelict tanks packed with explosive were fired but only one detonated leaving the culvert partly intact. Under small arms fire and air strafing, Second Lieutenant Bhagat broke cover to reignite the failed charge and completed the destruction of the culvert. Major Philbrick witnessed this incident and recommended him for a Military Cross (MC), but it seems that it was subsequently revised to a mention in despatches...

This action was followed up when Prem took part in a raid on the airfield at Metemma with the 3rd Frontier Force and carried out demolitions of aircraft and buildings.

For the next three months part of the 5th Indian Division remained around Gallabat to keep the Italian forces off balance while the remainder of the division, augmented by the arrival of the 4th Indian Infantry Division, launched an attack into Eritrea.

On 1 February 1941, the Italians abandoned Metemma and a mobile column was sent in pursuit, which included a detachment of 21 Field Company.

> The pursuit progressed well, but was frequently delayed by extensive minefields. Bhagat, the Sapper, led the column in a carrier, in which he stood next to the driver. He kept his eyes on the road, watching for any disturbance of the surface which might indicate a buried mine. All *wadi* beds – and they crossed many – were automatically suspect and examined minutely, since it was possible to bury mines under the uneven surface without leaving a trace. The outstanding performance of the detachment of Sappers during the advance was responsible for the award of the Victoria Cross to Second-Lieutenant Premindra Singh Bhagat. It was the first VC to be won by the Indian Army in the Second World War and the first to be earned by an Indian Commissioned Officer.

To quote from his citation:

> For a period of four days and over a distance of 55 miles this officer in the leading carrier led the column. He detected and supervised the clearing of 15 minefields. Speed being essential, he worked at high pressure from dawn to dusk each day. On two occasions when his carrier was blown up with casualties to others, and on a third occasion when ambushed and under close enemy fire, he himself carried straight on with his task. He refused relief when worn out with the strain and fatigue and with one eardrum punctured by an explosion, on the grounds that he was now better qualified to continue his task to the end.
>
> His coolness, persistence over a period of 96 hours and gallantry, not only in battle, but throughout the long period when the safety of the Column and the speed at which it could advance were dependent on his personal efforts, were of the highest order.

Two of the sappers who helped Prem were awarded the Indian Distinguished Service Medal (IDSM) and a *Jangi Inam* (a traditional reward in kind for distinguished service, normally a plot of land), respectively. In February, 21 Field Company moved with 9th Brigade, and Prem, now restored to fitness albeit with permanent damage to his ears, arrived back in March, in time to take part in the battle for Keren.

Premindra Singh Bhagat's gallantry was gazetted on 10 June 1941. In the same month, he was presented with the ribbon of his VC by General Wavell at a victory parade in Asmara. While the 21 Field Company sailed for the Mediterranean, Prem returned to India to a hero's welcome in India. He received his Cross on 10 November 1940 from the Viceroy, Lord Linlithgow, at the Red Fort in Delhi.

His rise through the ranks was swift. By 1943, he was a major and in 1945–46 he attended Staff College at Camberley. After Independence, he held several staff appointments and by 1959 he was Director of Military Intelligence. Elevated to lieutenant general in 1970, he was expected to become Commander of the Indian Army but instead a political appointment was made. In its place he was made GOC of Northern Command before retiring on 31 August 1974.

In less than a year he had contracted pneumonia and died at the age of fifty-six in the Calcutta Military Hospital on 23 May 1975.

Richpal Ram VC

Richal Ram was born on 20 August 1899 in Barda Village, Patiala State, to Mohar and Janki Singh. On 25 August 1920, he enlisted in the 4th Battalion, 123 Outram's Rifles, which two years later changed to the 6th Rajputana Rifles. He steadily rose up the promotion ladder and on 1 May 1936 he was appointed *jemedar* (lieutenant).

Raised in 1939 in Secundrabad, the 5th Indian Division was sent to the Sudan in 1940 and formed themselves into three brigades. The 6th Rajputana Rifles was part of the 4th Brigade that took part in the most decisive battle of the East African Campaign at the Eritrean town of Keren. In overall command was Lieutenant General William Platt and his leadership played a large part in the successful outcome of the battle.

Keren was the last Italian stronghold in Eritrea, having no built-in fortifications but forming a perfect defensive position as it was surrounded by a jumble of steep granite mountains and sharp ridges that gave the Italians a distinct advantage as they dominated the approaches to the town. The only road passed through a deep gorge with well-fortified ridges and mountains on either side: on these heights were positioned some 23,000 Italian infantry and artillery.

In order to bypass the main approach, the 6th Rajputana Rifles was tasked with crossing the open Happy Valley to the south-east of Keren to take the heights of Acqua Col. On the night of 7 February 1941, a company of the 6th Rajputana Rifles managed to capture the Col but ran out of ammunition. It was here that Acting Subadar Richpal Ram won his Victoria Cross. His citation published in *The London Gazette* dated 4 July 1941 describes the action:

> During the assault on enemy positions in front of Keren, Eritrea, on the night of 7–8th February 1941, Subadar Richpal Ram, who was second-in-command of a leading company, insisted on accompanying the forward platoon and led its attack on the first objective with great dash and gallantry. His company commander being then wounded, he assumed command of the company, and led the attack of the remaining two platoons to the final objective. In the face of heavy fire, some thirty men with this officer at their head rushed the objective with the bayonet and captured it. The company was completely isolated, but under the inspiring leadership of Subadar Richpal Ram, it beat back six enemy counter-attacks between midnight and 0430 hours. By now, ammunition had run out, and this officer extricated his command and fought his way back to his battalion with a handful of survivors (nine) through the surrounding enemy.
>
> Again, in attack on the same position on 12th February, this officer led the attack of his company. He pressed on fearlessly and determinedly in the face of heavy and accurate fire, and his personal example inspired his company with his resolute spirit until his right foot was blown off. He then suffered further wounds from which he died. While lying wounded he continued to wave his men on, and his final words were 'We'll capture the objective.' The heroism, determination and devolution to duty shown by this officer were beyond praise, and provided an inspiration to all who saw him.

His Cross was presented to his widow by Lord Linlithgow on 10 November 1941 at the Red Fort, Delhi. Also present was the new Commander-in-Chief, General Wavell.

It took fifty-three days and many casualties before Keren fell on 27 March. Massawa was then entered on 8 April. Although Platt's objectives in Eritrea had been effectively accomplished by early April, there was still some way to go before the Italians were ejected from East Africa. While Platt was struggling in the Keren gorge, Lieutenant General Alan Cunningham was advancing from Kenya into Italian Somaliland. Mogadishu fell on 25 February and by mid-March Nigerian troops had crossed the Ogaden desert and entered Jijiga. Cunningham's force then closed in on Addis Ababa from the east and south as the Italians evacuated the city in order to concentrate against Platt's force in northern Abyssinia. There they held out in the mountain stronghold of Amba Alagi until Cunningham's force reached them from the south and further resistance became impracticable. The war in East Africa was still not over; it was to take another eight months and cost more casualties than had been incurred to date to finally evict the Italians.

It was with General Cunningham's advance that the final Victoria Cross of the Abyssinian Campaign was awarded to an NCO of the King's African Rifles.

Nigel Leakey VC

Nigel Grey Leakey was born on 1 January 1913 at Kiganjo, Kenya. His father, Arundell Grey Leakey, was a missionary who was later murdered by the Mau Mau during the 1950s. Nigel's grandfather was the famous paleoanthropologist and archaeologist, Dr Louis Leakey, who proved that Africa and not Asia was the place of human origin.

Leakey attended Nairobi High School until he was thirteen, when he was sent to Bromsgrove School in Worcestershire. Part of the reason for the latter was that his uncle was a housemaster and his cousins attended the school. Although he was not an outstanding scholar, he did distinguish himself as a member of the shooting team.

Leaving Bromsgrove School at seventeen, he returned to Kenya and worked at various coffee and sisal estates before buying his own farm at Londiani. With the outbreak of war, he joined the Kenya Regiment before being attached as a sergeant in the 1/6th King's African Rifles (KAR). It was part of the force commanded by Lieutenant General Alan Cunningham, who was directed to advance through Italian Somaliland, retake British Somaliland and enter Abyssinia from the south and link up with General Platt's command. Cunningham's campaign was swift, which made safe the lower Red Sea for Allied shipping. In the process, he captured 50,000 prisoners with the loss of only 500 of his men.

In heavy rain, the Italians pulled back into Abyssinia and put up a stiff resistance at the Battle of the Lakes, 120 miles south of Addis Ababa. On 19 May 1941, Cunningham's men encountered a strong force near the village of Kulito on the River Billate. By 8.30 am the village was captured but the Italians had blown up the nearby bridge and were holding the opposite bank. Around midday, two platoons of the KAR had formed a human bridge by holding hands and crossed the 40ft-wide river without opposition. Sergeant Leakey had provided covering fire from a 3in mortar but, running out of ammunition, he decided to cross the river to add his support. He found the two under-manned platoons isolated in their precarious bridgehead without hope of immediate reinforcement.

Lieutenant Philip Thorne of the 1/6th KAR described the scene:

> Not jungle as such but a great big kind of bush-trees and tremendous anthills going up twelve, fifteen feet, which the Italians had made into machine-gun posts: good shelter and jolly good camouflage. Well by that time my platoon strength was down to fifteen Africans. We came to a road. I was told to take up a position as well on this road.

Then they heard the sound of engines approaching. The Italians had hidden their tanks in the thick bush and were advancing down the road with only a small platoon to oppose them. On hearing the engines, Leakey shouted to his men: 'Come on! I can hear some lorries trying to get away. Let's stop them.' Quickly it became apparent these were not lorries but light and medium tanks. With no anti-tank guns to oppose them, the KAR was in a desperate situation.

Leakey immediately advanced through the thick bush and stalked the nearest tank. He managed to clamber on it and the tank accelerated with its cannon and machine gun firing wildly in an attempt to shake Leakey off. After 100 yards, with Leakey straddling the machine gun, he managed to open the hatch and fire off four or five shots with his revolver. The tank stopped immediately and Leakey leapt off and took the only survivor, the driver, captive. He handed him over to an Askari to guard him while he attempted to fire the cannon to attack the other tanks. Unable to work out the mechanics, Leakey was forced to continue on foot.

In company with an Askari sergeant and two others he crossed ground swept by cannon fire from the other tanks. He attempted to climb on two but they were travelling too fast, although he managed to mount a third. Opening the hatch, he fired into the interior, killing a crewman. What happened next is something of a mystery for he was killed and his body never recovered.

What is not in dispute is that Leakey's action broke up the Italian tank attack having killed the Italian commander. A recommendation for the Victoria Cross was submitted with the three Askaris as witnesses. In Michael Crook's *Evolution of the Victoria Cross*, Nigel Leakey's file shows the witness statements translated from Swahili and signed by their thumbprints.

Although the Chief of the Imperial Staff and the Permanent-Under-Secretary thought the act was of VC standard, the Military Secretary, General Arthur Floyer-Acland, disagreed. When it was presented to King George, he sided with the Military Secretary and it appeared that Leakey's gallantry would go unrecognised. When it was resubmitted after the war by the Kenyan administration with further witness evidence it was granted and the citation appeared in *The London Gazette* of 15 November 1945. Leakey's father and brother flew to London and on 9 June 1946 accepted the posthumous Cross from the King. It is of note that Nigel's brother, Arundell Rea Leakey, was awarded the DSO and MC and bar at the same time.

There still remains the mystery of Leakey's death. Was he shot by a fourth tank or was he a victim of friendly fire from the KAR?

Major General William Platt was Commandant of the Sudan Defence Force who had to face the possibility of an Italian invasion from neighbouring Abyssinia. He was reinforced with both the 4th and 5th Indian Infantry Division and promoted to lieutenant general. Having seen two border towns (Kassala and Gallabat) captured by the Italians, he launched an invasion into Italian-held Eritrea. In early 1941, his force advanced to capture Argordat and the difficult terrain of Keren, which finally fell on 1 April 1941.

With Lieutenant General Alan Cunningham's force advancing from Kenya, the Duke of Aosta was forced to surrender his army on 18 May and the East African Campaign was all but over.

Chapter 2

The Greek VCs

The Desert Campaign started well for the British. The numerically superior Italians lacked sufficient armour and the surrender of the 10th Italian Army meant that Cyrenaica (Eastern Libya) was in British hands. Despite the victory, the British were forced to withdraw to refit and re-equip as most of their fighting vehicles were worn out.

The arrival of the Afrika Korps under the command of General Erwin Rommel added steel to the over-cautious Italians. By April, the Axis was once again on the Egyptian border. This was in main due to Winston Churchill ordering General Wavell to denude his Western Desert Force by sending a considerable number of troops to help the Greeks fight the invading Germans. This was in reality a political gesture that was doomed before it began. Churchill, for all his outstanding leadership, was not a good strategist, as witnessed by the ventures in Antwerp and Gallipoli in the First World War.

The Italian invasion of Albania on 7–12 April 1940 saw this small country become part of the Italian Empire. This easy victory did nothing to reduce Il Duce's chagrin over his own lack of conquests compared with Hitler's overrunning of most of Europe. Using Albania as a springboard, Mussolini sent his troops into Greece in October 1940. It was a foolish move as the weather bogged down the invading army and the Greek army swept the Italians back to their starting position on the Albanian frontier.

General Wavell reluctantly complied by sending to Greece the 6th Australian Division, a British armoured brigade and the 2/New Zealand Division to join forces with the Greeks. Hitler had already occupied the Balkans and felt he had to support his ally and prevent Britain establishing a foothold on his southern flank. The weak Anglo–

Greek force had to confront twenty German divisions and face 1,100 Axis aircraft with just eighty of its own.

With his eyes firmly on the forthcoming invasion of Soviet Russia, Hitler sought a speedy victory in Greece. This he achieved but he felt that the Allied troops who had fled to Crete could still create problems.

Even at the point of surrender, the Allies could look to the outstanding gallantry of a tough Kiwi whose refusal to quit won New Zealand its first VC.

John Hinton VC

John (Jack) Daniel saw the light of day on 17 September 1909 at Colac Bay on the southern tip of South Island, New Zealand, one of seven children born to Harry and Elizabeth Hinton. He was educated at a local school but, before lessons started, he had to milk forty cows. When he was twelve, he ran away from home after an argument with his father, a former sergeant who had fought in the Boer War.

He found work as a delivery boy for a grocer in a neighbouring town before, at the age of thirteen, signing on as a galley hand on the Norwegian factory ship, *C.A. Larson*. Jack Hinton spent nine months in Antarctica hunting whales in the freezing Ross Sea. When he left the ship he had earned £380; a small fortune for a young teenager.

He was reconciled with his family and worked as a shepherd before boredom set in and he looked for a more adventurous occupation. In the 1930s, he moved to the west coast of South Island, working as a gold miner on the black sands of the West Coast beaches. From there he drifted from one job to another, working as a labourer, picking fruit, hauling coal and working in a sawmill. He found regular work in the government's public works department, building bridges and roads. In 1937, he invested his savings in the lease of a pub, an experience that would later hold him in good stead.

With the outbreak of war, Hinton enlisted in the 2nd New Zealand Division (2/NZD), which had been raised for service abroad. He was posted to the 20th Battalion under the command of Lieutenant Colonel Kippenberger, later to become Major General Sir Howard Kippenberger. When Hinton was promoted to sergeant, his father sent him his old Boer War stripes. After training, the 20th departed for the Middle East on 5 January 1940 but had to wait a year on garrison duty before it saw action.

In March 1941, the 2/NZD was sent to Greece to counter the expected invasion by the Italian and German troops. When the invasion began on

6 April, Hinton was in Athens with the division's reinforcement unit and did not take part in the retreat south through the country. Instead he joined the thousands of allied troops awaiting evacuation from the fishing port of Kalamata. On 26 April, in chaotic scenes, some 7,000 Australian troops were taken off by Royal Navy destroyers. For political reasons, Churchill had ordered that the Australian troops should get priority.

The following day no ships appeared. By that time the Germans were close by and on 28 April they entered the port. Sergeant Hinton went to the headquarters of Brigadier Leonard Parrington, the officer in charge of evacuation, to find out what was happening. On being told he must surrender by the brigadier, Hinton exploded: 'Surrender? Go and jump in the bloody lake!'

'I'll have you court martialled for speaking to me like that!' replied the affronted officer.

'If you're not careful I'll have you court martialled for talking surrender!'

Hinton stormed off and, armed with a rifle, bayonet and hand grenades, he met a major from the 3 Royal Tank Regiment (3 RTR) commanding a machine gun post near the beach. The officer promised to give covering fire as Hinton gathered together a dozen New Zealand soldiers and led them back into the town. Ignoring an order from an officer to retreat, Hinton charged on to the waterfront, hurling a grenade into a German machine gun post and killing the crew. He then went to attack a self-propelled 6in gun, which was fired at him but missed. Another grenade killed all the crew.

With covering fire from the 3 RTR machine gun, Hinton threw his remaining grenade at another self-propelled gun, which the German crew quickly abandoned. They ran into nearby houses followed by Jack Hinton's Kiwis, who killed them. Having caused mayhem, Hinton momentarily relaxed, only to be shot in the stomach by a German sub-machine gun.

Inspired by Hinton's unexpected show of gallantry, the allied soldiers recaptured the town and waterfront for a few hours. Unfortunately the Royal Navy did not come again as the naval liaison officer had been killed and no message was sent. In the early hours of the 29th, the Germans re-entered Kalamata to accept Brigadier Parrington's surrender and Jack Hinton, along with 6,000 Allied troops, went into captivity for the remainder of the war.

Major George Thompson, the Senior Medical Officer, with ten other officer witnesses wrote a recommendation for the Victoria Cross to be awarded to Hinton. It came in the form of a letter to the War Office through the International Red Cross. Thompson had already been captured by the Germans and was advancing into Kalamata with their column. He had witnessed Hinton's one-man attack on the German guns and later recognised him in the Prisoner of War Hospital at Kokkinia as he tended his wounds.

When Hinton recovered he was sent to Stalag IXC near Bad Sulza in Germany. His citation was announced on 14 October 1941, but Hinton was in solitary confinement for trying to escape. The camp commandant had Hinton brought from the cells and in a parade before the rest of the prisoners, announced the award and presented Hinton with a red ribbon.

The citation read:

> On the night of 28–29th April 1941, during the fighting in Greece, a column of German armoured forces entered Kalamata, this column which contained several armoured cars, 2' guns and 3' mortars, and two 6' guns, rapidly converged on a large force of British and New Zealand troops awaiting embarkation on the beach.
>
> When the order to retreat to cover was given, Sergeant Hinton shouting 'to Hell with this, who'll come with me,' ran to within several yards of the nearest gun, the gun fired, missing him, and he hurled two grenades which completely wiped out the crew. He then came on with the bayonet followed by a crowd of New Zealanders. German troops abandoned the first 6' gun and retreated into two houses. Sergeant Hinton smashed the window and then the door of the first house and dealt with the garrison with the bayonet. He repeated the performance in the second house and as a result, until overwhelming German forces arrived, the New Zealanders held the guns. Sergeant Hinton then fell with a bullet wound through the lower abdomen and was taken prisoner.

Hinton hated being a POW and made life difficult for his captors. He made a second attempt to escape and remained at liberty for two weeks before he was recaptured. Instead of being returned to camp, he was put in the tender hands of the Gestapo, by whom he was beaten and interrogated.

By April 1945, the Allied advance into Germany neared Hinton's POW camp and the prisoners were evacuated. Hinton feigned sickness and remained behind with other sick prisoners. He managed to find the keys to the gates and let himself out. He soon made contact with the

US 6th Armoured Division, who treated him with suspicion as Hinton was dressed in civilian clothes. Finally convinced that he was a POW, he was given an American uniform and, after some persuasion, went forward with the 44th Infantry Division to help capture three villages and round up surrendering Germans. When some senior American officers discovered his presence he was sent to England.

He arrived on 12 April 1945 and stayed for three months before being repatriated to New Zealand. During this time he received his Victoria Cross on 11 May from the King at Buckingham Palace. He was joined by a comrade from the 20th Battalion, Charles Upham, who received a bar to his own VC.

Hinton arrived back in New Zealand on 4 August 1945 and was demobbed. He struggled to adapt to civilian life and was very reticent about his Victoria Cross. Drawing from his public house experiences before the war, he joined the Dominion Breweries group and managed some of its hotels. In the late 1940s, he received a mention in despatches for his escape attempts while a POW. He was married to Eunice Henriksen from 1950 until her death in 1968. He married again, to Molly Schumacher, and when he retired they moved to Christchurch. He died there on 28 June 1997, the last surviving Kiwi VC.

His Victoria Cross medal group was loaned to the Army Museum at Waioura. On 2 December 2007 it was one of nine VCs among hundreds of medals stolen from the museum. Ten weeks later all the medals had been recovered thanks to a NZ$300,000 reward offered by Lord Ashcroft and New Zealand businessman Tom Sturgess.

Crete was a short distance from Greece but nearly 400 miles from the nearest British base at Alexandria. From east to west it was 160 miles long with an average width of 35 miles. As far as the New Zealand garrison commander Major General Bernard Freyberg was concerned, Crete faced the wrong way. The north side nearest Greece had all the ports and airfields, while the south was dominated by mountains, gullies and cliffs. Crete was a very picturesque island with olive groves, vineyards, patches of cornfields and tall spires of cypress. There was only one good road that linked the north coastal towns and it was here that Freyberg concentrated the 30,000 troops he had at his disposal. Apart from the 14th Infantry Brigade stationed there, the balance was made up of units who had escaped from Greece; 2nd NZD, 19th Australian Brigade, about 2,000 Royal Marines and some 11,000 largely untrained Greek soldiers.

The German assault began at dawn on 20 May 1940 and was concentrated on the west of the island in the Maleme and Suda areas, which had airfields and were largely defended by the New Zealanders. Hitler had decided that a swift, decisive victory could be delivered by his elite airborne regiments and had given their commander, General Kurt Student, just twenty days to prepare for the landing on an unfamiliar island. A total of 500 Junkers Ju 52 transport planes had to be gathered in haste to convey 8,000 men in the initial drop. Once the airfields had been captured then more troops would be flown in and the expected victory would be won.

Fleets of the corrugated-bodied, three engined Junkers Ju52 roared over the Cretan coast disgorging hundreds of paratroopers, who were picked off by the waiting defenders. The anti-aircraft fire caused so many casualties to the transports that General Student and his staff doubted the wisdom of continuing with an airborne attack. Hitler concurred and vetoed any further massed parachute attacks.

With the heavy losses to the transport planes, no heavy equipment or ammunition could be delivered except by sea. A convoy was despatched but intercepted by the Royal Navy, which tore into the unprotected ships and destroyed them. There followed a period of relative calm while Germany reorganised its forces.

The Germans had total superiority in the air and began placing its aircraft on neighbouring Greek islands. From there they attacked the Royal Navy, sinking and damaging eight ships and turning the tide of the battle for Crete. During the course of this battle, two more New Zealand VCs were awarded and one to a Royal Navy petty officer.

Arthur Clive Hulme VC

Arthur Clive Hulme was born in Dunedin on 24 January 1911 and was educated at Eastern Hutt School. Clive, as he preferred to be called, was a tough and powerfully built youth who developed into a talented wrestler. In 1934, he married Rona Marjorie (née Murcot) and they had two children, Anita and Denny. Working as a farm labourer in Nelson, he enlisted in the 2nd New Zealand Expeditionary Force (2/NZEF) and was posted to the 23rd Battalion (Canterbury Regiment).

Sent to the Eastern Mediterranean, he was appointed provost sergeant to the 2nd New Zealand Division's field punishment centre at Platanias on the island of Crete. The precipitous retreat from Greece to Crete, some 60 miles from the mainland, was thought to be a staging point on their way back to Egypt. With no air cover or artillery, about 32,000 soldiers, including the bulk of 2nd New Zealand Division, learned that they were to spend more time on Crete than that for which they had prepared. The New Zealand soldiers were responsible for the western sector of the island, which included the all-important Maleme airfield and the towns of Platanias and Canea, and the village of Galatas. For nearly a month the troops anticipated an attack. On the morning of 20 May 1941, at the Platanias field punishment centre, the Kiwi prisoners were having breakfast when the German airborne assault began. Quickly issuing rifles and ammunition, the prisoners were released to join in the fight against the German invaders with the promise that those who survived would be granted the remission of their sentence.

Sergeant Hulme joined the 23rd Battalion as it battled the German paratroopers who jumped from the dozens of Junkers Ju 52s that filled the sky over Maleme airfield. He led several groups and succeeded in keeping the Germans at bay, killing some 100 troops. In an interview after the war, Hulme admitted that he was haunted by the killing of one particular German paratrooper he found rummaging among the papers at the punishment centre. Hulme shot him between the eyes and for some reason, given the numbers he killed, this affected him: 'I never felt so sorry to kill a German.'

Hulme took possession of the paratrooper's camouflage blouse and cap. He also acquired a Mauser sniper's rifle equipped with telescopic sights and also picked up a couple of Luger pistols. Now suitably equipped, he started to stalk the Germans, even if it meant suffering summary execution if caught. While he was moving about behind enemy lines, he came across a small party of New Zealand engineers who had been captured and were guarded by a single sentry. Wearing his paratrooper's smock and cap, Hulme approached the unsuspecting guard and quietly despatched him with his bayonet.

After a two-day fight, the New Zealanders were forced to relinquish the Malema airfield, which gave the Germans a supply base to push east and squeeze the Allies from the island. On 25 May, the Germans attacked the strategically important village of Galatas and soon occupied it. Despite increasing casualties, Brigadier Kippenberger organised a counter-attack, in which Hulme took part. With the support of two British light tanks, the New Zealanders pushed their way back into the village. The advance was held up by a machine gun in a schoolhouse. Hulme went forward alone and attacked the building with hand grenades, which either killed the Germans or caused them to retreat.

Following up with another soldier, Hulme saw a German run into a nearby house and gave chase. When they entered they could not find the German but noticed that a trapdoor in the floor was slightly opened. While the other soldier held open the door, Hulme threw in a couple of grenades. Tragically, the cellar was occupied by the village women and children, who were either killed or wounded. It was to have a deep and lasting impression on Hulme for the rest of his life.

The next day, 26 May, Hulme learned of the death of his brother, Corporal 'Blondie' Hulme of the 19th Battalion. Filled with a need to avenge his brother's death, Hulme stayed hidden as the 23rd Battalion withdrew from Galatas. He took up a position overlooking a food dump and waited until an enemy patrol appeared, shooting three and forcing the rest to withdraw.

Later, the 23rd acted as rearguard and, after a gruelling march, reached Stylos, where the weary men slumped to the ground in exhaustion. A couple of officers made a quick reconnaissance and spotted a party of Germans approaching about 400 yards away. The company commander called Sergeant Hulme to lead his men up the hill before the Germans could reach the summit. Hulme sprinted ahead and beat the Germans by 15 yards. Hurling grenades and firing, Hulme drove off the enemy but was wounded in the arm. The battalion's history records:

> Hulme was to be seen sitting side-saddle on the stone wall, shooting at the enemy on the lower slopes. His example did much to maintain the morale of the men whose reserves of nervous and physical energy were nearly exhausted.

The next day, German snipers fired at some senior officers at 5 Brigade headquarters and Hulme volunteered to go out and deal with them. Donning his German disguise, he managed to climb undetected until he was behind the five snipers, pretending to be part of their group. Singling out the leader, Hulme shot him. The other four snipers looked round to see where the shot had come from. Hulme also turned his head as if searching for the shooter and then shot and killed two more in quick succession. The other two snipers, realising they were the next targets attempted to escape, but Hulme killed them as well. All this was witnessed by Hulme's company commander, Major H.H. Thompson, who was following the action through his binoculars.

Another withdrawal followed with a further daring act by Hulme. The Germans began shelling the rearguard with a heavy mortar as they held an important ridge. Once again Hulme penetrated the German lines, killing the mortar crew and putting the weapon out of action. On the same day he killed three more snipers, bringing his tally to thirty-three in one week.

While he stalking another sniper, he was shot through the shoulder and forced to go to the rear. The wound was serious but he stayed in the Stylos area, directing traffic and organising stragglers into section groups. By now the Allies were making their way over the mountains that divided Crete to the evacuation port of Sphakia. On 30 May, Hulme was on his way back to Egypt and his short war was over.

His outstanding solo actions during the retreat had been noted by four officers, including Brigadier Hargest, who wrote:

> Sgt. Hulme, during the whole of the fighting up till the moment of being wounded, conducted himself with such courage that the story of his exploits were on everyone's lips. From my own personal observation I knew he showed such a complete contempt for danger that it amounted to recklessness... The effect his actions had on all the men in his unit is incalculable, and he at once became almost legendary. I sincerely hope that the recommendation will be accepted.

The recommendation was accepted and appeared in *The London Gazette* on 10 October 1941. Sergeant Hulme received his Victoria Cross on 7 November 1941 from the Governor-General of New Zealand, at Nelson.

As a result of his wound, Hulme was medically discharged in 1942. The wound subsequently wasted the muscles in his forearm, but it was the post-traumatic stress that caused him the most torment, particularly the incident of the grenades in the cellar at Galatas. After the war he lived at Pongakawa near Te Puke on the north coast of North Island, running a small farm and trucking business.

His son, Denny, learned to drive a truck while sitting on his father's lap and by the age of six was driving solo. Clive encouraged Denny's passion for driving and was rewarded when his son won the Formula One World Driver's Championship in 1967.

Decades after the battle for Crete, one of New Zealand's VC heroes was accused of war crimes by three academics. Sadly it has become the norm these days to resurrect events that may have been acceptable at the time but are now frowned upon. In 2006, a book by two military historians was published that attacked Hulme for committing 'acts of perfidy' in winning the Victoria Cross. The claim gained support among fellow academics and one even stated that Hulme's actions were 'unsanctioned murder' and that the New Zealand government should apologise to the families of the Germans he killed: 'Killing soldiers while wearing their uniform was prima facie a war crime.' The New Zealand public thought otherwise and the furore soon died down.

Hulme died on 2 September 1982 and his medal was among the nine VCs stolen from the QEII Army Museum, Waiouru, in 2007 but subsequently recovered as a result of a reward being offered.

Charles Upham VC

Charles Hazlitt Upham was born in Christchurch on 21 September 1908, the son of John Hazlitt Upham, a lawyer, and his wife, Agatha Mary (née Coates). He boarded at Waihi School, Winchester, South Canterbury, between 1917 and 1922 and Christ's College, Christchurch, from 1923 to 1927. From an early age he was a quiet and unusually determined boy, which gained him respect. Upham was keen to pursue a farming career and completed a diploma of agriculture at Canterbury Agricultural College, Lincoln, in 1930. For the next six years he worked on high country sheep stations in Canterbury. In 1937 he joined the Valuation Department as assistant district valuer in Timaru, and the following year he became engaged to Mary (Molly) Eileen McTamney. In 1939 he returned to Lincoln to complete a diploma in valuation and farm management.

Upham enlisted in the 2nd New Zealand Expeditionary Force (2NZEF) in September 1939 and was posted to the 20th (Canterbury–Otago) Battalion. He was of average height, with a wiry build, flashing blue eyes and great powers of endurance. From the beginning of his military service he displayed tactical flair and an intense desire to master the practical skills of the soldier's craft. He was soon promoted to temporary lance corporal, but he declined a place in an Officer Cadet Training Unit (OCTU), fearing that it would delay his departure overseas. In December he was promoted to sergeant and a week later sailed for Egypt with an advance party.

In July 1940 he was persuaded to join an OCTU. He was commissioned as a second lieutenant on 2 November and given command of a platoon in 20th Battalion that consisted mainly of tough West Coasters, including Sergeant Jack Hinton. As a capable officer he was greatly concerned for their safety and comfort.

He sailed for Greece in March 1941 but saw little fighting. He contracted dysentery that was to plague him throughout the Greek/Crete Campaign. Upham, through a superhuman effort, managed to suppress this debilitating sickness enough to embark on the first of his series of VC actions.

Evacuated to Crete, the 2/NZD defended the western end of the island that housed the all-important airfields of Maleme and Suda. On 20 May, a vast fleet of German Ju 52 transports took off from Greek airfields and delivered the elite German *Luftlande Sturmregiment* over Maleme airfield, where the 21st and 23rd Battalions of the New Zealand 5th Infantry Brigade was waiting. They held their fire until the parachutists were at tree height and then opened up, inflicting terrible losses. One German unit recorded losing all but two of the 136 paratroopers dropped.

More successful were the glider-borne troops of the *Fallschirmjäger*, who managed to capture a bridge and knock out some of the anti-aircraft positions around the airfield. Despite these small victories, things were looking bleak for the Germans with casualties mounting and many small groups being pinned down. The German commander, General Student, did not know of this and ordered in a second wave. Delays caused the *Fallschirmjäger* to be dropped over a wide area but they were able to reorganise themselves before taking on the defenders.

By the end of the first day, the Germans were just about holding on. The New Zealand commander, General Bernard Freyburg, was getting reports that landings had been made all along the north coast and that all his garrisons were under attack simultaneously, which caused some dismay. He saw his first priority as reinforcing his men fighting for control of Maleme airfield.

At 3.30 am on 21 May, the 20th Battalion and the 28th (Maori) Battalion launched a counter-attack. Charles Upham led 15 Platoon, C Company towards the airfield. As they crossed an open field a German heavy machine gun opened fire from a range of 60 yards, hitting four of the platoon. One of its members recalled the action:

> We edged forward on our stomachs until we were within 20 yards of the Nazis, who were tucked away behind a large tree, and then (we) opened fire with our one Tommy gun, one Bren gun and eight rifles. As we kept up the fire the platoon officer (Upham) cautiously crawled round to the side and slightly to the rear of the tree. Although it was still dark, we could tell by the way the Jerries were shouting to each other that they didn't like the look of the

24

situation. When he got round the tree the platoon officer jumped to his feet and hurled three Mills bombs, one right after the other, into the nest and then jumped forward with his revolver blazing. Single-handed he wiped out seven Jerries with their machine-guns ... Two machine-gunners managed to hobble away in the darkness, but we got them later.

Moving on, 15 Platoon soon came under fire from two machine gun positions. One was firing from a house and the other from a nearby shed. With covering fire from the Bren, Upham moved at a crouch to the shed and threw in a grenade. Calling his men forward, they captured eight wounded and a half a dozen dazed Germans who surrendered. Turning his attention to the house, Upham ran forward and threw a grenade through the window, killing the machine gun crew.

They then came upon the village of Pirgos, held by some 200 Germans of the 2nd Parachute Regiment. A platoon member recalled:

Jerry had taken up vantage points in the houses. We slowly blasted our way from house to house, wiping out one nest after another, while the snipers kept up a constant deadly fire.

Upham could hear a captured Bofors gun firing. Cautiously they approached and managed to keep the gunner's head down with a stream of fire. Upham crawled forward until he was in range and lobbed in a grenade that killed the gunner and damaged the gun. Upham wrote a vivid account of the action:

Went on meeting resistance in depth – in ditches, behind hedges, in the top and bottom stories of village buildings, fields and gardens on road beside the drome. The wire of 5 Brigade hindered our advance. There were also mines and booby traps which got a few of us. We did not know they were there.

There was Tommy gun and pistol fire and plenty of grenades and a lot of bayonet work which you don't often get in war. The amount of machinegun fire was never equalled. Fortunately a lot of it was high and the tracers enabled us to pick our way up and throw in grenades. We had heavy casualties but the Germans had much heavier. They were unprepared. Some were without trousers, some had no boots on. The Germans were hopeless in the dark. With another hour we could have reached the far side of the drome. We captured, as it was, a lot of machineguns, 2 Bofors were overrun and the guns destroyed. The POWs went back to 5 Brigade.

The village had been cleared but it was now daylight and the airfield had not been captured. Outnumbered, the New Zealanders were forced to withdraw. During the attack, D Company had become isolated and had not heard the order to fall back. Upham and his sergeant volunteered to go looking for the missing company. Making their way through about 600 yards of enemy-held ground, they found that D Company had already retired but on the return they found some men of B Company, who had been isolated, and brought them safely back.

Upham's day was not yet done. Despite being weakened by sickness, he and his men twice went into Pirgos looking for wounded soldiers and brought some of the badly wounded back carried on wooden doors. In the afternoon, to add to his dysentery, he was wounded in the shoulder by a piece of shrapnel from a mortar bomb. After refusing to go to the field hospital, he allowed a fellow soldier to cut it out with a knife. Only then did he allow the medics to patch him up but he was unable to shoulder a rifle.

Six days later, the order came for a further retreat. Upham was on his way to warn other troops that they were in danger of being cut off. In view of his men, he was seen to fall after being shot at by two Germans hiding in an olive grove. Feigning death, he waited as the Germans approached. With one wounded arm in a sling, he used the crook of a tree to support his rifle. He shot one assailant and reloaded awkwardly as the German closed in on him. He managed to kill the second, who was close enough to fall on the barrel of Upham's rifle.

With no artillery or aircraft, the belated order came to evacuate the island. For Upham it must have been agony as he climbed the 40 miles over the White Mountains to the south and the small port of Sphakia. There is a photograph of him riding a donkey, which was probably his mode of transport on this harrowing journey.

The track they took was steep and rough. The Germans harried them all the way with unopposed strafing runs, which resulted in many casualties. The more serious wounded had to be left behind in caves to hope for humane treatment from the enemy soldiers.

On reaching Sphakia, Upham was once again called into action. On 30 May, about fifty heavily armed Germans managed to outflank the New Zealanders and travel down a narrow ravine lined with rhododendron bushes towards the evacuation beach. They began shooting in an effort to panic the troops. Colonel Kippenberger quickly countered this attack, sending 18th Battalion to the eastern side of the ravine while A Company of the 20th Battalion blocked the ravine's mouth. Upham was ordered to take C Company on to the western slope to attack the enemy's flank.

It took them nearly two hours to cover 2 miles of hard climbing to reach their position. Upham was still suffering from sickness and added to this was a bullet that had lodged in his foot a week before. The party worked above and around the trapped Germans and began firing down on them. With little cover, the enemy were wiped out. The sides of the ravine were so steep that the Bren gunner had to be held by the legs so he could lean over far enough to fire his gun.

That night and the following night the evacuations continued but not all the men could be taken off the beaches and some 6,500 went into captivity. Priority was given to the New Zealanders and Australians and many British soldiers were left behind. General Mark Clark wrote in his book, *Calculated Risk*:

> Dominion troops who are very jealous of their prerogatives ... have always been given special consideration by the British ... The British were exceedingly careful in the handling of New Zealand forces because they were territorial troops responsible only to their home government and it was necessary to use tact to work harmoniously with them.

One man who had been left behind made a remarkable escape. Gathering a small party of eighteen together, Royal Marine Major Ralph Garrett put to sea in an abandoned landing craft, which after ten gruelling days reached Egypt.

A very sick Charles Upham returned to Egypt, where his condition could be treated properly. Colonel Kippenberger drafted a recommendation for a VC based on many eyewitness statements and Upham's citation appeared in *The London Gazette* on 10 October 1941.

General Sir Claude Auchinleck presented Upham with his VC ribbon at a ceremonial parade in early November. Careless with his appearance to the last, it was noted that Upham was wearing yellow socks instead of the regulation issue. He also forgot to salute Auchinleck as he marched off the parade ground.

Upham did not enjoy his status as a VC recipient and refused to wear his ribbon until Kippenberger ordered him to do so. For someone so self-effacing, within a year he was again awarded a second Victoria Cross.

Alfred Sephton VC

Alfred Edward Sephton was born on 19 April 1911 at 30 Collier Street, Warrington, Lancashire, one of six children to Alfred Joseph Sephton, a journeyman blacksmith and his wife, Annie (née Ryder). When he was one year old, the family moved to Wolverhampton, where Alfred was educated at the Council School. When he was seventeen, he joined the Royal Navy as a boy and by 1939 he had risen to petty officer.

He joined HMS *Coventry*, a First World War light cruiser, which was a ship with colourful past. During the 1920s she was the flagship of Rear Admiral Andrew Cunningham, later Second World War Commander-in-Chief Mediterranean Fleet. In Gibraltar during 1923, an accidental torpedo explosion caused two deaths and some damage. While serving off the Shetlands at the outbreak of the war, she was damaged by German bombers and had to have a refit.

In an effort to prevent the German troops reaching Crete by sea, the Royal Navy sent cruisers and destroyers to block such a move. The consequence was that the Luftwaffe, with its superior numbers of aircraft, sank eight British warships during May; the light cruisers *Gloucester* and *Fiji*, and the destroyers *Kelly*, *Greyhound*, *Kashmir*, *Hereward*, *Imperial* and *Juno*. Seven other ships were damaged, including the battleships *Warspite* and *Valiant* and the light cruiser *Orion*. In all, nearly 2,000 sailors died.

During her refit, HMS *Coventry* had been converted to an anti-aircraft ship armed with ten 4in high-angled guns, several pom-poms and Oerlikons, making her into a formidable floating flak battery. Her guns were directed at incoming aircraft by two director-towers, which calculated speed, course and range and passed the information to the guns' crews. Both director-towers were in exposed positions, one of which contained a crew of Lieutenant J.M. Robb, C.P.O. Davenport, P.O. Alfred Sephton, Able Seaman Fisher and Marine Corporal Symmons.

The Navy ships were also covering the evacuation of Crete, which was under constant Axis attack from land and air. On 18 May while patrolling off Crete, *Coventry* along with HMS *Phoebe*, received an SOS message that the hospital ship, *Aba*, was being attacked south-east of Crete by dive bombers despite displaying red crosses. The Luftwaffe had already sunk four hospital ships and machine-gunned survivors struggling in the sea so the men on *Coventry* were determined to see off this heinous attack on a humanitarian vessel.

The two vessels reached *Aba* at 1745 hours as another wave of Junkers Ju 87 Stukas started their attack. As they approached, some of the dive-bombers broke off their attack and headed for the *Coventry*. Attacking in pairs, the Stukas went into a 375mph dive to the accompaniment of their terrifying wailing sirens, dubbed 'Jericho's trumpet'. The *Coventry*'s captain threw his ship violently side to side while every gun put up a terrific barrage. The first direct attack came from astern and the Stuka sprayed the ship with machine gun fire while its bomb landed close to port.

P.O. Sephton was a layer in 'B' director-tower, just behind the mainmast. The machine gun burst had penetrated the vulnerable director-tower and fatally wounded Sephton, with the bullet passing through his body and injuring A.B. Fisher sitting behind him.

Sephton reported to Lieutenant Robb that he had been hit but could carry on. Despite the great pain, blood loss and being partially blinded, Sephton knew he had been mortally wounded but the cramped space in the director-tower meant he could not be recovered until after the action. Stoically, he remained at his post and carried on his gun-laying duty until the Stukas flew away. Throughout the action the *Coventry* avoided being hit. Sephton was the only fatality but he insisted that Fisher be taken to the sickbay first.

Ten minutes after the attack, Sephton was relieved but no one knew how badly he had been wounded. He refused any assistance as he climbed out of the director tower but on reaching the deck, he collapsed. Taken to the sickbay, it was obvious that nothing could be done except to make Sephton as comfortable as possible. He died the next day from extensive internal injuries and was buried at sea.

Alfred Sephton was recommended for a Victoria Cross and his citation appeared in *The London Gazette* dated 2 December 1941. The final line of the citation read:

> His high example inspired his shipmates and will live in their memory.

His parents collected his posthumous Cross on 23 June 1942 from the King at Buckingham Palace. After the war, when Coventry Cathedral had been rebuilt within its ruins, Sephton's Victoria Cross was put on display in its precincts. Pointlessly, it was stolen on 25 September 1990 and has never been recovered. It has still not dawned on thieves that stealing a Victoria Cross will not benefit them as the award is so special and well-known that no collector would be tempted to add it to their collection.

Chapter 3

The Syrian VCs

One of the least known of the North African operations involved
the Australian 7th Division, which was stationed in Palestine. It
was there for a dual purpose; keeping an eye on the tense situation
between Arab and Jew and training for the Desert Campaign. The
campaign was fought in Lebanon and Syria against the erstwhile
ally, France, which had been granted a League of Nations mandate
over the area in 1919. When the French surrendered to the Germans,
an armistice was signed on 22 June 1940 establishing a German
occupation zone in northern and western France encompassing the
Atlantic and English Channel ports and leaving the remainder 'free'
to be governed by the French.

The pro-German French chose the small spa town of Vichy as their
administration centre, a situation that lasted until the Allied invasion
in 1944. All French colonies were governed by Vichy France, including
Syria and Lebanon, which were acting as *de facto* client states of
Germany.

The British invasion of Syria and Lebanon was aimed at preventing
Nazi Germany from using the Vichy French-controlled Syrian Republic
and French Lebanon for attacks on Egypt. In addition, the leaders of a
nationalist uprising in neighbouring Iraq appealed for help from the
Nazis who, with Vichy French consent, sent several aircraft to Syria.
The British government became concerned about German influence
creeping into the Middle East and Churchill ordered General Wavell to
send men from his Western Desert Force to occupy Syria and Lebanon.
Wavell was reluctant to further weaken his army, which was occupied
in clearing the Italians from Cyrenaica. He had already complied with
Churchill's orders in sending men to Greece only for that to end in
disaster with many troops being captured.

Unbeknown to Britain, Hitler had suspended any further operations in the Middle East – or least until he had dealt with the invasion of Russia. He had also considered the huge casualties the Germans had suffered in the Cretan Campaign for an island he considered unimportant compared with the mainland.

General Wavell did send a mixed force of 34,000 men from British, Indian and Free French units, but the largest force was 9,000 men from the 7th Australian Division. Commanding the expedition was British General Henry Maitland Wilson, who planned a three-pronged advance. The 21st Australian Brigade would advance north from Palestine, up the Lebanese coast with Beirut as its objective. The 25th Australian Brigade would advance on the large airfield at Rayak, while further east the 5th Indian Brigade and Free French Force would march on Damascus. The latter force must have been somewhat reluctant to enter into combat with their erstwhile comrades, even if they did follow a different doctrine. Once these three objectives had been attained, an advance on Tripoli, Homs and Palmyra would commence.

The invasion began on the night of 7 June with the expectancy that the Vichy French would quickly capitulate. In fact, shored up by the French Foreign Legion and tough colonial troops, the Allies met stiff resistance. Despite support offshore from naval ships, the coastal advance was held up on the Litani River. Inland progress was slowed by rugged terrain so that Wilson decided to transfer the bulk of his force to the coast.

The most rapid advance was by the Indian Brigade and the Free French as they progressed towards Damascus. This came to halt when the Vichy French launched attacks on their communication lines as they approached the city. A further transfer of forces finally led to the capture of Damascus, which fell on 21 June.

The towns of Ezraa, Kuneitra and Merdjayoun were recaptured by the Vichy French and it took a fierce fight before the Allies retook the first two on 18 June, although the latter remained in enemy hands. Emphasis was again centred on the coastal advance and the climactic battle of Damour, fought between 5 and 9 July. The Allies were only 10km from Beirut and the end of the fighting was in sight. On 12 July, the Vichy French Commander, General Henry Dentz, signed the armistice that brought the resistance to an end.

In this campaign, in which no one wanted to fight, two Victoria Crosses were awarded to members of the Australian force.

Roden Cutler VC

Arthur Roden Cutler was born on 24 May 1916 in the Sydney suburb of Manly, New South Wales (NSW), to Arthur William and Ruby (née Pope). He was educated at Sydney High School and graduated to the University of Sydney. Leaving with a law degree, he was employed by the NSW Justice Department. While at university, he had joined the Sydney University Regiment and with the outbreak of war was commissioned as a lieutenant in the 2/5th Field Regiment of the 7th Divisional Artillery.

On 19 October 1940 the regiment sailed for training in Egypt and Palestine. On 18 June 1941, the 7th Australian Division advanced north from Palestine along the coastal road towards Beirut. The following day the infantry attacked French positions at Merdjayoun. Cutler led an artillery forward observation team attached to the 2/25th Battalion that pushed forward under enemy machine gun fire to establish an outpost in an isolated hut.

Cutler went out to mend a telephone line that had been cut but when he returned his team came under an intense attack from Vichy French infantry and two tanks. His Bren gunner was killed and another was mortally wounded. Returning fire with anti-tank rifles, which were ineffective, they used the Bren gun to greater effect and succeeded in driving the attackers back.

The withdrawal was only temporary as the French returned, with their tanks putting down a heavy fire. Cutler took up the anti-tank rifle and managed to hit a tank's turret and then its tracks. Once again, this forced the French to retreat. Taking the opportunity to escape the unequal contest, Cutler supervised the evacuation of the wounded.

With his small party, he hid among rocks just north-west of the town, from which the Foreign Legion were keeping the Australian infantry at bay. Although he was operating within the enemy's position, he directed his battery's fire on to it. His determination to pinpoint the enemy was crucial in forcing them to retreat. Under cover of darkness, Cutler was able to make his way back through the enemy lines to his battery.

On the night of 23–24 June, Lieutenant Cutler was in charge of a 25-pounder that was sent forward in front of the Australian infantry to deal with a troublesome anti-tank gun that was holding up the advance. Accurate fire destroyed the gun, which opened the way for the recapture of Merdjayoun.

Two weeks later, Cutler was attached to the 2/16th Battalion as a forward observation officer at the deciding battle of Damour. The Australians outflanked the Vichy French and established a roadblock on the road north towards Beirut. When his infantry's wireless would not work in the hilly country, Cutler volunteered to carry the telephone line to a forward position. On the way he was shot and severely injured in the leg. He lay isolated and exposed for twenty-six hours before he was found, by which time his leg had turned septic. Under guard, Vichy French prisoners carried him to the medical base, where there was no alternative but to amputate his gangrenous limb.

The battle for Damour was the last battle of the Syrian Campaign and on 12 July the Vichy French commander General Henri Dentz sought an armistice.

After he was invalided home, Cutler received his Victoria Cross from the Governor-General Lord Gowrie, a VC from the 1898 Sudan War. He first became State Secretary for the Returned Sailors', Soldiers' and Airmen's Imperial League of Australia and moved on to Assistant Deputy Director of the Australian Security Service.

After the war, Cutler began a long career in the diplomatic service, including several high-ranking positions such as Australian High Commissioner for New Zealand and Minister to Egypt. In the latter position he was present during the Suez Crisis and took the precaution of sending home all but four of his staff. The British Embassy was slower off the mark and became cut off and short of food. Cutler and his commercial secretary drove to the bazaar and bought rice and a whole sheep, which they smuggled into the embassy.

In December 1965 he was knighted by the Queen in what was his final diplomatic post. He returned to take up the position of Governor of New South Wales, which he served for fifteen years. When he retired, he served on the boards of several prominent businesses, including the State Bank of New South Wales. He was also the vice-chairman of the VC and GC Association and later the president from 1991. Towards the end of his life, he suffered from ill health and died on 22 February 2002. He was accorded the rare honour of a state funeral by the Government of New South Wales.

James Gordon VC

James Hanna (Heather) Gordon was born at Rockingham, Western Australia, on 7 March 1909, one of eight children born to William

Beattie Gordon, a state parliamentarian, and his wife, Harriet (née Scott). Growing up in rural Western Australia, Jim Gordon left school and worked at several jobs including droving, farming and gold mining.

On 26 April 1940, at the age of thirty-one, he lied about his age to join the Australian Imperial Force (AIF) so he could serve overseas. For some reason he also falsely gave his middle name as 'Heather' instead of 'Hanna'. Soon after, he married a local girl rejoicing in the name Myrtle Anzac Troy. He trained for five months before being sent to the Middle East in September 1940. In February 1941, he was assigned to 2/31st Battalion as part of the 7th Australian Division sent to prevent Nazi Germany using the Vichy French countries of Syria and Lebanon to ferment trouble in neighbouring Iraq. It was a campaign that was not well reported, mainly because it was fought against the French who until very recently had been the allies of the British.

On the night of 10 July in the last fight of the campaign, the 2/31st was confronted with an impossible situation. Just north of the town of Djezzine, in an area known for its waterfalls and pine forests, the terrain was rugged and easy to defend. Code-named 'Greenhill', this height rose almost sheer for 600ft; a formidable feature that overlooked the villages of Amatour and Badarane. Below was an 800ft wide dry *wadi* with no cover.

The approach was criss-crossed with gorges and precipices and it was about 2.30 am when the 2/31st arrived about 400 yards from Badarene to be met by heavy machinegun fire. This fire split the two leading platoons. The left platoon took cover in an olive grove but lost three men, including its officer. The one on the right, which included Gordon, were pinned down in the open, unable to move. The attack seemed to be in danger of stalling.

In a VC action that has been repeated several times by men in a lowly rank, Gordon decided that something needed to be done. He slithered forward on his stomach under machine gun bullets that passed over him and grenades that were thrown at him. With a deep breath, he rose and charged full tilt at the machine gun nest.

The crew, who were Senegalese colonial soldiers, lost their nerve at the sight of a single Australian soldier charging with a fixed bayonet. Before they could recover, Gordon had jumped into the gunner's position and bayoneted all four crew. With the main obstacle neutralised and the rest of the enemy demoralised, the 2/31st took Greenhill and this fierce firefight was over.

34

Gordon was recommended for the Victoria Cross, which was announced on 28 October 1941, and his investiture was held on 26 September 1942.

Gordon's war was not over. In March 1943, the 2/31st returned to Australia to take part in the grim fighting in Owen Stanley's campaign in Papua New Guinea. He was promoted to acting sergeant in July. During the advance on Lae on the Huon Peninsular of New Guinea in September, he led a charge against a machine gun nest. He was probably considered for a further decoration, possibly a VC, but no award was forthcoming. Instead, Gordon was phlegmatic about it, saying: 'Imagine what my cobbers would have called me then.'

Further service in the Markham and Ramu valleys followed but bouts of malaria brought him back to Australia and a lengthy spell of hospitalisation. He was finally discharged in February 1947. Life in 'civvy street' did not suit him and he re-joined the army in December 1947. He became an instructor and finally retired from the army in 1968 with the rank of warrant officer II. Even in retirement, he still retained connection with the army by acting as groundsman at Campbell Barracks, Swanbourne. He died on 19 July 1986 and was cremated with full military honours.

With the surrender of the Vichy French government, the Allies gained control of Lebanon and absorbed many of the many of the former enemy fighting units into the Free French Forces. As well as bringing to an end Lebanon and Syria involvement in the Second World War, it led directly to the recognition of independence for both these countries in 1943 and 1944 respectively.

The hard campaign had resulted in many casualties; the Allies 4,652 and the Vichy French an estimated 8,912.

Chapter 4

Early Victory and the Siege of Tobruk

While the Abyssinian Campaign was being played out, the Italians were massing in Cyrenaica on the Egyptian border. General Wavell had command of about 86,000 troops spread thinly throughout Iraq, Palestine, Iran, East Africa and on the Libyan frontier. The focus fell on the last mentioned, where just 36,000 British, New Zealand and Indian troops faced nearly 250,000 Italians under Marshal Rodolfo Graziani. In fact, the British chose their forward position at the easier defended position at the coastal town of Mersa Matruh, set back 120 miles inside the Egyptian frontier.

It took Graziani a month after being instructed by Mussolini to advance into Egypt. On 13 September 1940, with some reluctance he ordered six divisions forward until they reached Sidi Barrani, just short of Mersa Matruh. Here he halted to establish a chain of fortified camps, which were too widely separated to support each other. Wavell decided to penetrate the gaps and attack the camps from the west, the undefended side. Rather than a sustained offensive, these were large-scale raids aimed at unsettling the Italians, who had not expected being attacked from their rear.

After the threat of a German invasion on Britain had eased, Wavell began to receive the reinforcements he had craved. An additional 126,000 Commonwealth troops arrived in Egypt from Britain, Australia, New Zealand and India, together with tanks and artillery. On 9 December 1940, the Western Desert Force under the command of Lieutenant General Richard O'Connor attacked the Italians at Sidi Barrani and pushed them back into Cyrenaica. O'Connor felt confident of totally defeating the Italian army now the British were equipped

36

with fifty heavily armoured Matilda tanks that could outclass the Italians' lightly armoured tanks and were impervious to their anti-tank weapons.

By 22 January 1941, the British forces were within 20 miles of Derna and it was becoming clear that the Italians were preparing to leave Cyrenaica. With Wavell's blessing, General O'Connor launched Operation *Compass*. In a master stroke, he sent a flying column from the 7th Armoured Division in a wide flanking sweep into the desert and established a roadblock at the Beda Fomm–Sidi Salah area to the south of Benghazi. At the same time he would press the retreating Italians back along the coastal route.

On 5 February the Italians were staggered to find their way blocked by a force numbering just 2,000. Instead of trying to outflank them, the Italians resorted to a frontal attack. In a battle that lasted until 9 February, the Italians surrendered 20,000 of their soldiers and great quantities of weapons and supplies. In just thirty hours, the 7th Armoured, 'the Desert Rats', had advanced across 150 miles of unmapped desert. Short of water, petrol and without hope of reinforcements, they fought and destroyed an army many times their number. Alluding to their passion for hunting, O'Connor sent a message to Wavell: 'Fox killed in the open!'

The further west the British travelled the more extended became their supply line. Their tanks and wheeled vehicles were wearing out in the sandy conditions and in urgent need of a refit. Two months later the tide had completely turned, with the enemy once again on the Egyptian border.

On the point of the Allies finally expelling the Italians from Libya, Hitler stepped in to shore up his ally. Two German divisions crossed from Italy into Libya, becoming known as the famed Afrika Korps, and placed under the command of Brigadier General Erwin Rommel. In addition, a further two Italian divisions were sent. By the end of March 1941, Rommel attacked El Agheila and from there embarked on Operation *Sonnenblume*, to expel the British from Libya and, hopefully, capture Cairo.

To exacerbate the fragility of the British position, Churchill ordered Wavell to withdraw many of his troops from Cyrenaica and send them to Greece. Reluctantly complying with his political master, Wavell oversaw the rapid retreat of the seemingly victorious British army back to the Egyptian border.

General O'Connor was replaced by Lieutenant General Philip Neame VC as commander of the Western Desert Force, but his tenure was brief. On the night of 6 April, along with O'Connor who had been sent to brief him, the two generals were captured by the Germans in their unescorted staff car.

The Western Desert Force on its sweep west through Libya had captured the small port of Tobruk just 60 miles inside the Libyan border. It was decided to reinforce and garrison the port to deprive the Axis of a supply port closer to the Egyptian border than Benghazi, some 550 miles further west. The siege, which lasted for 241 days from 10 April to 27 November, tied up enemy troops needed at the frontier. It became a heroic symbol for the Allies and an irritant to the Axis.

Under the command of Major General Morshead, Tobruk with its 35-mile perimeter was manned by British tanks, artillery, infantry and also the 9th Australian Division. It was not possible to operate aircraft from there as they would be destroyed within minutes of landing by Axis aircraft from El Adem airfield, just five minutes away. So close indeed, that those on the perimeter could hear the aircraft warming up.

Tobruk town was a maze of broken, tottering buildings. Shells fell constantly among the wrecks in the harbour. All supplies by sea were carried and delivered at night, as were the swapping of reliefs at the front. There were some 25,000 men within the perimeter, who were supplied with everything from ammunition to cigarettes by the naval and merchant ships.

Three days into the siege saw the awarding of the first Second World War Victoria Cross to an Australian and for the North African Campaign.

John Edmondson VC

John Hurst Edmondson was born at Wagga Wagga in New South Wales on 8 October 1914 to Joseph William and Maude Elizabeth. The family bought a farm when John was a child and moved to Liverpool, 20 miles south-west of Sydney. When he left school, John worked on the farm until the age of twenty-six. In 1939, at the start of the war, he joined the 4th Battalion Australian Rifles of the Citizen Military Force. This was but a step to enlisting in the 2/17th Battalion the following year. He was promoted to corporal and sailed for Palestine on 19 October 1940.

In January 1941, the battalion moved to Port Said for guard duty on the Suez Canal before joining the 20th Brigade of the 9th Australian

Division and moving to the British front at Mersa Matruh. From there they joined General O'Connor's advance into Libya and replaced the 7th Australian Division, which was part of the army sent to Greece. The forward movement was brief, for Rommel and the Afrika Korps quickly reversed the momentum and the 2/17th Battalion, along with the rest of the 20th Brigade, withdrew to Tobruk.

The siege began on 11 April. The Australians were supported by the tanks, engineers and artillery of the British Army. Tobruk was not just an all-military garrison for there were 6,000 prisoners of war and refugees to care for, although most were shipped out by sea over the next few weeks.

In anticipation of an attack, John Edmondson and D Company 2/17th were positioned behind the wire south-west of Tobruk town. On Easter Sunday, 13 April, about thirty Germans quietly broke through the wire and set up a good firing position to cover the tanks that would be following them through the gap. They were armed with at least six machine guns, mortars and two small field pieces. Spotted by D Company, its platoon commander, Lieutenant Mackell decided to break up the German party with a bayonet charge.

Silently, the platoon moved to take the enemy's flank, but was spotted and the Germans put down a heavy machine gun fire. With cover fire from those left behind, Mackell led his yelling men in a bayonet and grenade charge. Met with almost point-blank firing, Corporal Edmondson was twice wounded, in the stomach and neck, but pure adrenaline kept him moving forward until the platoons closed with the Germans. In the noisy, deadly brawl that followed, Edmondson killed one of the enemy and was tussling with another when he heard Mackell call out: 'Jack'. The officer was on the ground fighting with a German who had been bayoneted. Another German was coming at him with a pistol and in a moment Mackell would be dead.

Edmondson, despite his painful wounds, moved quickly and bayoneted both Germans. By this time the Australians had so disorganised the Germans that they fled, leaving twelve dead. Two hours later, the Germans launched another attack with armour and a desperate tank, artillery and infantry battle was fought inside the wire. Gradually the enemy was forced back and the gap closed.

Edmondson had been mortally wounded and there was little the medics could do for him. He died the next morning and was buried in the Tobruk Cemetery. He was recommended for the Victoria Cross, which ran into the objections of the aforementioned Military Secretary, Major

General Floyer-Acland, who was suspicious of spontaneous displays of gallantry as opposed to long, sustained courage and endurance. In the event, his views were not upheld and Edmondson's citation appeared in *The London Gazette* on 4 July 1941. His Cross was presented to his mother on 27 September 1941 by the Governor-General, Lord Gowrie. John Edmondson's Cross is displayed at the Australian War Memorial in Canberra.

Chapter 5

Disastrous Prelude – Operation Flipper

General Wavell put in motion Operation *Battleaxe* to clear the enemy from eastern Cyrenaica and to relieve the defenders of Tobruk. The operation failed because Rommel had built a strong defensive position that broke the British attack. The 7th Armoured Division spread its tanks across a wide front and on the first day of the battle the British lost half of them. They had taken possession of the new A15 Crusader tank with its ineffective 2-pounder gun, which proved no match for the German Panzers and the 88mm anti-tank guns. On the second day the British managed to repulse a big German counter-attack but on the third day they narrowly avoided annihilation before returning to their original position in Egypt.

It came as little surprise to Wavell that he was replaced by Lieutenant General Claude Auchinleck. In fact, the two swapped roles and Wavell took over as Commander-in-Chief India. After the initial and unexpected successes against the Italians in North Africa, the British Army had been pushed out of Libya. By November 1941, the main British army was holding a defensive position along the Italian-built double-wire fence known as 'the Wire' along the Egyptian–Libyan frontier. The Western Desert Force was rebranded with the new title of Eighth Army. This was commanded by Lieutenant General Sir Alan Cunningham, rewarded for his successful Abyssinian Campaign. His opposite number was General Erwin Rommel, who was to be responsible for the high turnover of British commanders in the next couple of years. He had been sent by Hitler ten months earlier, together with a huge force of tanks, infantry and aircraft. Although preoccupied with his Russian venture, Hitler felt duty-bound to help his Italian allies, who had suffered a humiliating defeat at the hands of a much smaller British army.

General Auchinleck mounted Operation *Crusader* to disrupt and destroy the Axis forces before they could begin their anticipated invasion of Egypt. Sixty miles from the border lay the beleaguered port of Tobruk, whose determined defence was delaying Rommel's invasion plans. Cunningham's strategy was to send an armoured force through the Wire and sweep round the open southern flank and head north towards Sidi Rezegh, an area of stepped plateaus about 10 miles from the coast. At a given signal, the British 70th Division, holding Tobruk, would advance and endeavour to link up with the 7th Armoured Division. The New Zealand Division was then to advance from the northern area of the frontier.

In tandem with this operation was an audacious plan to further disrupt the Axis, which resulted in the awarding of a posthumous Victoria Cross.

Geoffrey Keyes VC

Geoffrey Charles Tasker Keyes was born on 18 May 1917 at Aberdour in Fife. After the birth of three girls, he was the son Rear Admiral Roger Keyes and his wife, Eva (nèe Bowlby), hoped for. He was joined by a brother, Roger, in 1919. Geoffrey's father, who was one of the leading seamen on his day, had masterminded the famous St George's Day raid on Zeebrugge in 1918. The family moved in elevated circles as Admiral Keyes served as a naval aide-de-camp to the King George V and rose to be Deputy Chief of Naval Staff, a Member of Parliament for Portsmouth, a baronet and, in the Second World War, Deputy of Combined Operations.

Geoffrey began his education at King's Mead preparatory school in Seaford, Sussex, before passing his exams for Eton in 1929. During his time at Eton he caught a severe case of measles, which affected his hearing. Added to this he also had myopia, forcing him to wear spectacles, and he developed a curvature of the spine, which restricted his ability to carry heavy objects. To his father's disappointment, these problems meant he was unable to join the Navy. In 1935, with possible paternal help, it was something of a surprise that Geoffrey managed to pass his medical and won a scholarship to RMC Sandhurst.

Geoffrey developed into a good horseman at the college. He was earmarked for joining the Royal Scots Greys when he qualified, which he did by finishing fourth in his year. He was duly commissioned into the Scots Greys and so followed his uncle, who had been killed in 1916, into the regiment. He found that his uncle's full dress uniform, which had hardly been worn, fitted him perfectly and was a better quality than contemporarily materials. His father, already disappointed that his son had failed to follow him into the Navy, was further disapproving that he had joined the Scots Greys, whose officers he felt were the sons of businessmen and therefore 'trade'. Further, he felt it would have been far more acceptable for him to have joined the Life Guards.

Peacetime soldiering was a cavalryman's paradise: hunting, gymkhanas, polo, and exercises against other cavalry regiments, usually ending in a free-for-all. This came to an end when the regiment was sent to Palestine in 1938 to try to keep the Arabs and Jews from slaughtering each other. When the Second World War began in September 1939, Keyes wanted to become more involved and even contemplated taking part in the Winter War in Finland but this ended before he could do so. Instead, he applied as a liaison officer to the French Chasseurs Alpins in the Anglo–French intervention in Norway.

The French arrived on 26 April and were involved in several skirmishes with the Germans, culminating in the fight for Narvik. Without artillery and adequate air cover, the Allies stood little chance against the Germans, who could call on superior reinforcements. News of Belgium's surrender and the dire situation in France decided the Allies to evacuate from Norway. Although brief, Keyes' Norwegian service had proved that he wanted to be involved in any action and he was not just a dilettante cavalry officer.

After the withdrawal from France, Britain stood alone with a large and ill-equipped Army. General Sir John Dill, Chief of the Imperial General Staff, declared: 'We must find some way of helping the Army to exercise its offensive spirit once again.' Winston Churchill suggested that there should be irregular troops to mount lightning raids to boost morale at home and with the subjugated Europeans. Churchill called on his old friend to organise this and to Admiral Keyes' delight, he was appointed Director of Combined Operations (DCO). He took charge of all Commandos and independent companies and their first success was an operation in the Lofoten Islands off Norway.

After his brief liaison appointment in Norway, Geoffrey sought to join the Commandos and wrote to his father about his wish. Admiral Keyes wrote back:

> I have given instructions that you are to be entered. Isn't it marvellous, my best beloved first born; but I am glad you started it not I … fortunately W (Winston) is placing his faith in me.

Geoffrey joined the 11th Scottish Commandos, taking with him a troop of Scots Greys and Royals, which he called his 'Cavaliers'. The training on Annan was hard and rigorous but there was still no objective in sight. After a while, some of the men asked to re-join their units so they could take part in the fighting in the Middle East. Geoffrey wrote in his letter to his father:

> It is all disappointing, so please fix us up Pop.

With little to keep them in Britain, the Commandos were sent to the Middle East as part of 'Layforce' under the command of Acting Brigadier Robert Laycock, a fiercely ambitious soldier.

11th Scottish Commandos' first taste of action was the invasion of Lebanon and Syria, which was now in the hands of the Vichy French, Britain's erstwhile ally. With the Australians advancing from Palestine, the Commandos put in a sea-borne attack on the Litani River to link up with them. One of the officers of No.7 Troop was Lieutenant Paddy Mayne, later to gain fame as a leader of the newly formed Special Air Service (SAS). In the stiff battle on the Litani, Geoffrey led an attack across the river, for which he was awarded the Military Cross (MC). At the age of twenty-four, Keyes was also promoted to lieutenant colonel, the youngest in the British Army.

Despite their success in Syria, the Commandos of Layforce began to be disbanded, with many joining the Long Range Desert Group (LRDG) and the Special Air Service. Geoffrey appealed to his father to retain a small unit of 110 volunteers while he looked around for a target to vindicate the existence of his group. In the meantime, his Scottish Commandos languished on Cyprus until there was a change of heart by the Chiefs of Staff with some prompting from Churchill. One of the objections the Chiefs of Staff voiced was that Admiral Keyes was too old and too senior to command shock troops in a modern war. To the chagrin of the senior Keyes, Churchill replaced him and appointed Lord Louis Mountbatten as Chief of Combined Operations.

About this time, Lieutenant Colonel Keyes had the idea of mounting a raid to destroy the enemy's leadership by capturing or killing Erwin Rommel. He learned from an officer he had known in the Scots Greys, who was now with the Special Operation Executive (SOE), that Rommel had been seen at an Afrika Korps headquarters in Beda Littoria near the coast about 250 miles from the front line. Armed with this sketchy information, Keyes went to see Lieutenant General Sir Alan Cunningham, commander of the Western Desert Forces. Keyes' valuable connections gained him access to Cunningham, who was won over by the audacious plan that, if successful, could shorten the North African Campaign.

Another SOE officer disguised as an Arab had spied out Beda Littoria from Jebel al-Akhdar, a heavily forested mountainous plateau that significantly has the heaviest rainfall in Libya. Through binoculars, officers who bore a resemblance to Rommel were seen around the building that was the German HQ. A reconnaissance of the beach was made by submarine and a small team was landed. Unfortunately, when they returned to the rendezvous point, a navigation error had placed the submarine in the wrong bay. Both the team and their boats were discovered, so another location for landing had to be made.

General Auchinleck's Operation *Crusader* was due to start on 18 November 1941 and at the same time two operations were mounted to cause the enemy maximum disruption.

One of the first operations carried out by David Stirling's SAS was an airborne raid on five enemy airfields. Instead of being driven in by the LRDG, the SAS would parachute close to the targets and destroy as many enemy aircraft as possible, so reducing the air threat to Operation *Crusader*. In one of the worst storms seen in Libya for sixty years, the pilot misjudged the drop zone and the parachutists were blown over a wide area along with their equipment. Unable to mount any sort of attack, the operation was called off.

Keyes's operation, code-named *Flipper*, timed to coordinate with Stirling's airdrop was badly affected by the same storm. Leaving in late afternoon on 10 November from Alexandria, the submarines HMS's *Torbay* and *Talisman* carrying Keyes, Captain Robin Campbell and Colonel Laycock with their Commandos arrived off the landing beach at Khashm-al-Kalib on the night of 13 November. The high wind and heavy seas made a successful landing an impossibility; several folboats (collapsible kayaks) were swept away from *Torbay*'s side, thus reducing the number of men that could be taken ashore. After six hours of struggle, Keyes arrived on the beach with Captain Robin Campbell and seventeen Commandos. Laycock, who had elected to remain and secure the beach, landed with a dozen men from *Talisman*. As less than half of his men had been able to land, Keyes was forced to amend his plans: instead of attacking four targets, he reduced them to two. No.2 Detachment was to sabotage the telephone and telecommunications at the Cyrene Cross Roads while No.1 Detachment went ahead with their raid on Rommel's villa at German Headquarters.

With about 18 miles to travel to their target, Keyes' party set off to cross the 3,000ft Jebel al-Akhdar range in the teeth of freezing wind and rain. The going was very tough over slippery, rock-strewn goat tracks and it did not help when the guide left them at midnight as he was afraid being caught in their company. Guided by poor maps and a compass, they rested for the following day in their sodden clothes before resuming their difficult night trek.

Finally, they reached a position where they surveyed Beda Littoria between lightning flashes and another deluge. Although they could not know it, intelligence was received in Cairo that Rommel was in Rome and was about to return to Libya. In any event, he would not have gone to Beda Littoria, which was too far from his front-line units, but to his HQ near Tobruk. Ignorant of this, No.1 Detachment's target was no longer the 'Desert Fox' but a Colonel Schleusener, the chief quartermaster of the Afrika Korps.

It was now midnight on a dark and stormy night when the attack went in. Captain Robin Campbell later recalled what happened:

> Geoffrey then led us through a hedge into the garden and we found ourselves at the back of the house. He posted Corporal Kearney and Private Hughes at the back door, which he had already tried and found locked. All the ground floor windows were high up and barred with heavy wooden shutters, so it was impossible to get in that way. There was no alternative but to use the front door. We followed him round the building on to a gravel sweep in front of the house. The front door was set back inside the porch, at the top of a flight of stone steps. Geoffrey ran up the steps. He was carrying a Colt, and I knocked on the door for him, demanding loudly in German to be let in. The door opened on a second pair of glass doors, and we were confronted by a German (officer I think) in a steel helmet and overcoat. Geoffrey at once closed with him, covering him with his Colt. The man seized the muzzle of Geoffrey's revolver and tried to wrest it from him. Before I or (Sgt) Terry could get round behind him he retreated, still holding on to Geoffrey, to a position with his back to the wall, and his either side protected by the first and second pair of doors at the entrance. He started to shout. Geoffrey could not draw a knife and neither I nor Terry could get around Geoffrey, as the doors were in the way, so

I shot the man with my .38 revolver, which I thought would make less noise than Geoffrey's Colt. Geoffrey then gave the order to use Tommy guns and grenades, since we had to presume that my revolver shots had been heard. (Geoffrey said that his arm had gone numb; perhaps the shots had chipped his elbow, or it may have been the wrestling match with the German had damaged it.)

We found ourselves, when we had time to look around, in a large hall with a stone floor; it had a stone stairway leading to the upper stories on the right.

The hall was dimly lit by a single bulb but Terry spotted a gleam of light from a doorway before it was hastily closed. At the same time, a man came clattering down the stairs and as his feet appeared, a burst from one of the Tommy guns sent him scampering back.

Geoffrey had been flinging open the doors on either side of the hall. We looked inside and found the rooms empty. He pointed to a light shining through the crack under the next door and inside were about ten Germans with steel helmets, some sitting and some standing. He fired two or three rounds with his Colt .45 automatic. I said 'Wait, I'll throw a grenade in.'

He slammed the door shut and held it while I got the pin out of the grenade (Sgt. Terry, who had closed the door behind them, afterwards said he heard the sound of heavy breathing inside the room.)

I said 'Right' and Geoffrey opened the door. I threw in the grenade, which I saw roll in the middle of the room, and Sergeant Terry gave a burst with his Tommy-gun. Before Geoffrey (who said 'Well done' as he saw the grenade go in) could shut the door the Germans fired. A bullet struck him just over the heart and he fell unconscious at the feet of myself and Terry.

Campbell dragged Keyes out of the house but found that he was already dead. He then made his way to the back of the house, forgetting he had ordered the sentries to shoot anyone coming that way. The two Commandos at the rear shot Campbell in the leg, breaking a bone. Now the raiding party was without an officer. Campbell was propped against a tree to await capture while Sergeant Terry was put in charge to take the rest of the men back to the beach.

Michael Asher, in his book *Get Rommel*, provides a different version of these events. He suggests that Keyes was accidentally shot by Campbell as he struggled with the German at the front door.

A non-propaganda German report states that both officers (Keyes and Campbell) were shot by their own men as the Germans only fired one shot during the raid.

Sergeant Terry managed to bring away the rest of the group and, after a difficult journey back over the Jebel al-Akhdar, they reached Colonel Laycock near the beach. The weather was still stormy and the sea too rough for HMS *Torbay* to collect the men. With German and Italian search parties closing in, Laycock finally ordered the men to split into small groups and try and make it back to their own lines. Some disappeared, presumed dead, and most were captured. Laycock, Terry and an SBS soldier survived in the Jebel until they were finally picked up by the British after forty days; the only ones to return safely.

Rommel, who had never stayed at Beda Littoria, sent his chaplain to organise a funeral for Keyes and four other dead Commandos. In a ceremony, the five were buried with full military honours: another reason for a sneaking admiration of the enemy's commander.

On returning to Cairo, Laycock recommended both Keyes and Terry for the Victoria Cross, even though he was not a witness to any of the action. In the event, Keyes received a posthumous Cross and Terry the Distinguished Conduct Medal. Although news of the raid generated much excitement among the British public hungry for some positive news, it does raise the question of why Keyes was awarded the highest gallantry award for leading a shambolic raid in appalling weather, which reduced his fighting strength, on the wrong target. As Terry faced the same odds as Keyes and brought the Commandos safely back to the beach, why was he awarded a lesser decoration?

There were enough outstanding raids behind enemy lines conducted by the LRDG and the newly formed SAS that went largely unrewarded. Doubtless Keyes was a brave officer but, as his father until weeks before had been the Director of Combined Operations, it did smack of nepotism and can be compared with the awarded of the Cross to Lieutenant Harry Havelock by his father General Havelock during the Indian Mutiny. Possibly at that time it was felt that the Commandos of Layforce needed the highest award to give them credibility to fend off disbandment.

Rather in the manner in which the defenders of Rorke's Drift were lavished with Victoria Crosses to divert attention from the mismanaged battle of Isandlwana, Keyes's VC deflected attention away from the costly failure of the raid. It also beggars the question why an act of gallantry has to be witnessed by officers when the only officer to recommend Keyes was 18 miles away?

Chapter 6

Operation Crusader (1)

Operation *Crusader*, with its huge series of battles, is one of the least known conflicts of the Second World War. It was to last from 17 November, when the British passed through the Wire, until 1 December, when the last brigade withdrew. It was a sprawling and confusing battle that was fought over an area roughly the size of East Anglia. Fought in winter conditions of bitterly cold winds that whipped up dense sandstorms, with sleet and rain that often turned the desert into a morass, it was an operation that very nearly defeated Rommel.

It was important to occupy the ground at Sidi Rezegh as it dominated the vital line of communication and threatened Rommel's assault on Tobruk. At this point, the desert descended to sea level in three giant steps, the risers of which constituted steep escarpments. This middle step, which contained an important Axis airfield, was 2½ miles wide and 7 miles long. Along the northern edge was a low rocky ridge. Below that on the third step was the Trig Capuzzo, the main communication road.

This account will concentrate on the main action at Sidi Rezegh, which involved 7th Support Group and the awarding of three Victoria Crosses to its members.

John Campbell VC

John Charles Campbell was born at Thurso, Caithness, on 10 January 1894 to Daniel and his wife, Marion, (née MacKay). He was educated at Sedbergh School and on the first day of the First World War, Jock as he was better known, volunteered for the Honourable Artillery Company. He was put forward for a commission and in July 1915 passed as a second lieutenant in the Royal Horse Artillery (RHA).

49

He was twice wounded in February and May 1916 and ended the war as a captain with a Military Cross. Campbell was an outstanding horseman and between the wars he served as an instructor at the Cavalry and Artillery Establishment for Equitation training at Weedon in Northamptonshire. This had been set up in 1922 despite the obvious vulnerability of horses on the battlefields of the First World War. Campbell was able to indulge his passion for hunting with the nearby Pytchley Hunt, ride point-to-point and play polo. He met and married a Northamptonshire resident, Rosamund Rhodes, a relative of Sir Cecil Rhodes, and together they produced two daughters. He was also put in charge of the British Equestrian Team at the 1936 Berlin Olympics.

The outbreak of the Second World War found Jock serving as a major in command of 'C' Battery, 4th Regiment RHA, in Egypt. The following year he succeeded to command the regiment and was soon able to distinguish himself under fire. His regiment was the artillery component of 7th Armoured Division's Support Group under command of Brigadier William 'Strafer' Gott. In September 1940, when the Italians began to advance, he handled his guns boldly during the retreat. He organised a number of mobile columns named 'Jock Columns' that attacked the Italian communications and were later used against the Afrika Korps. He was rewarded with the Distinguished Service Order (DSO). When the tide turned and the British chased the Italians back across Libya and, in turn, were chased back to Egypt, Jock was awarded a bar to his DSO for his readiness in covering the withdrawal.

In the autumn of 1941, Gott was appointed to command 7th Armoured Division (the original 'Desert Rats') and Jock was promoted to brigadier to take over command of 7th Support Group (SG). The 7th SG was composed of infantry and artillery and its purpose was to provide support for the armoured brigades and to hold ground. Campbell was charismatic, inspirational and popular with his men. One later commented: 'Whenever he was near me, I felt a brave man.'

Like most 'old Desert Hands' he dressed unconventionally, wearing corduroy trousers and a coloured scarf around his neck. In the coming battle, he would tie this to a walking stick, serving as a battle standard.

When Operation *Crusader* began in November 1941, Campbell's force followed the 7th Armoured Division as it moved across the Wire. On 19 November, the tanks of 7th Armoured arrived at the rim overlooking the middle step and beheld twenty-two Italian aircraft on the airfield below. Quickly descending, they captured the airfield and took prisoner the pilots and ground crew. Three planes did manage to take off but the remaining nineteen were put out of action by the simple method of driving the tanks over them.

On the morning of the 20th, the enemy occupied the ridge on the northern rim and the Germans opened a heavy barrage from more distant positions, including Ed Duda, the next objective. As the tanks could not hold the ground without infantry, the 7th Support Group was ordered to take over on the Sidi Rezegh shelf, while the tanks withdrew to the top plateau.

Ignoring the almost continuous fire, Campbell rode about in an open top staff car and set about disposing his command. It was stretched thinly over a distance of 5 miles with little cover. The ground was too rocky for digging trenches and it was fortunate that the enemy did not attack. Instead they contented themselves with heavy artillery fire and attacks by Stuka dive-bombers.

War correspondent Alan Moorhead witnessed the battle and in particular Campbell's role in it:

> In the east the Germans were counterattacking the airfield and Jock Campbell was like a man berserk. He led his tanks into action riding in an open unarmoured staff car, and as he stood there, hanging onto its windscreen, a huge well-built man with the English officer's stiff good looks, he shouted, 'There they come. Let them have it.' When the car began to fall behind, he leaped onto the side of a tank as it went forward and directed the battle from there. He turned aside through the enemy barrage to his own twenty-five pounder guns and urged the men on to faster loading and quicker firing. He shouted to his gunners, 'How are you doing? And was answered, 'Doing our best, sir.' He shouted back, grinning, 'Not good enough.'
>
> They say Campbell won the VC half a dozen times that day. The men loved this Elizabethan figure. He was the reality of all the pirate yarns and the tales of high adventure, and in the extremes of fear and courage of the battle he had only courage. He went laughing into the fighting.

The following day, the 7th Armoured Division planned to fight its way to the Ed Duda ridge, 6 miles to the north-west, and meet up with the 70th Division, which was to break out of Tobruk simultaneously. In the meantime, Rommel had recovered from the initial surprise of the British incursion behind his lines and had rushed reinforcements to the area. This included the 15th and 21st Panzers, who were approaching from the south, thus encircling Sidi Rezegh.

Just before dawn on 21st, Campbell's men advanced into battle positions before they could be observed by the enemy. In order for the advance on Ed Duda to begin, the low broken ridge along the northern rim had to be cleared by the infantry.

For Brigadier Jock Campbell, the battle was only halfway through. He had driven to whatever part of the Sidi Rezegh plateau was in the greatest danger. Now that the morning's fighting had died down, the Support Group removed the wounded, grabbed a quick meal and waited for the next assault. This came at 1515 hours and again from the east. This time two battalions of German infantry backed by the 8th Panzer Brigade advanced against a company of the Rifle Brigade. Because of the thick smoke and dust, they managed to get to within 1,000 yards of Campbell's command post. Driving to the remnants of 6th Royal Tank Regiment (RTR) and finding them under fire and with their turrets closed, he went along rapping on their hulls with his stick and ordering them to counter-attack.

Calling for them to follow, he led the tanks through shellfire, standing up in his open car and holding aloft his blue scarf. Within minutes, seven of the fourteen German tanks were on fire. The suddenness of the counter-attack surprised the Germans, who thought that dust clouds must conceal a much larger force of tanks. They halted and then withdrew. They were not to know that there were only twelve tanks left at Sidi Rezegh.

The following day the Germans captured the Sidi Rezegh ridge by moving in from the eastern and western flanks. That night, the 7th (SG) withdrew to the upper escarpment. Campbell was to again lead tanks into battle the following day. He also twice manned guns when the crews became casualties. During this fight, he received a wound in the upper arm.

In the ten days that followed, the men of 70th Division from Tobruk captured the Ed Duda ridge and linked up with the New Zealand Brigade. Conceding that they had lost too many tanks and that the Germans were receiving reinforcements, the British called off Operation *Crusader*, retreating behind the Wire, and the briefly liberated 70th Division returned to Tobruk.

Campbell was recommended for the Victoria Cross for his inspiring leadership that enabled his Support Group to withstand repeated attacks by superior forces and to inflict great losses on the enemy.

On 3 February 1942, his citation appeared in *The London Gazette* and he received his VC ribbon from General Auchinleck. He was also appointed to command the 7th Armoured Division with the rank of major general, but these two accolades quickly faded. Just three weeks later, on 26 February, Campbell died in a most mundane manner. Travelling near Bug, east of Tobruk, his staff car overturned in wet conditions and he was killed.

His Victoria Cross is held by the Royal Artillery Museum.

John Beeley VC

John Beeley was one of twin boys born in Openshaw, Manchester, on 8 February 1918 to William, who had served in the Lancashire Fusiliers in the First World War. After leaving Wheeler Street School, John trained as a stonemason before enlisting in The King's Royal Rifle Corps (KRRC) on 4 August 1938. He trained at the corps' base in Winchester and married a local girl, Betty Davy, who was serving in the Auxiliary Territorial Service (ATS).

At the beginning of the war, he was posted to Egypt with 1/KRRC as a Bren gunner in A Company. In November, his regiment made up part of the 7th Support Group under the command of Jock Campbell. As 400 men of three companies of the KRRC and a company of the Rifle Brigade picked their way through the wreckage on the Sidi Rezegh airfield they made their way towards the low ridge to the north. They were ordered to cross 2,000 yards of flat stony ground without cover and capture a 2-mile stretch of the ridge to allow the armour to get through.

Soon the German and Italian defenders opened up with machine guns and mortars and the riflemen took heavy casualties. After three and a half hours, supported by artillery and helped by smoke and dust, the soldiers managed to get within 100 yards of the ridge. A Company was opposite the most strongly held enemy position and pinned down by heavy fire. It was at this point that Rifleman Beeley performed his VC exploit.

Beeley had gone into battle pre-occupied with bad news from home, which may have prompted his extraordinary action. Pinned down by a strong point that contained an anti-tank gun and two machineguns, any advance seemed suicidal. Suddenly, Rifleman Beeley leapt to his feet and ran straight at the strong point, firing Bren gun bursts from the hip. Clambering among the rocks, he was hit but it did not stop him. Pausing 20 yards from the nest, he coolly aimed and opened fire, killing all seven Germans. He was almost immediately killed by fire from other positions.

His remarkable action spurred his comrades into charging forward and carrying the ridge, capturing about 800 prisoners. Beeley's single-handed action had enabled this important feature to be captured and was recognised with the posthumous awarding of the Victoria Cross. His widow received his Cross on 20 October 1942 from the King at Buckingham Palace. It is displayed at the Royal Green Jackets Museum, Winchester.

With the ridge taken, two squadrons of the 6th Royal Tank Regiment advanced down the second escarpment and headed for Ed Duda. They knocked out six enemy tanks before they advanced up the slope of Belhamed. As they breasted the rise, they were met with devastating fire from the assembled anti-tank guns, including the fearsome 88mm guns. The British Cruiser and Honey tanks were out-gunned and too lightly armoured, losing thirty of their number. When they withdrew, all that remained of 6RTR were seventeen tanks.

The infantry was left in a vulnerable position with the advancing armour and when the Germans counter-attacked the following day, they were overwhelmed. Only five officers and fifty other ranks managed to escape; the rest were captured.

While this was taking place, another desperate struggle was being fought out 4 miles to the east. Having advanced from the south-east, the 200 tanks of the German 15th and 21st Panzers had all but destroyed the 7th Hussars and 2RTR. Rommel had sent orders that they should hurry to counter the breakout from Tobruk by the 70th Division. In order to achieve this, they had to destroy the 7th Support Group on Sidi Rezegh.

While the main German armour had paused to replenish its ammunition and fuel, sixteen Panzers drove forward to ascertain the opposition. As they appeared over a rise, they were met with accurate fire from the gunners. Four of the tanks were set on fire and the remainder quickly retreated. During this phase in the battle there was another Victoria Cross action.

George Gunn VC

George Ward Gunn was born on 26 July 1912 at his grandparents' home of Calf Hall, Muggleswick, County Durham. His father had been born in Australia but had returned to England, qualifying as a doctor and surgeon. Soon after George's birth the family moved into their new home built at Church Road, Neston, on the Wirral. George was first educated at Mostyn House School, where his father was, among other institutions, the medical officer. Later George and his three brothers were sent to board at Sedbergh School in Yorkshire, where they collectively became known prophetically as the 'Gunn Battery'. George became one of four Sedbergh School VCs. The others were Kenneth Campbell, Robert Digby-Jones and Gunn's CO, Jock Campbell.

After leaving school, Gunn trained to be a chartered accountant and passed his finals in 1938. He joined the firm Sissons & Co in the City of London as an accountant and company secretary. This did not last long for he joined the Royal Artillery on in December 1939. In August 1940 he was commissioned and posted to the 3rd Regiment RHA. He was described as of slight build, good looking, charming and sporting a fashionable moustache with turned up ends.

His regiment was sent out to the Middle East and during the retreat from Benghazi Gunn found himself in beleaguered Tobruk in January 1941, where he won the Military Cross and his citation was published in *The London Gazette* dated 6 May 1941:

> He displayed sustained gallantry and coolness which inspired all ranks under heavy and close enemy fire on a number of occasions, and participated on January 4th and 5th as one of the heroic Tobruk garrison.

His regiment was evacuated by sea on 21 September 1941 and re-joined 3 RHA. As part of Jock Campbell's 7th Support Group, 'A' Troop, 'J' Battery RHA was commanded by twenty-nine year old 2nd Lieutenant George Ward Gunn. He had acquired the *panache* of a horse-gunner and wore a silk scarf and the colourful RA mess cap rather than regulation khaki. On 21 November, Gunn's 'A' Troop was positioned near the foot of the upper escarpment when some fifty Panzers appeared. They were brought to a surprised halt by the fire from the 25-pounders of the 60th Field Regiment. Standing off at a range of about 2,000 yards and supported by their artillery, the Germans began to pound the British gunners. The RHA then attempted to get close enough to get within effective range and also to distract the enemy's aim. So began one of the greatest anti-tank contests of the war.

The RHA were equipped with 2-pounders mounted on 'portees', the flatbeds of open, low-slung Chevrolet lorries. Gunn's troop began to manoeuvre his guns forward to reduce the range, which invited a concentration of enemy fire. The four trucks were set on fire but the gunners continued to fire, change position and open fire again. One by one, the 2-pounders were taken out of action as their crews were killed or wounded. Gunn was riding from gun to gun in a small command truck, directing fire and encouraging his men.

Finally, all but one of the crew of the surviving gun was killed and a Sergeant Grey began to drive the portee away. The commander of 'J' Battery, Major Bernard Pinney, shouted to Gunn to stop the portee, which he did. Pulling aside the dead crew, Gunn and Grey manned the gun themselves, the former serving the gun and the latter acting as loader. Despite the portee being on fire, Gunn scored two hits, setting the enemy tanks alight. Meanwhile, Major Pinney attempted to fight the fire.

Ignoring the heavy enemy fire from the front and the flames threatening to ignite the ammunition behind, Gunn fired off about fifty rounds before being shot through the forehead. Pinney pulled Gunn aside and fired off a few more rounds until the gun was hit and put out of action. Unable to do continue fighting, Pinney then drove the portee away.

The following day, Major Pinney was struck by shrapnel and killed. Both he and Gunn were recommended for the Victoria Cross, but only Gunn was awarded it. It is also interesting that Pinney's role, which witnesses say was significant, is hardly alluded to in Gunn's citation. Gunn's daring and aggression was contributory to the Panzers withdrawing and leaving the 7th Support Group still in possession of Sidi Rezegh. Gunn's VC was presented to his parents on 20 October 1942 by the King and is now part of the Royal Artillery Museum's collection.

J Battery was further honoured with a change of title to 'Sidi Rezegh Battery' and in honour of Gunn's VC the cipher is backed by VC crimson.

Two of his brothers had interesting military careers. His younger brother was a medical officer who served in the SAS until he was killed in a car accident in 1944. Another brother served as a doctor with the Chindits in Burma and went to become an eminent orthopaedic surgeon after the war.

Chapter 7

Operation Crusader (2)

The second aim of Operation *Crusader* was to link up the 70th Division inserted into Tobruk in September. The 2nd New Zealand Division crossed the Wire in the north and successfully managed to link up with the 70th on 26 November. It was a meeting that lasted for just four days before Rommel launched a ferocious attack on the Kiwis that drove them back eastwards to their original position. It was the most costly in terms of casualties for the Kiwis, who had 878 men killed and 1,700 wounded.

The 70th Division was not strong enough to withstand the Germans and returned to its former positions around Tobruk. In the course of the link-up, two Victoria Crosses were awarded.

Philip Gardner VC

Philip John Gardner was born on Christmas Day 1914 at 37 Trewsbury Road, Sydenham, London. He had two older sisters and his father, Stanley, who ran the family engineering firm, J. Gardner & Co. Ltd., would have been delighted to have an heir to carry on the business. Philip, or Pip as he was usually known, was educated as a day-boy at Dulwich College, where his best subjects were maths and science, which enabled him to study engineering. He was an enthusiastic rugby player and also won prizes for rifle-shooting. He also enjoyed his involvement in the school's Officer Training Corps.

Without any coercion, Pip joined the family business, having a love and aptitude for engineering. As with most sons of proprietors, he began on the factory floor and graduated to the drawing office. By January 1934, he was experienced enough to be working as draughtsman in charge of a large building in Oxford Street. It was as a result of the competent way he handled this project that his father offered him a job in Hong Kong overseeing the installation of air conditioning in the new Hong Kong and Shanghai Bank building. This was the first such installation on the island. Gardner was to engineer the ducting, which was a considerable responsibility for a nineteen-year-old.

Leaving by steamer in May, the journey took five weeks. Soon after he arrived, he was told that the skilled metal worker from England who was to set up a small factory to produce the sheet metalwork was not coming. It then fell to Gardner to start up a factory that eventually employed more than 100 workers: a true baptism of fire for the teenager.

Gardener spent eighteen months in Hong Kong and enjoyed a full social life. He joined the Hong Kong Volunteers as a member of the Armoured Car Section; a precursor of things to come. By November 1935, his work in Hong Kong had come to an end and Gardner decided to make his way back home by completing a circuit of the world. The young man travelled by train through China, Manchuria and Korea. He crossed to Japan, which he explored by train, before catching a boat to Honolulu and then to California. After seeing Hollywood in its heyday, Gardner boarded a ship that took him through the Panama Canal to Cuba and then on to New York. He sailed for England and reached home in time to celebrate his twenty-first birthday, having experienced an opportunity granted to few men of his age.

When Hitler annexed Austria and half of Czechoslovakia there was a movement in Britain to join the Territorial Army. Gardner, with his engineering bent and previous experience in Hong Kong, joined an armoured unit, the Westminster Dragoons.

On 3 June 1939, Gardner married Renée Sheburn and they honeymooned in Paris. Married life had to be suspended when he reported to the Westminster Dragoons depot on 3 September. Four days later he was at Blackdown Barracks, training to become an officer in the Royal Tank Regiment. In March 1940, he was commissioned as a subaltern but became frustrated because there were no tanks available for him to man. As a consequence, he found himself on an anti-aircraft site in Dorset.

With little immediate prospect of commanding a tank, Gardner volunteered for the newly formed Commandos. He was appointed to 4 Commando and sent to Scotland for training. At the beginning of December instructions were received that trained Royal Armoured Corps personnel were recalled to their units as replacement tanks were starting to arrive in significant numbers. Gardner's commando days were over and he was about to revert to what he had been trained for – tank warfare.

With the threat of invasion abated after the heroics of Fighter Command during the autumn of 1940, it was decided to send the tanks and armoured cars to where they could be effectively employed, which was against the Axis forces in North Africa.

Gardner embarked on a troopship on 3 January 1941 and after the long voyage around the African coast, arrived in Egypt on 10 March. He was assigned to the 4th Royal Tank Regiment and given command of a troop of Matilda tanks.

In December 1940, General Sir Archibald Wavell had started the campaign that had spectacularly pushed the Italians west across Libya until virtually the whole of Cyrenaica was in British hands. Unfortunately, by the time Gardner and his comrades arrived, the situation had undergone a considerable change.

In February 1941, the Afrika Korps under the command of Rommel, arrived in Tripoli to bolster crumbling Italian resistance. At the end of March, he had turned the tide and, by the end of April, Rommel had pushed Wavell's army back to the Libyan–Egyptian border. During Rommel's initial advance, a large number of British and Commonwealth prisoners were taken, including no fewer than four of Wavell's generals; Lieutenant General Philip Neame VC, Major General Carton de Wiart VC, Lieutenant General Richard O'Connor and Major General Gambier-Parry.

The only Libyan foothold retained by the British was the port of Tobruk, some 70–80 miles behind enemy-held territory.

Against his better judgement, General Wavell was put under strong pressure to relieve the Tobruk garrison and return to Cyrenaica. His first aim was to attack Fort Capuzzo, which barred the way to Bardia and ultimately to Tobruk. Part of the plan was for a frontal assault on Halfaya Pass, which was to be carried out by the 11th Indian Brigade. Tank support was provided by two troops from 4th RTC totalling six Matilda tanks, each troop commanded by Lieutenant Tom Rowe and Second Lieutenant Pip Gardner.

As the six tanks moved forward to their starting point, they were attacked by Stuka dive-bombers, which swooped down making a frightening wail as they dropped their bombs. Fortunately the Matildas weathered the attack unscathed.

At dawn the six Matildas crossed the start-line and advanced towards the unseen enemy across the flat desert ahead. Very soon they came under heavy bombardment and returned the fire in the direction from which it was coming. Unfortunately they had not been warned of a minefield that lay in their path and all six tanks set off mines. They found themselves immobilised, with their tracks blown off. Unable to move, they were sitting ducks but managed to continue firing.

Soon Gardner's tank received a direct hit that killed his driver and put the 2-pounder out of action. Lieutenant Rowe got out of his tank and ran across to Gardner to find out if they could repair the broken tracks. Halfway across, he was hit and mortally wounded. Gardner grabbed a first-aid kit and ran to the stricken officer, but there was nothing that could be done.

Gardner was now in command and he ordered that all tanks should try and repair their tracks but they were all too badly damaged. When night fell, Gardner decided to abandon the damaged tanks and lead the crews back to safety. He shouted instructions that all crews should walk back along their tracks with care in order to avoid treading on more mines. In this way he managed to assemble them safely and bring them back to headquarters.

The following morning, Gardner returned and carefully picked his way through the minefield. He then immobilised all the tank's guns and collected papers and personal items from the dead crews. For his cool handling of a difficult situation, he was awarded the Military Cross.

Rommel's forces had driven the Allies back to the Egyptian border, but had left the garrison of Tobruk isolated and under siege. The defenders consisted of the Australian 9th Division, the Australian 18th Brigade and some British tanks and artillery. The defences had been strengthened along the 30-mile perimeter, which enclosed an area about the same size as the Isle of Wight. Thanks to the supremacy of the Royal Navy, the garrison was able to be supplied and reinforced by sea.

Rommel viewed the Allies' occupation of this valuable deep water port with great irritation and resolved to capture it. Afrika Korps panzers, supported by Italian infantry, made their first attack on Tobruk on 13 April 1941 and again on 24th and 30th, but they were beaten back. Attempts by Wavell were made during May and June to reach and relieve the garrison but these also failed. Gardner's tanks were involved but found the German 88mm guns devastating and had to pull back. Gardner and his comrades were withdrawn for two months while they were re-equipped. His inability to relieve Tobruk spelt the end for General Wavell and he was replaced by General Claude Auchinleck.

In September, the Australians were relieved by a large force made up of the British 70th Division, the Polish Carpathian Brigade and the 32nd Army Tank Brigade, of which the 4/RTR was part. In a bold move, this large force was inserted by sea into Tobruk and the Australians taken back to Alexandria.

Auchinleck planned a concerted attack on Rommel as he prepared a push towards Alexandria and Cairo. The intention in Operation *Crusader* was to destroy the Axis forces where they stood and for the 70th Division to break out of Tobruk and link up with the main force and drive the enemy out of Cyrenaica.

The main attack was launched on 18 November, three days before the breakout in order to catch the enemy in the rear and to draw away much of his armour. On the night of the 20th, Royal Engineers removed mines and cleared gaps in the wire so that on the morning of the 21st, the British armour sped through the gaps and fanned out. Their targets were strong points, which were taken from an enemy astonished to be attacked by tanks coming from inside the Tobruk perimeter. After a day's fierce fighting, during which Gardner's tank was put out of action, more than 1,000 prisoners were taken. With nightfall, 4 Royal Tanks went into open laager to await fresh orders.

Just before they were to move off on the morning of the 22nd, word was received that two Marmond Herrington armoured cars of the King's Dragoon Guards were trapped in no-man's-land about a mile away and under heavy enemy fire. The squadron leader, Major Jack Prichard, ordered the Matildas of Lieutenants Paul Gearing and Acting/Captain Pip Gardner to go and render assistance.

The tanks passed the forward infantry position and began a gradual descent down the forward slope. The tank crews felt totally exposed as they entered this huge amphitheatre. They soon came under heavy fire and could see that the two armoured cars were being smashed to pieces at very close range.

Gardner later wrote to his parents about the action:

> I took one other tank with me and set off. When I got near the cars I found that some of the crews had managed to get out and had crawled away to some trenches and were lying 'doggo' there, waiting for a chance to make a run for it, as they were under very heavy fire.
>
> I passed them and went on to the front car, only to be greeted at very short range with heavy anti-tank and machine-gun fire. We managed to back the tank up to the car and I hopped out to get it

on tow: I found behind the car a badly wounded officer (Lieutenant Peter Beames) with his legs blown off ... I got the chap into his car again and got the car on tow and started off; but as luck would have it the rope broke, and so we had to go back again and get the chap out of the car and on to the tank. During all this we had been under heavy fire and my guns were put out of action, and the tank with me was unable to give us much covering fire, as his guns were damaged.

Well, I had to leave the car and started back again, only to discover that, while I had been outside, the top of my turret had been shot away and my loader dead. Well, to cut a long story short, we picked up the rest of the boys on the way back and got out of it. I then found that I had stopped a few small pieces of metal in my leg, neck and arm, but nothing serious.

Gardner was taken back to Tobruk to a field hospital but after three days he discharged himself and returned to his squadron. For the next thirteen days there were twelve distinct tank battles. Having linked up with General Freyberg's New Zealanders at Ed Duda, the Tobruk force was under repeated attack. On 30 November, Rommel delivered a concentrated blow against the New Zealanders, which drove them back leaving the Tobruk garrison cut off once more. They did manage to hold on to Ed Duda until they saw signs that the Axis forces were retreating westward. The siege of Tobruk was finally raised on 9 December and Cyrenaica was once again in Allied hands.

Gardner was sent to a rest camp in Alexandria and had his captaincy confirmed. He was transferred to the 32nd Army Tank Brigade staff as a liaison officer and moved to Palestine. Soon after arriving he heard on the radio that he had been awarded the Victoria Cross and his citation appeared in *The London Gazette* on 10 February 1942, which read:

On the morning of November 23rd, 1941, Captain Gardner was ordered to take two tanks to the assistance of two armoured cars of the King's Dragoon Guards which were out of action and under fire in close proximity to the enemy, south-east of Tobruk. He found the two cars halted two hundred yards apart, being heavily fired on at close range and gradually smashed to pieces. Ordering the other tank to give him covering fire, Captain Gardner manoeuvred his own close up to the foremost car; he then dismounted in the face of intense anti-tank and machine-gun fire and secured a tow-rope to the car; seeing an officer lying beside it with his legs blown off, he lifted him into the car and gave the order to tow. The tow-rope, however, broke and Captain

Gardner returned to the armoured car, being immediately wounded in arm and leg; despite his wounds he lifted the other officer out of the car and carried him back to the tank, placing him on the back engine louvres and climbing alongside to hold him on. While the tank was being driven back to safety it was subjected to heavy shell fire and the loader was killed.

Pip Gardner's obituary in *The Times* indicates a different version:

Gardner dismounted and tried to unhitch one of his tow-ropes, to tow the car away. The one stowed along the side of his tank jammed, so he loosened the one at the rear and signalled to his driver to turn about. In order to keep the main gun facing towards the enemy, the gunner began to traverse his turret and in doing so accidentally killed the wireless operator/loader who most unfortunately chose that moment to put out his head to see what was happening. The gunner had to ease the body clear before he could complete the gun traverse and, having done so, saw Gardner lifting Lieutenant Beame ... back into his armoured car ...

There was little that could be done for Lieutenant Beame and he died of his terrible wounds soon after his rescue.

By mid-April, it was time to leave Palestine and return to Egypt to take over the arrival of new tanks. Before leaving, there was a full parade of the 4th Royal Tanks at which Gardner was decorated with the VC ribbon by General Auchinleck. Captain Gardner's days as a tank commander were over as he was now the brigade liaison officer.

On 26 May 1942, Rommel began his all-out attack to once more push the Allies out of Libya. By 18 June, he had succeeded in reaching Gazala, about 50 miles west of Tobruk. Pip had been carrying out his duties with the 50 Division and prepared to retreat eastwards. He then received a message from Brigadier Willison in command of 32 Army Tank Brigade to join them at Tobruk.

Rommel continued his rapid advance and this time he was not going to have the irritation of an Allied-occupied Tobruk in his rear. Gardner had just been reunited with his old comrades when they received the shocking news that the South African commander of the Tobruk garrison had surrendered. In the meantime, the Allied retreat continued until they reached their prepared defensive line at El Alamein.

Brigadier Willison decided that, despite the official surrender, he would allow his men to make their way eastwards in the hope of reaching their lines. Under cover of darkness, Gardner and a group of officers passed through the surrounding enemy lines and walked for three days. By the end of the third day, they were out of food and water. With little hope of regaining their lines they were captured by a lorry-load of Italians, who drove them back to Tobruk and a crowded prisoner of war cage.

A week after capture, the officers were separated and a group, including Gardner, were sent to an airfield where they were flown to Italy to begin their new lives as POWs.

Gardner's first permanent camp was at Chieti, west of Pescara on the Adriatic side of Italy. After enduring a cold Italian winter, the prisoners' thoughts turned to escaping. Gardner joined a team of tunnellers but before their tunnel reached the wire, it had been discovered. Gardner and his comrades were punished with a fortnight in the 'cooler' and then transferred further north to a punishment camp near Genoa. To their relief they arrived, not at the grim punishment camp, but at Campo di Concentramento No.9 near Palma. This turned out be a great improvement to the Chieta camp and they even had bed sheets that were regularly laundered at a nearby nunnery.

By 16 May 1943, the last of the Axis forces had been driven out of North Africa and soon the Allies had captured Sicily. Then the welcome news reached the prisoners that Mussolini had been deposed. This was followed with even greater tidings that the first Allied troops had landed in Italy.

The senior British officer (SBO) in the camp broke the sensational news that Italy had agreed on an armistice with the Allies. Like all SBOs in other camps, Lieutenant Colonel de Burgh had received instruction through the channels of MI9 that the prisoners should not be let loose to roam the countryside but to stay put until relieved by the Allied forces. Most SBOs followed this instruction with dire results as it was highly unlikely that the Germans would allow so many Allied prisoners to be repatriated. Lieutenant Colonel de Burgh had other plans.

On 9 September, it was discovered that the Germans had established themselves in the district and would probably attempt to move the prisoners to Germany. De Burgh warned the prisoners to gather their kit and prepare to break away from the camp. The Italians, who had so recently been their jailers, now actively sent out patrols to keep an eye on the Germans.

Finally, several hundred prisoners left the camp in one big group led by Italian soldiers to a hiding place in a vineyard well hidden from the highway. For a couple of days they observed several German convoys mostly heading in the direction of Genoa. Gardner and a couple of friends decided to make a break for it and try to reach the Allied lines. There were many rumours as to where the Allies had landed including Genoa, Milan and even the Brenner Pass. In fact, the Salerno landing had taken place, more than 600 miles to the south.

On 11 September, they set off with haversacks full of bully beef, service biscuits and slabs of chocolate. Over the following weeks they cautiously made their way south, staying with friendly farmers for days at a time. They were sure that the Allies would be landing at Genoa, so they kept moving around in that general region. Although the Italians had surrendered, there were still many Fascists who could turn in any escaped POW they found. The Germans were offering 1,500 lire for information leading to the capture of a POW and were shooting out of hand anyone found giving shelter to escaped prisoners.

On 30 September, they received firm news that the nearest Allies were at Salerno, south of Rome. After weeks of indecision and waiting, they now had a goal – albeit hundreds of miles away. They had now acquired civilian clothing and could pass as Italian farm workers but they still kept away from roads as much as possible. On one occasion, they stayed on a farm and helped with the grape harvest and joined in treading the grapes.

They steered a course that was taking them south-east and when they had skirted Bologna, they turned south towards Florence. So far, they had been walking for three weeks, averaging about 10 miles a day. They had begun to resemble a trio of tramps and when they were walking near a village a man approached them and asked if they were British soldiers. Although they denied this, the man led them to his home, where they were fed and given new clothes. Their luck was increased when it turned out that their benefactor was a bicycle manufacturer and he supplied the three astonished escapees with new bikes. When it came time to depart, they were almost overwhelmed when the Italian thrust wads of lire in their hands.

With their new mode of transport they felt confident to cycle through the middle of Florence. Later, when they got into the mountains, they found the going very difficult. Once when they were labouring up a particularly steep hill, a lorry-load of Germans pulled up and the driver got out. Thinking that they were about to be captured, they were astonished when a German driver offered to tie a rope to the back of the lorry and tow them up the hill. The cyclists grabbed the rope, one behind the other and were pulled effortlessly to the top.

The three realised that they were no longer in cycling country. Their problem was solved when they stayed at a village inn and the owner suggested they swap their bikes for walking shoes.

It was now late October and the first signs of winter appeared in the mountains. One day they were walking a road when a couple of rough-looking men sprang out from behind a tree brandishing pistols. Instead of being confronted by *banditti*, they had made contact with partisans.

For the next few weeks, they were passed from one group to another. Then one day while they were hiding in a mountain hut, a partisan called and asked for Captain Philip Gardner and handed him a note. It was from Major Sam Derry, who had known him at Chieti Camp. In it, Derry invited Gardner to Rome, where they could make plans to reach the Allied line. The only condition was that only one prisoner at a time could travel. The others would follow at later dates.

Accompanied by the partisan, Gardner caught a bus that reached Rome in seven hours. The long journey was enlivened when an American fighter swooped over them with machine guns blazing. Fortunately, all it hit was the gravel in the road ahead.

When they reached Rome, Pip was taken to a flat near the Vatican, where he joined another British fugitive. Pip discovered that he was in the hands of the Rome Organisation, which looked after escaped prisoners and was administrated by Sam Derry. It was the British Minister in residence at the Vatican, Sir D'Arcy Osborne, who set up the Rome Organisation and had appointed Derry to run it. When the Allies finally reached Rome on 4 June 1944, they found there were 3,925 escapers of various nationalities on the books of the Rome Organisation.

Gardner could have sought sanctuary in the Vatican but he was determined to reach the British lines. New Year's Day 1944 was memorable because Gardner and his companion obtained tickets for the opera. That evening they saw Benjamino Gigli and his daughter, Rine, in *La Traviata*. Despite being surrounded by German and Italian Fascist officers, they were able to sit back and enjoy the opera.

On 8 January 1944, Gardner's four months of freedom came to an end. During the past few weeks, there had been increasing activity from the security forces. The Germans had taken control of Rome and the Gestapo and Fascist police had cracked down hard on any subversive activity. One of the Italian resistance workers involved in the Rome

Organisation had been arrested and tortured. From the information divulged, the Gestapo was able to plant a Fascist agent in the group and soon there were many arrests, including Gardner and two fellow fugitives.

They were taken to Rome's main prison, euphemistically named Regina Coeli (Queen of Heaven) and shut in separate cells. It was soul-destroying to have reached so close to the British lines at Monte Cassino only to have their freedom snatched away.

After three very unpleasant weeks, the prisoners were herded on to coaches and driven to a transit camp north-east of the city. From there they were marched to a small railway station and herded into cattle trucks to begin the long and uncomfortable journey north to Germany.

After an ordeal lasting four days, the prisoners arrived at a camp north of Munich. Their stay here was brief and they were once again on the move north, this time on a passenger train. Next morning they arrived at Luckenwald, about 60 miles south of Berlin. Here they marched to a most forbidding prison where Gardner was put in solitary confinement. This lasted for a week and he was again in transit to another prison: this time in Czechoslovakia. Housed in a former Czech military academy, Oflag VIII F was luxury compared with what had gone before.

As the Russian Spring Offensive gradually pushed the Germans back to their borders, so the prisoners were moved back into the heart of Germany. On 28 April 1944, Gardner and his fellow POWs boarded yet another train, this time in cattle trucks. To prevent any thoughts of escape, each prisoner was handcuffed. All this did was to present a challenge and within a short time, the prisoners had managed to pick the locks and dispose of the cuffs through a ventilator, a slops bucket or solemnly hand them back to the sheepish-looking guards.

The journey took two days and on 1 May the prisoners arrived at Oflag 79, 5 miles from the town of Brunswick. The camp was well established and in that respect it was more tolerable than others in which Gardner had been incarcerated. The downside was that it was built on the edge of Brunswick aerodrome, which had a nearby Luftwaffe barracks and a large underground aircraft engine works. As such, it made it a plumb target for Allied bombers.

The increasing number of air raids on Germany meant that there was a reduction in the amount of food for the prisoners. This was offset by the news received from a concealed radio that the Allies were advancing on Germany from all sides. It was also the time when Hitler unleashed the V-rockets on London. Despite the prisoners suffering stress from hunger, cold and air raids it was decided it would be beneficial if they could focus their attention on those civilians, particularly the young, who were suffering from the Blitz. It was an idea that was received with enthusiasm and a 'Boys' Club Office' was set up to accept pledges of donations. Gardner was one of the founders of this scheme and was elected to a board of trustees.

By the time Oflag 79 had been liberated by the Americans on 14 April 1945, the POWs of Brunswick had raised pledges of £13,000.

Gardner returned home and was reunited with Renée. On 18 May 1945, Pip and his wife attended Buckingham Palace, when he was presented with his Cross by the King. Resuming civilian life, Gardner returned to the family business, rising to managing director and finally chairman.

He also devoted much time and energy in starting the Brunswick Boy's Club with the money raised by the Oflag 79 prisoners. A site was purchased in Fulham and a club premises built, which was opened by the Duke of Edinburgh in 1948. It was rebuilt in 1970 and reopened by the Duke and further extended in 1977. In 1985, Gardner was elected president, something of which he was immensely proud and richly deserved. Other voluntary appointments he undertook were honorary secretary of the VC & GC Association and a governor of his old school, Dulwich College.

When retired, he and Renée moved to Hove, where he died on 13 February 2003 aged eighty-eight. He was cremated and a memorial plaque was placed in St Andrew's Churchyard, Hove. His VC group is now on display in the Ashcroft Gallery at the Imperial War Museum.

James Jackman VC

James Joseph Bernard Jackman was born on 19 March 1916 at Glenageary, County Dublin, the only son of Dr and Mrs J.J. Jackman. At the age of twelve he left his preparatory education and was sent to board at the Roman Catholic Stonyhurst College in Lancashire. One of his fellow pupils was Harold Marcus Ervine-Andrews, who was awarded the Victoria Cross during the retreat to Dunkirk. As fellow Irishmen, they journeyed together back to Ireland during the holidays. He remained there until he was eighteen before entering the Royal Military College at Sandhurst. On 27 August 1936, he received his commission and joined the Royal Northumberland Fusiliers (RNF).

The following year he joined the 1st Battalion in Egypt, which was being converted from an infantry unit to a motorised machine gun battalion. With the Arabs and Jews still in conflict in Palestine, 1st Battalion reverted to infantry as it spent a year trying to keep the peace.

With the outbreak of war, the battalion changed back to a machine gun unit and was sent to the Libyan border. In the summer of 1940, the 1st Battalion joined General Wavell's advance against the Italians and much to their surprise pushed the enemy 350 miles back to Benghazi. On the point of a remarkable victory, Wavell's force was stripped with a good proportion of manpower and equipment sent to defend Greece. Unfortunately, instead of the foe being the Italians, it was the mighty German Army and Luftwaffe that confronted them and the brief campaign ended in an ignoble defeat.

A similar situation arose in North Africa when Hitler sent Rommel to command the Afrika Korps to prop up his defeat-minded ally. Disembarking at Tripoli in the spring of 1941, the Afrika Korps completely reversed all the gains made by the Western Desert Force. Now involved in a fighting retreat, the British Army fell back. On the night of 9 April, 1/RNF arrived in Tobruk with orders to defend the valuable port, little realising that they were to spend eight months under siege until Operation *Crusader* started in November 1941.

When the Italians had first occupied Tobruk at the beginning of the war, they had fortified the perimeter with wire, deep anti-tank ditches and strong points; something for which the allied defenders were grateful. The Tobruk area was under almost constant bombardment from enemy artillery and Stuka dive bombers, which forced the defenders to live in dug-outs during the day and only move at night. Each morning the tracks made by relief parties and the evacuation of the wounded and sick had to be smoothed over and the dug-outs re-camouflaged with bits of scrub.

Lieutenant Jackman had been promoted to temporary captain in command of Z Company. The siege began on 10 April with a concerted attack by Rommel's Panzers, which 1/RNF helped repel. Jackman was regarded by his fellow soldiers as unflappable and good humoured. He never issued an order but rather made a suggestion and it was done.

When Operation *Crusader* began, the plan was for the defenders of Tobruk to break out of their defensive position, take some salient points from the enemy and link up with the 2/New Zealand Division. The first enemy strong points that had to be carried were the 'Corridor', which housed some twelve enemy strongholds, and the heavily defended Ed Duda Ridge on the El Adem escarpment.

On 20 November, the infantry supported by a squadron of tanks attacked one of the vital positions along the 'Corridor'. This was held by mostly Italians supported by anti-tank guns and machineguns secure behind wire and mines. The attack was halted, which stalled the rest of the advance.

Jackman summed up the situation and took the bold decision to lead No.14 Platoon in a flanking movement. Making a wide sweep through some heavy shellfire, he was able to position his men so they could fire on the enemy from their right flank. The main attack was able to advance once more and the position was taken leaving the advance on Ed Duda possible. Z Company's objective had been thoroughly planned during the weeks before as day after day they had studied sand models of the Ed Duda feature and even staged mock attacks.

On the morning of the 25th, the main attack on Ed Duda began led by Brigadier Willison. The Matilda tanks of the 32nd Army Tank Brigade with the RNF trucks in support advanced under an intense bombardment. The ridge overlooked the Trig Capuzzo, or what the British referred to as the 'Tobruk By-Pass'. The main metalled Via Balbia coastal road passed through Tobruk but since the occupation by the British the Axis had been forced to use a rough track that wound past Ed Duda.

As the tanks reached the crest of the ridge they slowed to the 'hull-down' position, using the ridge line to protect the hull of the tank but exposing the gun turret. Willison saw that the opposition was not from enemy tanks but from guns on the ground and ordered Captain Jackman to advance in his wooden-framed 15cwt Morris trucks and attack the enemy with his twelve Vickers machineguns. They drove past the stationary tanks, fanned out and began firing at the enemy positions.

Driving to a high point on the ridge, Jackman deployed his gun crews without the aid of a radio but using a flag. Incredibly this was achieved without sustaining any injuries from the heavy fire. The problems now came from enemy tanks and machine guns that were able to use Tobruk By-Pass and began firing into the exposed flank of Willison's tanks. Once again Jackman, under fire, manoeuvred his company so they gave support to the 32nd's Matildas.

After about an hour, Captain Jackman moved to 13th Platoon's position on the right flank. All three platoons had dug in and had an excellent field of fire on the enemy's main supply line along the Tobruk

By-Pass. A truck and motorcyclist were spotted approaching and Jackman gave the order to open fire. At that moment a mortar round exploded in front of his position, wounding three men and killing two. One of the latter was Captain Jackman. By ill-luck it was the only mortar bomb fired by the enemy to have landed in Z Company's area.

The RNF held on to its position until the next morning when it was joined by fresh troops from the Essex Regiment and a battery of anti-tank guns. The New Zealanders had fought their way through the devastation of Sidi Rezegh and joined forces with the 70th Division, albeit for a short time.

Jackman's valour was recognised in the citation that appeared in *The London Gazette* on 31 March 1942. His VC was presented to his mother by the King at an investiture on 20 October 1942 and is held by Stonyhurst College.

Operation *Crusader* was regarded as a confused and confusing battle fought over a wide area in which both sides lost men and much armour. The Italians and Germans were worn down by a disruptive supply route and they were at the limit of being succoured from their supply bases. The attack also brought together the 70th Division fighting their way out of Tobruk to occupy Ed Duda and General Freyberg's New Zealand Division advancing west on the north side of the battle.

Having destroyed much of the British armour at Sidi Rezegh, Rommel then turned his full might on the New Zealanders, who were forced to retreat on 1 December. The 70th had little option but to retreat back behind its defences at Tobruk. This besiegement was to last just a week. Rommel ordered a withdrawal from the Libyan border some 350 miles to the port of El Agheila, thus allowing the defenders of Tobruk to be relieved. The German commander had been advised by the Italians that the Axis losses could not made good for some weeks due to the Allied naval threat to the supply ships.

On balance, the battle was won by Rommel, who managed to extricate the bulk of his army before the British could close the trap. Also, with so much hardware scattered around Sidi Rezegh, the Germans' superior recovery system salvaged many tanks, lorries and guns that helped to make up for temporary shortage. As Alan Moorhead wrote in his history of the British North Africa campaign:

> All our tanks were outgunned and ... however many vehicles the Germans lost they were going to get a far greater number back into action than we could because of their efficient recovery system.

71

Chapter 8

Gazala

The apparent success of Operation *Crusader* inflated British hopes. Rommel pulled back to El Agheila, which he had previously fortified and used as a base for his operations. Following up, the Eighth Army reached El Agheila in January 1942, and encountered the same problem that Rommel's forces had on the Libyan–Egyptian border, namely long lines of communication that bedevilled logistical supply. The British troops were also exhausted and their equipment was in dire need of an overhaul. The extension of the war to the Far East also meant that urgently needed reinforcements had to be diverted to that theatre, so depleting the Eighth Army. Rommel now possessed shorter lines of communication and the accumulation of forces under his command proceeded rapidly. Three weeks into the New Year he launched a counter-offensive. By May 1942, the British had retreated to Gazala, 400km east of El Agheila and about 35 miles west of Tobruk.

The army was split into two corps; XXX Corps commanded by Lieutenant General Norrie contained the 1st and 7th Armoured Divisions, and XIII Corps under Lieutenant General Gott contained most of the infantry. The latter was made up of 50th Northumbrian Division under Major General Ramsden, and 1st and 2nd South African Divisions commanded respectively by Generals Pienaar and Klopper. The Corps was supported by the 1st and 32nd Army Tank Brigades. In total the British had 100,000 men and 849 tanks with 145 in reserve.

The Battle of Gazala is considered the greatest victory of Rommel's career. Operation *Crusader* had exhausted both sides but Rommel's tactical withdrawal hundreds of miles west was not a sign of defeat but a time to re-equip his force. This moment coincided with the arrival of *Fliegerkorps II* in Sicily, which had neutralised Allied air and naval forces in Malta, thus allowing the flow of supplies into Tripoli. The Allies, on the other hand, had not had time to reorganise their army and were now at the fullest extent of their supply line.

They also suffered a severe intelligence leak. The American military attaché, Colonel Bonner Fellers, had been given access to British intelligence information, which he innocently passed on to his superiors in the United States. Unbeknown to the Americans, the code had been stolen by the Italians from the US Embassy in Rome in the summer of 1941. The Germans had also cracked the code and from mid-December 1941 until 29 June 1942, the Axis learned of the Allies' movements, including British convoys to Malta that were heavily attacked. Now greatly outnumbered in the air, the British were hard-pressed to defend Malta. Even raids on airfields by the LRDG and the SAS were compromised with the enemy garrisons alerted. This information about the numbers and condition of the British forces facing him provided Rommel with the knowledge with which to plan his counter-attack.

Reaching the limit of their supply line, the Allies were further affected by the terrible weather that had hit Libya. Troops huddled in their greatcoats as the camps became flooded. Traffic from the east was greatly affected by the glutinous red mud and the RAF was grounded as its airstrips disappeared beneath the muddy water. Some troops further south reported the fall of snow, something of a rarity in the desert. British intelligence was at fault when it reported to Auchinleck that the Axis fighting strength was 35,000, when in reality it about 80,000. The Eighth Army shivered in its camps and waited for February, when the men were told they could expect to sweep aside the weakened enemy and push on to Tripoli.

On 21 January, Rommel sent out three strong armoured columns to make a tactical reconnaissance and found only the thinnest of screens. He quickly ordered a full-scale offensive, recapturing Benghazi and pushing the British back to Gazala.

The Axis advanced through Cyrenaica and occupied the coastal village of Timimi, about 45 miles west of the British position at Gazala. The Gazala Line extended from the coast, about 30 miles west of Tobruk, to Bir Hakeim, 50 miles to the south. The line was not continuous but a series of defensive boxes with extensive minefields between them. Here the British were able to concentrate their forces to turn and fight. The British had started to receive new equipment from the Americans in the Lend-Lease agreement; the new M3 Grant tanks with the larger 75mm guns and 6-pounder anti-tank guns. The Axis recognised that with America's entry into the war they had to inflict a defeat to push the Allies back into Egypt and the Gazala Line presented the ideal place for victory.

Fought between 26 May and 21 June, the twenty-five day battle saw two men awarded the Victoria Cross.

Quentin Smythe VC

Quentin George Murray Smythe was born on 6 August 1916 in Nottingham Road, Natal, South Africa. He was one of eleven children born to Edric Smythe, whose father Charles Smythe had been Prime Minister of Natal (1905–06) and Chief Administrator. Nottingham Road was town about 35 miles north-west of Pietermaritzberg and named after the Nottinghamshire Regiment stationed there during the nineteenth century.

Smythe attended Estcourt High School and had ambitions of becoming a veterinary surgeon but with five brothers and five sisters, his parents could not afford the training. He then settled on farming and attended the Weston Farm Training school before becoming assistant farm manager near Richmond, Natal. Just before the war, Smythe had volunteered for local regiment, the Natal Carbineers. When war was declared he was called up to join the 1/Royal Natal Carbineers, 1st South African Infantry Division (1/SA). The first place he sent was to serve in the East African campaign under General Alan Cunningham in 1940–41.

With the defeat of the Italians, On 12 June 1941, the 1/SA sailed from Massawa to Egypt. The troops were kept back from the front line and given support duties, which led to much discontent. The South Africans suffered from a lack of equipment and trained soldiers. The general feeling was that they were not yet strong enough; the division made up of just 5,570 men was not the divisional strength of 23,187. A compromise was found with the 1st and 2nd Brigades sent forward to Tobruk and the Gazala Line.

By 10 February 1942, the 1/SA formed the northern box closest to the sea. The unit lost its commander, General Brink, who injured his back, and was replaced by Major General Dan Pinaar. On 26 May, Pinaar warned his division (now built up to three brigades) that they could expect an attack on its front.

Smythe had been promoted to sergeant and was second in command of a platoon commanded by Lieutenant K.H. Douglas. In the early hours of 5 June, to the distant rumble of artillery in the south, three platoons moved carefully through the minefield protecting their Alem Hamza box. Emerging into no-man's land, the officers counted off the number of paces they needed to take to reach the enemy stronghold. In the tradition of First World War warfare, this was a raid to neutralise a troublesome enemy strong point.

At 5.20, the artillery opened its barrage and ten minutes later, Douglas gave the order to fix bayonets. Reaching top of a slight rise, the men gave the Zulu war cry and charged the enemy salient. Smythe saw Douglas fall and took command. In a vicious hand-to-hand fight, Smythe shot one and bayoneted a second. As he withdrew his bayonet, it parted from his rifle. The strong point had been taken and Smythe turned his attention on the next machine gun nest.

As he charged towards it a grenade was thrown and burst close to him and a splinter lodged in his skull just above the right eye, causing his eyes to fill with blood. Another grenade exploded nearby and a splinter tore into his ankle. Ignoring his wounds, he gathered together some grenades and, ordering his men to give him covering fire, charged the enemy position, hurling a grenade that wiped out the whole crew.

Returning to his men, he rallied them and led a charge of the final target; a 47mm anti-tank gun. As they charged, the gun was fired and Smythe was near enough to see the flash and feel the blast. Although weak from loss of blood, he told his men to remain under cover as he went forward and shot two of the crew, taking the remaining three prisoners.

Sergeant Smythe then set about consolidating the position until daylight. He fired off his Very pistol to let the battalion HQ know he had captured the position. Receiving no response, he fired off another signal but still received no answer. When dawn broke, he found that the other platoons had withdrawn and the enemy was closing in. After half an hour, the enemy fire was so hot that he ordered his men to pull back, which was successfully completed even with several prisoners. The raid had been a success with only one killed and seven wounded.

The South Africans retreated to Tobruk and soon surrendered, much to the dismay of most of the defenders. On the night of 21–22 June, Smythe managed to evade capture by hitch-hiking to Mersa Matruh.

Lieutenant Douglas recommended Smythe for the Victoria Cross, which was gazetted on 11 September 1942. The first South African VC of the Second World War, Smythe received his crimson ribbon from General Pinaar. He returned to South Africa and received his Cross from the Natal Administrator on 1 September 1943. His war was over when his appendix burst and the complications that followed meant a long stay in hospital.

At the war's end, Smythe returned to farming and became a stock inspector. He applied to join as an officer instructor with the Department of Defence but was rejected on the grounds that he 'failed to meet certain requirements of an officer'. The unpopular decision was later reversed and he was commissioned and served from 1970 to 1981. He retired as captain and returned to farming.

In 1945, he married Dale Griffiths and had three sons and one daughter. They divorced in 1970 and he married Margareth Shatwell, who died in 1980. He married a third time to Patricia Stamper in 1984.

His grandson, Adrian Smythe, served in the South African Army on the Mozambique border from 1993 to 1999 before moving the England. An injury has left him blind and he took part in the Blind Veteran's UK 100k race in July 2017 from London to Brighton.

On 22 October 1997, Quentin Smythe died of cancer and was cremated at Durban Crematorium. His VC group was sold the following year and is on display at Lord Ashcroft's Gallery in London.

The Axis had defeated the British counter-attack on 5 and 6 June in the north and turned their attention to the Free French-held box of Bir Hakeim. The French managed to hold out for a day until weight of numbers and firepower forced them to retreat.

On 13 June, the Afrika Korps demonstrated superiority in tactics, combining tanks and anti-tank guns while on the offensive. By the end of the day, the British tank strength had been reduced from 300 tanks to about seventy, the heaviest ever defeat of British armour. When the two sides clashed the superior firepower of the Panzers and the 88mm anti-tank guns mauled the British tanks, littering the desert with blazing wrecks. Lieutenant General Willoughby-Norrie, in command of XXX Corps, launched Operation *Aberdeen*, which was severely criticised for his 'cavalry' approach to modern warfare and Auchinleck replaced him the following month.

The Battle of Gazala was lost on that day. The remnants of the armoured brigades withdrew northwards to a backstop box called 'Knightsbridge', where a lieutenant colonel of the 7th Royal Tank Regiment (7/RTR) by skilful leadership, fought off the Panzer attack for a day, allowing the British to withdraw. For this outstanding feat of leadership he was awarded the Victoria Cross.

Henry Foote VC

Henry Robert Bowreman Foote was born on 5 December 1904 in Ishapur, India, where his father, Lieutenant Colonel Henry Bruce Foote, was the superintendent of a rifle factory. His mother died when he was two and he returned to England with his father. Educated at St Cyprian's School, Eastbourne, and Bedford School, he sat his exams and entered Sandhurst in 1923.

In 1925, Bob Foote, as he was better known, was commissioned in the Royal Tank Corps and posted to India. In 1939 he entered Staff College, was promoted to Major 10th Armoured Division and sent to Palestine. He was then appointed Acting Lieutenant Colonel in the 7th RTR and joined the Eighth Army that advanced into Libya. He was awarded the Distinguished Service Order for his action at the Sidra Ridge. When his tank was disabled by a mine, and ignoring the bullets flying around, he went by foot to each tank and issued his orders. Soon after, he would repeat this cool disregard for incoming fire under even graver conditions.

The remnants of the 2nd and 4th Armoured Brigade fell back on the Knightsbridge Box closely pursued by Panzers, so that by 13 June, the box was virtually surrounded. The brigade's tanks were roughly lined between Knightsbridge and Rigel Ridge with little hope of either inflicting damage or escaping. The Queen's Bays were holding ground nearest the Rigel Ridge but had exhausted their ammunition and appeared doomed.

At about 10 am, the twenty-five Matildas of 7 RTR arrived and replaced the Bays. Foote looked to the east and saw the tanks and anti-tank guns of the fifteen Panzers standing about 800 yards away, already firing red tracer. Behind him he was reassured by a troop of 6-pounders keeping the Germans at a distance. Unfortunately the distance was too great for the Matildas' puny 2-pounders to do much damage.

Very soon, Foote's tank was hit, so he dismounted and walked through heavy fire to his other tanks, giving them instructions and emphasising that they must try and hold the ground for the rest of the day before a planned night-time withdrawal. They were helped by a dense sandstorm blowing in from the Sahara that obscured the battlefield for three hours.

When it had passed, Foote ordered the artillery to lay down a smokescreen, which gave them some extra cover. By this time there was only about ninety minutes of daylight left. The Germans were determined to capture the Guards Brigade garrisoning Knightsbridge before nightfall and increased their pressure. The ground was dead flat with no chance of Foote's tanks taking a hull-down defensive position. The Panzers and the 88mm subjected Foote's Matildas to a merciless bombardment and the leading tanks went up in flames.

Foote deployed his remaining two squadrons and, standing in his turret, he ordered them to follow his lead. Firing the Matildas' smoke projectors, the squadrons moved forward a few hundred yards, which threw out the enemy's range. Once the Germans had recalculated and began to hit the British, Foote ordered another smokescreen and retired. Once again the Germans had to readjust their range. Once they had, they hit Foote's tank twenty-nine times, which destroyed his weapons. He was still able to lay down a smokescreen and edge his squadrons forward and backwards until nightfall.

They had held the ground all day but at the expense of eighteen tanks. The Guards Brigade garrison was saved and was able to escape the German encirclement. By skilful use of his inferior armour, Foote had kept a superior Panzer force at bay for a whole day.

The Eighth Army fell back to its prepared positions at El Alamein but still kept a holding force at Tobruk. Churchill decided at the last moment that the fall of this thorn in the side of the Axis would be detrimental to British morale. One of the units to be left at Tobruk was Bob Foote's 7/RTR.

The 2nd South Africa Division had moved into Tobruk at the end of March under the command of Major General R.B. Klopper. With the retreat to Egypt, the garrison was increased to 33,000 men prepared to withstand another onslaught by the Axis. To many of the defenders they felt they could stand fast as they had done on many previous attacks, so it came as a shock of disbelief when Klopper surrendered to Rommel on 21 June 1942.

Foote was one who decided he was not going to be captured but during his attempt to escape he broke his leg and went into captivity. Along with most Desert POWs, Foote was incarcerated in Italy. In 1943, he and some other prisoners managed to escape over the wire and make for the mountains. Helped by villagers, they eventually joined the partisans, who helped them cross into Switzerland, where Foote was interned. He was allowed to work at the British Legation, where he learned that he had been awarded the Victoria Cross.

Once he was free to leave Switzerland, he was appointed General Staff Officer at Allied Forces Headquarters in 1944 and, in 1945, second-in-command of the 9th Armoured Brigade. On 12 December 1944, Foote received his VC and DSO from the King at Buckingham Palace. With the war's end, Foote was flying to Berlin to take part in a Victory Parade when he bailed out of the aircraft which suffered engine failure. This entitled him to become a member of the Caterpillar Club for those saved from death by means of a parachute.

Promoted to brigadier, Foote was in command of the Royal Armoured Corps, Middle East, from 1945 to 1947 before taking command of 2nd Royal Tank Regiment from 1947 to 1948. He commanded the 7th Armoured Brigade and then the 11th Armoured Division. In 1953, he was elevated to Director of the Royal Armoured Corps at the War Office before retiring in 1958 with the rank of major general.

He became chairman of the trustees of The Tank Museum at Bovington in Dorset and was a keen golfer with the appropriately named Ironsides Golf Society. On 22 October 1986, he appeared on the popular TV programme *This Is Your Life*.

He died at Pulborough, West Sussex, on 11 November 1993 and was buried at St Mary's Church, West Chiltington. His medals are displayed at The Tank Museum.

Chapter 9

The Submarine VCs

The Second World War in the Mediterranean saw the largest naval warfare actions outside the Pacific. They were mostly centred on the central and eastern end of the Mediterranean (the Latin for 'inland sea'), in particular the vital island of Malta and the Axis supply routes from Italy. It was these shipping lanes that the Royal Navy's submarines concentrated their activities on to prevent the Axis in North Africa receiving supplies. Simply stated, if the Axis could bring their supplies over a comparatively short distance then defeat for the British was certain. Malta created great problems for the Axis and it seemed certain that they would send in an invading force. Instead, they chose to capture Crete and lost many men in the process. The British struggled to supply and defend Malta but the proximity of the Axis air forces in Sicily forced the submarine fleet to operate out of the less well-equipped port of Alexandria hundreds of miles to the east.

At the beginning of the war with Italy in 1940, the Royal Navy lost several submarines due to the superior Italian anti-submarine forces. The large aging submarines used were not suited to the Mediterranean with its clear waters and shallow depth, especially to the south of Sicily. The new U-class was a smaller 630-ton, 196ft-long submarine used for training purposes but now converted to a fully armed warship. The Royal Navy ordered 49 U-class vessels and twelve operated out of Malta, first as Malta Force Submarines and then as the 10th Submarine Flotilla, under the command of Captain George Simpson. One of the most celebrated of this group went on to become the first submariner to be awarded the Victoria Cross in the Second World War.

David Wanklyn VC

Malcolm David Wanklyn was born on 28 June 1911 in Calcutta, the third son to William and Marjorie Wanklyn. His father was Argentinean-born of Scottish descent and was working as chief engineer at the Port Engineering Company based near Calcutta. David, as he was better known, was brought up in some affluence and his parents were at the height of their material and social success. In 1911, they were invited to the Delhi Durbar, attended by George V and Queen Mary. When the family returned to England, David was sent to Parkfield Preparatory School near Haywards Heath, Sussex.

He was greatly influenced by his uncle, who had commanded a destroyer in the First World War that had rammed a U-boat off Ireland. Determined to join the Royal Navy, he passed his entrance exam at the age of fourteen but ran into trouble with the medical. It was discovered that he was colour blind, a disorder that would normally have ended his career. Fortunately, the chief medical officer was a patient man and coached him to differentiate between what he was seeing and what was a congenital illusion. Negotiating the Admiralty Interview Board, he entered Dartmouth Naval College, where he excelled at mathematics and science. Something of a loner but well-liked by his fellow cadets, he did well in exams and, by 1929, he was senior midshipman of the battlecruiser *Renown*. He was regarded as quiet and studious and it was little surprise that when he took his exams for sub-lieutenant that he gained five first-class passes.

In 1933, he was promoted to lieutenant and volunteered for submarines, joining HMS *Oberon* in the Mediterranean Fleet. From 1934 to 1939, he served on *L.56*, *H.50*, *Porpoise* and *Otway*. While serving in Malta on the new S-class *Shark*, he met and fell in love with Elspeth (Betty) Kinlock. She had gone to the Mediterranean to care for an old woman and met Wanklyn on a picnic. They married on 5 May 1938 and had a son in 1939.

Wanklyn returned to England to take the Commanding Officers' Qualifying Course, known as 'The Perisher', as the use of the periscope was one of the hardest tests to sit. He passed and was given his first command, He passed and was given command of *H.31*.

His success was rewarded with command of *Upholder*, which he sailed to join the Malta Submarine force, later named the 10th Submarine Flotilla. While en route, he helped provide cover for Operation *Excess*,

81

a series of British supply convoys to Malta in which all merchantmen reached their destination safely.

The waters in which the Malta submarines operated were confined and dangerous. They were heavily patrolled by the Italian Navy, while above the *Regia Aeronautica* had command of the skies. In the previous seven months nine Royal Navy submarines had been lost; a poor exchange for the sinking of ten Italian merchant ships totalling 45,000 tons. Most of these submarines were the large, older vessels transferred from the Far East and unsuited for the Mediterranean.

In January 1941, newly promoted Lieutenant Commander Wanklyn took his new ship on its first patrol. His first attack on two supply ships ended with misses but later he sank another. Two days later he torpedoed a supply ship but was then depth-charged by an escort. Returning to Malta, he was reasonably pleased but the next three patrols yielded no targets and he was regarded as a slow starter. A fourth aborted attack that wasted eight torpedoes raised suspicions about his competence. Despite the disappointment of *Upholder*'s failure to sight or sink any more enemy ships, the crew of three officers and thirty-four ratings had every confidence in their captain. He exuded a calming influence on his crew, even at the height of a depth charge attack.

Their faith in Wanklyn was repaid on the next patrol. Three days out, he sighted a convoy and picked out the 5,428-ton *Antonietta Laura*. Closing to 700 yards, he fired two torpedoes that scored direct hits and sank the ship. The next assignment was tricky. An Italian destroyer and German merchant ship had been abandoned on a shoal and *Upholder* had been ordered to finish them off. Approaching in shallow water with little chance of escape if discovered, Wanklyn managed to pull alongside the merchant ship, search her and then set her on fire. With the smoke of the burning ship seen for miles around, there were moments of anxiety as the sub grounded on the shoal. Calmly, Wanklyn manoeuvred *Upholder* to deeper water.

A few days later in rough seas, Wanklyn spotted a convoy of five merchant ships guarded by no fewer than four destroyers. Creeping closer, he fired off a salvo of four torpedoes, scoring three hits, sinking one ship and badly damaging another. The destroyers immediately steamed to *Upholder*'s position and began to depth charge but Wanklyn had moved away.

With two torpedoes remaining, he reloaded his tubes and approached the damaged ship and sank her. He then returned to

Richipal Ram – posthumous VC at the Battle of Keren, Eritrea 1941.

Nigel Leakey – possibly killed by friendly fire.

Eric Wilson – given a posthumous VC citation until liberated from a PoW camp.

Alfred Sephton – carried on his duty despite being mortally wounded.

Jack Hinton – belatedly received his VC at Buckingham Palace after years as a PoW.

Alfred Clive Hulme – stalked the enemy on Crete and was accused of war crimes years after his death.

Double VC
Charles Upham
with Colonel
Kippenburger.

Roden Cutler – lost
a leg in battle
against the Vichy
French in Syria.

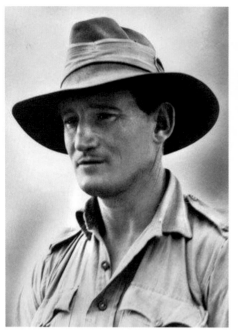

James Gordon – single-handedly
attacked machine-gun nests.

Thomas Gould.

Malcom Wanklyn (with beard) poses with his crew on HMS *Upholder*.

Peter Roberts – jointly removed two enemy 100lb bombs from the deck of HMS *Thresher*.

Anthony Miers – the fiery commander of HMS *Torbay*.

John Linton – lost with all hands at the height of his success.

George Gunn – one of the
Sidi Rezegh heroes.

John Edmundson – Tobruk VC.

Geoffrey Keyes –
killed in abortive raid
on Rommel's HQ.

Thomas Gould VC surveying damage caused by two German bombs (A & A1).

John Beeley – single-handedly destroyed machine-gun nest and opened the way for his comrades to advance.

Jock Campbell – flamboyant leader
of the 7th Armoured Brigade.

Philip Gardner – saved
crew of armoured car
under heavy enemy
fire.

Henry Foote – clever tactics delayed the German armour for a day enabling the infantry to escape.

James Jackman – led successful breakout from Tobruk but was killed on point of victory.

Quentin Smythe – the first South African desert VC.

Adam Wakenshaw – the remains of his anti-tank gun.

Charles Upham – a sick but resolute
fighter riding a donkey on Crete.

Keith Elliott – the
hero of Ruweisat
Ridge.

Arthur Gurney – charged a series of enemy machine-gun posts enabling his company to press forward.

William Kibby – El Alamein VC.

Victor Turner – surrounded by
the enemy at El Alamein, he
inspired his men to hold the
position for a day and destroyed
thirty-five tanks.

Herbert Le Patourel – the
first Tunisian VC.

Frederick Peters – sailed the former US Coastguard Cutter HMS *Walney* into a heavily-
defended Oran Harbour in an attempt to capture the port.

Moananui-a-Kiwa Ngarimu – Tebaga Gap VC.

Hugh Malcolm – the only RAF VC of the Desert Campaign.

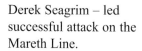

Derek Seagrim – led successful attack on the Mareth Line.

John Anderson – captured Longstop Hill only to be killed later in Italy.

Lorne Campbell – inspirational commander of Argyll & Sutherland Highlanders.

Wilwood Sandys-Clarke – single-handedly attacked and destroyed three machine-gun posts, but was killed attacking a forth.

Charles Lord Lyell – buried beside the 88mm gun he captured.

John Kenneally – the 'Brummie-Irishman' who twice attacked the enemy despite being wounded.

Malta for maintenance and rest. The island had serious limitations as it was under almost continuous bombardment. The submarine base was particularly singled out and the accurate bombing forced the submarines to submerge during the daylight hours.

The next patrol two weeks later was bedevilled with problems. A torpedo already loaded into its tube sprang a leak and had to be changed; a tricky operation. More concerning was the sub's Asdic apparatus, which had failed leaving Wanklyn to rely on the periscope to locate enemy shipping.

The following day he sighted a convoy sailing against the backdrop of land and almost invisible. Without the aid of Asdic, he fired off three torpedoes and scored a hit. The following day he attacked another heavily defended convoy and again successfully sank a ship. There followed the inevitable nerve-shattering depth-charging. One would have thought that his score was creditable without the aid of Asdic but Wanklyn had two torpedoes left and wanted to use them.

Patrolling off the coast of Sicily, on the evening of 24 May, he spotted three large ships surrounded by several destroyers. The size told him that they were troop carriers. Without Asdic he could only estimate their speed and course, something made even more difficult as the ships were zig-zagging. *Upholder* was well positioned ahead of the approaching convoy, which was travelling at an estimated speed of 20 knots. Wanklyn aimed at the centre of the three ships and sent his two torpedoes on their way.

As he gave the order he spotted a destroyer dead ahead and quickly dived to 150ft. The crew heard the satisfying crump of two explosions and braced themselves for hours of being hunted by the enemy destroyers. All motors were stopped and the crew remained silent as the depth charges came ever closer. Their sound was like a hammer blow to the hull and the shock waves shattered lamps and the cork insulation fell from the bulkhead. A total of thirty-seven depth charges were dropped in twenty minutes.

Unexpectedly the attack moved away and after a while Wanklyn brought the sub to the surface. Although they could not see anything, there was a strong smell of oil fuel. Later it was discovered that *Upholder* had sunk the 18,000-ton former liner *Conte Rosso* filled with troops travelling from Naples to Tripoli. Of the 2,729 soldiers and crew aboard, 1,300 were drowned. The rest of the convoy turned about and returned to Naples.

This patrol had been particularly successful and David Wanklyn was recommended for the Victoria Cross, the first submariner in the

Second World War to be honoured. The citation appeared in *The London Gazette* on 1 December 1941. However, the *Upholder*'s exploits had only just begun.

There was a similarity between air force pilots and the skippers of submarines about the number of operations they could safely undertake. Wanklyn was the leading Allied 'ace' and was beginning to show signs of strain. Commander Simpson, his commanding officer, ordered that he be taken off patrols for a month.

When he had rested he took out his next patrol on 30 June. Within twenty-four hours he spotted and attacked a liner but the Italian captain skilfully avoided the torpedoes. On 3 July his patience was rewarded when a 4,000-ton tanker was spotted but was forced to break off when it changed course around a headland. Three hours later he spotted three ships escorted by a destroyer. Picking a vessel named *Laura C* laden with wooden packing cases, he sank her, but endured nineteen depth charges from the destroyer.

On 19 July *Upholder* left Malta to help guard an incoming convoy to the island. From there Wanklyn moved to the western tip of Sicily and on 24 July he was rewarded. Firing three torpedoes from long range, he crippled the 5,000-ton *Dandalo*. On 28 July in thick fog, he spotted two cruisers supported by destroyers. One of them was identified as the *Giuseppe Garibaldi* travelling at 28 knots. At 4,000 yards *Upholder* fired a spread of four 35-knot Mark IV torpedoes at twelve-second intervals.

The obligatory depth-charging, in which thirty-eight were dropped, meant that Wanklyn could not tell if they had been successful. It was later learned that the cruiser had sustained two hits and was badly damaged.

It was noticed how vulnerable Italian coastal railways were to attack and on 15 August, *Upholder* sailed to the Marettimo area of western Sicily to land a party of saboteurs. Before that he was directed to two convoys, both of which he missed. On 20 August he moved to the San Vito lo Capo area and spotted a cargo ship and an anti-submarine trawler. Firing off two torpedoes, he sank the *Enotria* and avoided the trawler's depth charges.

Two days later three tankers were spotted under an escort of three destroyers and a flying boat. Waiting until the seaplane had flown to the far side of the convoy and the nearest destroyer had moved to the rear of three of the tankers, Wanklyn move in for a kill. He chose the *Lussin* painted in mauve and khaki dazzle camouflage carrying three large drums on deck. Two torpedoes struck the tanker and she keeled over and sank. Wanklyn counted forty-three depth charges dropped in eight minutes but noted the Italian destroyers began their attacks at high speed and overshot the sub by 200 yards.

On 24 August, Wanklyn attacked another convoy escorted by six destroyers, two cruisers and a battleship. Unable to catch the merchant ships, he fired his last two torpedoes at a cruiser, heard an explosion and claimed a hit.

Now all his torpedoes had been fired, he dropped a landing party near Palermo. Unfortunately they could not locate their target and, running from an Italian patrol, were collected by Wanklyn. There was another abortive raid during the next patrol, but during it he spotted three irresistible targets – the three 19,000-ton liner-transports *Neptunia*, *Oceania* and *Marco Polo*. He fired off all his torpedoes but missed. Just fifteen days later he would engage two of these vessels again.

When the *Upholder* returned to port Wanklyn learned that he had been awarded the Victoria Cross, although it would be several months before it was gazetted. Several of his crew received awards for the attack on the *Conte Rosso*. In addition, Wanklyn was awarded a bar to his DSO.

Leaving Malta on 16 September with three other submarines sent to intercept a convoy bound for Tripoli, Wanklyn received a message from *Unbeaten* two days later informing him it had spotted a convoy but it was too far away to attack. Wanklyn was in a better position to attack and at 3.40 am he saw three large ships carrying troops and with a large destroyer escort.

Wanklyn decided to remain on the surface and closed in on the convoy's bow. All four tubes were ready and Wanklyn ordered the full salvo to be fired. It was a difficult shot as the large transports were travelling at high speed. He clambered down the conning tower, the submarine levelled off below the surface and four minutes later two explosions were heard. A large hole had crippled the *Neptunia* and she started to limp back to port. The *Oceania* was badly damaged and had come to a dead stop with her propellers destroyed. Instead of the destroyers attacking *Upholder*, they went to the assistance of both ships.

Wanklyn dived deep to reload his tubes and decided to finish off the stricken troop ships. Closing in, he was forced to crash-dive because of the sudden appearance of a destroyer. Now too close to the *Oceania*, he dived under her and fired off a single torpedo, which blew the ship apart. Most of the troops, who were German, had already been rescued by the destroyers. Unbeknown to Wanklyn, *Unbeaten* had now reached the area, had also seen the crippled vessel and was on the point of firing off her torpedoes when *Upholder* beat her to it.

Wanklyn turned his attention to the *Neptunia*, which could only manage 5 knots. Two more torpedoes finally sank her. In a single attack, Wanklyn had accounted for nearly 40,000 tons.

A lean period followed but on the night of 8 November lookouts spotted an Italian submarine off the toe of Italy. *Upholder* fired four torpedoes and Wanklyn claimed a 'kill', but he had missed. Just thirty-six hours later *Upholder* witnessed the Battle of the Duisburg Convoy, a surface fight by Force K, a flotilla of destroyers under the command of Captain William Agnew. Wanklyn pitched in and sank the Italian destroyer *Libeccio* but missed a cruiser and another destroyer. There was one anxious moment when the gyro failed on one of the torpedoes, which ran in circles narrowly missing the sub.

In December, Wanklyn's citation appeared and was broadcast on the BBC. He became the hero of the moment for a nation hungry for good news. When asked what was needed in submarine warfare, he replied:

That's a nasty one, so I will use a long word: Imperturbability.

Soon after, as *Upholder* was entering harbour, she was suddenly strafed by a Messerschmitt Bf 109. Before she could dive, her new No.1 lieutenant was badly injured by a cannon shell that hit the conning tower, peppering the unfortunate officer with shell splinters. The enemy attacks on the island were increasing. On 7 February 1942 alone there were seventeen bombing attacks in twenty-four hours. It was small wonder that the submarine crews were glad to go on patrol to escape the relentless raids.

On 31 December, *Upholder* put to sea again and fired three torpedoes at a merchant ship off north-west Sicily, but all missed. Then, west of Palermo on 4 January 1942, he fired four torpedoes at the merchant ship *Sirio* and one found its mark. Wanklyn surfaced to finish off the damaged ship but was forced to dive as the Italian was armed with a deck gun. The following night, he sank the 1,500-ton Italian submarine *Ammiraglio Saint Bon*, thus winning a bar to his DSO.

Wanklyn was ordered to take a month's leave as he was showing signs of cumulative exhaustion. He returned on 14 March to take his ship on its twenty-fourth patrol. He was heading for the Italian port of Brindisi. On arriving, he noticed that the vessels seen entering and leaving the port were not following a swept channel, indicating that there were no mines. He moved closer and sighted a submarine on the surface. Firing off a spread of torpedoes, he sank the *Tricheco*, which was lost with all hands. This scalp brought him a second bar to his DSO.

Looking for a soft target, he found a trawler and four fishing smacks near St Cataldo Point. Surfacing, the crew was told to abandon their boat and it was sunk with gunfire.

The twenty-sixth patrol was to be *Upholder*'s last.

She was detailed to carry out a special operation off Libya. Departing on 6 April, she landed Captain 'Tug' Wilson, a Royal Marine officer, a lance corporal and two Arab agents, who were to sabotage a railway near Cathage, a raid that was successful. The two British soldiers were picked up and transferred to HMS *Unbeaten* on 11 April. Wilson was the last man to see the crew of *Upholder*.

Wanklyn was then sent to form a patrol line with *Thrasher* and *Urge* to intercept a convoy approaching Tripoli from the east. On 14 April a submarine was detected by two Messerschmitt Bf 110 aircraft and two Dornier 17s escorting the convoy. They attacked the submerged submarine and saw leaking oil on the surface.

Another explanation, which has since been discounted, was that *Upholder* was spotted by a reconnaissance seaplane and an Italian torpedo boat dropped depth charges. No debris surfaced and the seaplane later claimed that the attack was made on a dolphin!

HMS *Upholder* under the command of Lieutenant Wanklyn was the most successful submarine in the Second World War. In her sixteen-month operational career she carried out twenty-four patrols and sank around 119,000 tons of Axis shipping, three submarines, a destroyer and fifteen transport ships. She possibly also sank a cruiser and another destroyer.

Wanklyn's wife, Betty, and their son, Ian, received his Cross and DSO and two bars on 3 March 1943 from the King at Buckingham Palace.

April also saw Malta ceasing to be of value as a base for attacking Rommel's supply lines due to the frequency of the Axis aerial bombardment. The 10th Submarine Flotilla was sent to its new base at Alexandria. Sadly, on the way it lost another valued submarine, HMS *Urge*, which had just sunk the Italian cruiser *Bande Nere*. Although his name did not appear among the list of crew members, Bernard Gray of the *Sunday Pictorial* is known to have perished an 'unofficial submariner'; the only journalist to known to have been killed in a submarine. Ironically, he was not on an assignment but wanted a quick passage to Alexandria.

Thomas Gould VC and Peter Roberts VC

The story of Tommy Gould VC is one of a long attachment to the Royal Navy, the high point of which was the award of the Victoria Cross. This he won serving as a petty officer on board the submarine *HMS Thrasher* on 16 February 1942. He was born William Thomas at Dover, Kent, on 28 December 1914. His father, Reuben, was serving in the Army when he was killed in action during 1916. His widow later married Reuben's friend; a naval petty officer named Cheeseman.

After attending St James's School, Dover, young Tommy followed his stepfather's career and volunteered for the Royal Navy on 29 September 1933, seeing service in the Middle East with the cruisers *Emerald* and *Colombo*. In 1937, he volunteered for the Submarine Service and served in *Regent*, *Pandora* and *Regulus* so that by the outbreak of war in 1939 he was an experienced submariner. In August 1940, he was rated as acting petty officer and joined *HMS Thrasher* in the spring of 1941.

Peter Scawen Watkinson Roberts was born on 9 July 1917 at Chesham Bois, Buckinghamshire, the younger son of George Watkinson Roberts, an incorporated accountant, and Georgina (nèe Tinney). He attended Falconbury School, Bexhill, before moving to King's School, Canterbury. At the age of seventeen, he joined the Royal Navy in 1935 as a 'special entry' cadet (one who joins from public school instead of at thirteen going to the Naval College at Dartmouth). He trained on *Frobisher* and as Midshipman on HMS *Shropshire*, joining the submarine service in 1939.

He was promoted to lieutenant and was navigation officer on *H.32* and torpedo officer on *Tribune*. He joined HMS *Thrasher* as first lieutenant on her completion in 14 May 1941.

A month later, HMS *Thrasher*, under the command of Lieutenant Commander P.J. Cowell, departed from Holy Lock bound for Gibraltar. From there she would sail on to join the 1st Submarine Flotilla at Alexandria. On 22 July, she departed on her second patrol with a Royal Navy agent on board who was to be landed on Crete. While *Thresher* was there, she was to pick up any stranded troops and continue to patrol the Aegean Sea. In fact, she had to abandon any plans for the Aegean as she picked up seventy-eight Allied troops and had to return to Alexandria.

Lieutenant Commander Cowell took *Thrasher* out on four patrols but failed to hit any of the vessels he came upon. It would appear that he was replaced by Lieutenant Hugh Mackenzie, who did have better luck but nothing particularly spectacular

On the eighth patrol, on 16 February 1942, *Thrasher* spotted a heavily laden ship named the *Arkadia*, protected by five escorts and two aircraft circling overhead. Despite the enemy using Asdic, Mackenzie fired off a salvo of four torpedoes, none of which scored a hit.

Mackenzie gave the order to dive deep and was helped on his way by an explosion thought to have come from one of the accompanying aircraft. A series of thirty-three depth charges were dropped near the submarine, causing a few lights to shatter and cork insulation to fall to the deck.

Tommy Gould described the eerie sounds experienced by those on the receiving end of a depth charge attack:

> An explosion would happen on one side of the boat and the damage would appear on the other side, because you were pushed up against a wall of water. After that, when the metal of the hull expanded back to its normal size again it sounded like sand falling on the outer casing. Peculiar sounds – steel coming back to its normal shape.

When the depth charging petered out and darkness fell, Lieutenant Mackenzie decided to surface to recharge the batteries. In doing so, he altered course, which caused the boat roll in the swell. To the alarm of the crew, they heard the sound of heavy metal objects rolling about above them. A seaman who was on his way to take over watch duty heard a loud metallic sound coming from the casing below the deck gun. He reported this to Mackenzie on the conning tower, who could not hear it because of the sea sluicing over the saddle tanks. On inspection, it was discovered that two 100lb bombs had hit the *Thrasher* but failed to explode due to the fact that they had reached periscope depth at the moment of impact. Tommy Gould and First Lieutenant Peter Roberts were responsible for the exterior of the submarine and it fell to them to remove the bombs.

The time was about 02.00 hours on the morning of 17 February and, although pitch black, they were in enemy waters that were patrolled. The first bomb was dealt with quite easily. It was lying on the deck in front of the gun emplacement and was in full view. Tommy sent for a couple of sacks, in which he wrapped the bomb and secured with a couple of lines. He noticed how pristine was the bomb – not even a scratch on its shiny surface. As the bomb was too heavy to be thrown clear of the saddle tanks along the sides of the sub, Roberts and Gould carried it 100ft to the bow. Tommy signalled with a shaded torch to the conning tower and the sub moved astern, thus enabling the bomb to be dropped in safety over the bow.

The second bomb presented a far more difficult problem. It had penetrated the gun casing, being lodged beneath the deck casing and resting on the pressure hull. With only 2 or 3ft clearance, the two men had to lay flat in the pitch darkness as they worked out how to move the bomb, which was between 3 or 4ft long, 6in in diameter and weighed 100lb. In an interview Gould described the tense following hour:

> Down we went. I went first and I crawled through. I went through, got hold of the bomb, pointed it at the hole that it had made to get it in there but it wouldn't go back so I had to pass it through to Peter. That allowed me to get through to where he was. Then I took it from him, laid down, put it on my stomach, crawling headfirst on my back. And he was giving me a bit of help by pulling my shoulders.
>
> Inside there, you see, you've got angle irons to hold the casing together, to give it some kind of strength; then there are battery ventilations in there; also drop bollards: all that you've got to get by in darkness, there's not much room. And every time we moved there was a twanging noise as if of a broken spring, which was a bit upsetting, from inside the bomb. It sounded like a loose spring.
>
> They say, 'It must have been frightening,' but I don't think it was because we had a job to do, we were doing a job, and I don't think we gave any thought, at least I didn't, to the fact that it might go off at any minute. The first one did not go off, why would this? That would be the sub consciousness that was all on the work we were doing.
>
> I think people who suffered were those down in the boat who knew what was happening. 'Hurry up you silly buggers' was probably what they were saying; there were conscious of the time, we weren't. They were also thinking that the old man might have to dive at any minute but we didn't give that a thought. But the point was, had the enemy seen us, the captain would have dived to save the boat: he'd got a crew to think about.
>
> It took over an hour. The first lieutenant got out first, Lieutenant Roberts. I was left with the bomb then and I passed it up and it was

received by him and Sub Lieutenant Fitzgerald. Then, when we got up there, we wrapped it in cloth and put a couple of heaving irons around it and Roberts and I took it forward and the sub lieutenant went back to the bridge. We did the same thing with the same results: it didn't go off either.

Back in the submarine, Tommy recalled, with a twinkle, that Lieutenant Mackenzie advised him to change his underwear. In fact, very little was made of the duo's exploit in Mackenzie's report. Although he did commend them for their fortitude, he did not recommend them for any award.

It was Admiral Sir Andrew Cunningham, the C-in-C Mediterranean, who put forward both men for the Victoria Cross but the Honours and Awards Committee in London opposed this. They argued that the acts of bravery had not taken place in the presence of the enemy and that the award of the George Cross would be more appropriate. Cunningham won the argument by pointing out that the removal of two enemy bombs within sight of an enemy coastline constituted quite enough enemy presence.

Several months later, when *Thrasher* was on patrol, Tommy Gould and Peter Roberts were called to the wardroom, where all the ship's officers stood to attention as they entered. They were then told that they had been awarded the Victoria Cross. The citation appeared in *The London Gazette* on 9 June 1942.

Roberts left *Thrasher* in April 1942 and was awarded the Distinguished Service Cross for gallant and distinguished service in successful patrols while serving on the submarine. He sat a periscope course for submarine captains but was disappointed when he failed. He had married Brigid Lethbridge in Plymouth in February 1940 and they had a son and daughter. On 30 June 1943, Roberts received his Victoria Cross and DSC from the King at Buckingham Palace.

Despite his disappointment, he remained in the Royal Navy, serving mainly on shore with training establishments at Combined Operations base at Troon and HMS *Vernon* in Portsmouth. After the war he was promoted to lieutenant commander and served on a variety of ships, including the minelayer HMS *Apollo*, which served in the Korean War. He returned to shore duties and in July 1962 he retired. He and his family moved to Newton Ferres in Devon, where he died on 8 December 1979. His medals are displayed at Lord Ashcroft's Gallery in the Imperial War Museum.

There is some doubt as to when Gould received his Cross; some accounts state it was an undated day in March 1943 or with Peter Roberts on 30 June 1943. In a later interview with the Marquess of Donegal, Gould was asked what he was thinking while busy with the bombs. He received a rather trenchant reply, 'I was hoping the bloody things would not go off!' As often happens when a VC is awarded, other honours followed. On 13 January 1943, Gould was made an Honorary Freeman of Dover and, when he returned to his home in St Albans, he was given a civic reception.

He then transferred to another submarine, *HMS Truculent*, which was involved in that rare occurrence, the sinking of another submarine. On 4 June 1943, *Truculent* sank *U-308* off the Faroes, and part of the patrol report describes what happened:

> The first four torpedoes were fired by 'Aiming' and the last two by time-interval. The second torpedo hit with a vivid flash and a column of black smoke, nearly under the gun. A second hit was heard (4th torpedo) and the target enveloped in a dense pall of smoke. A third hit reported shortly afterwards was not heard by me. All H.E. ceased after the first hit. (Enemy had been doing 200 revs). It is regretted that accurate times of explosions were not taken due to an oversight. Three explosions were heard two minutes later. Quantities of shattered wooden wreckage, sea-boots, watch-coats and loaves of bread were found in the area of sinking as well as a large patch of oil fuel. There were no survivors.

Gould was among those whose actions were noted:

> P.O. Thomas William Gould VC. Mention in Despatches, already a holder of the highest award for bravery on the submarine HMS *Thrasher*. For outstanding zeal and efficiency in two patrols in *Truculent*. This was his first patrol as Coxwain and his example of devotion to duty contributed to a successful attack on a German U-Boat on 4th June 1943. The Admiral noted: 'Concur with Commanding Officer's remarks. On his first patrol as Coxswain, P.O. Gould has set a good example to his subordinates.'

After his discharge on 21 December 1945, Gould moved to Bromley, Kent, and maintained his links with the Navy by joining the Royal Naval Volunteer Reserve. He was commissioned as lieutenant and commanded the local Sea Cadet Corps on Bromley Common. Although not deeply religious, Gould never forgot his Jewish background. As the holder of the Victoria Cross, he was the centre of media attention when, in 1946, he took part in a march in London organised by the Anglo–Jewish community protesting against the British Government's policy towards Palestine.

After several moves, he once again settled down in Dover and, in the early 1950s became chief personnel manager with Great Universal Stores. Sadly, by May 1965, this association ended in acrimony when he lost his job due to a clash of personalities and the newspapers dubbed him as, 'a VC on the dole'. Tommy felt that his hard-won VC had become a liability:

> Incredible though it might seem people in top management seem to shy away from me. I think it might be because they are afraid that a man with such a record could show too much embarrassing initiative. If it is the VC, which is frightening people away from me, I wish they would forget it. Those days are over.

Gould subsequently ran several businesses of his own, with varying degrees of success. His other interests were life membership of the British Legion, the Royal Naval Association and several Masonic lodges. He was also President of the British Branch of the International Submarine Association and a founder member of the Victoria Cross and George Cross Association. In later life, Tommy sported a 'full-rig', a luxuriant beard that emphasised his naval connections.

In October 1987, Gould's VC group was put into Sotheby's auction. The Association of Jewish Ex-Servicemen made an appeal and raised enough to buy the medals for £44,000. Gould's financial worries were eased and he was still able to proudly wear his medals. When he died on 6 December 2001, more than 100 people, including former submariners, attended the funeral at Peterborough. A few months later, a memorial service was held at St Martins-in-the Field.

In a televised interview, Tommy had been asked to give his definition of courage: 'Doing what we were taught to do and having the wherewithal to carry it through under adverse conditions.'

The second most prominent British submarine in the Second World War was the T-Class submarine and one with an outstanding record. During the Mediterranean campaign, four Victoria Crosses were awarded to members of their crews. They were large (1,325 tons), 275ft in length and carried a formidable number of torpedoes, eleven tubes of 21in torpedoes. They were also vulnerable to air attack as they could easily be spotted in the clear waters of the Mediterranean. Following the exploits of HMS *Thrasher* came the extraordinary captain of one of the most celebrated submarines, HMS *Torbay*.

Anthony Miers VC

Anthony Cecil Capel Miers came from a Scottish military background. He was born at 'Birchwood', Drummond Crescent, Inverness, on 11 November 1906, the younger son of Captain Douglas Miers, an adjutant in the Queen's Own Cameron Highlanders and Margaret Annie (née Christie). Sadly, he did not have time to get to know his father as he was one of twenty-eight Camerons killed by enemy shellfire on 24 September 1914 on the River Aisne. His mother, a resilient woman who had lost three children in infancy, left Scotland and led a semi-nomadic life staying in hotels and boarding houses rather that settling down.

Anthony's first school was Stubbington House, a few miles out of Portsmouth. It was a school that prepared pupils for naval cadetships. This was followed by a short stay at Edinburgh Academy before being sent to The Oratory near Edgbaston. Finally, in 1920 he was sent as 'a son of a hero' to Wellington School in Berkshire. Here he found the sporting atmosphere he loved, excelling in cricket, athletics, tennis, squash and in particular rugby. He later played for London Scottish and even had a trial for the Scottish national team.

Despite being short-sighted in one eye and in danger of failing an eyesight test, his mother used her formidable personality to ensure her son joined the Navy. After all, Horatio Nelson coped very well with one eye. In 1924, he joined the Royal Navy as a special entry cadet on the training battleship HMS *Thunderer*.

By 1928, he was a sub-lieutenant and, after sitting the Lieutenant's Course, applied to join the Submarine Service. In 1930 he was posted to one of the Royal Navy's more bizarre submarines, the M-Class. Built at the end of the First World War, *M-2* was armed with a huge 12-in gun weighing 60 tons and taken from an obsolete battleship. Fortunately, it was never used in action and it was recognised as being more a threat to the crew than an enemy. Instead it was replaced by another hare-brained idea; a watertight hangar was built in front of the conning tower, which housed a two-seater sea biplane.

Lieutenant Miers served on this potential death trap from August 1929 until April 1931, when he was transferred to HMS *H28*. This was fortunate timing for Miers as *M-2* sank with all hands just ten months later.

In 1933, he was posted to the Fishery Protection ship *Dart* and had his first brush with authority. Feared for his volcanic temper, Miers had got into a late-night argument with the ship's stoker over Scottish players' lack of football skills, resulting in the former being punched by the latter. The next morning Miers apologised to the seaman and reported the incident. A court martial was held but the victim denied that Miers had hit him. Nevertheless, Lieutenant Miers was reprimanded and dismissed from the *Dart*.

A few months later he was sent to Hong Kong to join the submarine HMS *Rainbow* as part of the 4th Submarine Flotilla. With little to do, Miers concentrated on ensuring his crew were good sportsmen and that they collected the top prizes. In 1936 the submarines went on a show-the-flag trip to Malaya, Borneo, Singapore and the Dutch East Indies. It was during his stay in the Far East that he earned the nickname 'Gamp' from the lower deck. When on the conning tower, he carried a large umbrella as protection against sudden tropical storms. He was also given the less-acceptable sobriquet of 'Crap' by his officers, for presumably not taking any crap from anybody.

In 1936, Miers passed the periscope course and was given command of HMS *L-48* at Gosport. He soon made his ship one of the most efficient but still made sure he packed his crew with sportsmen. Competing with battleship and cruiser crews, he managed to place his submarine near the top of the sports competition. In 1937, he rounded off his time with *L-48* when his submarine appeared in the Coronation Review of the Fleet off Spithead.

Miers, with his overwhelming personality, naturally enjoyed acting and even performed at the Fortune Theatre in Drury Lane as a member of the Strolling Players.

For the following years he was given shore duties and when war was declared, pressed to re-join the Submarine Service. Although the Navy favoured younger submarine commanders, the thirty-four year old Miers was given command of the large T-Class vessel, HMS *Torbay*, which was being fitted out at Chatham. Lieutenant Commander Miers was not averse to sacking those officers and crew that did not measure up to his high standards but he was not without his own faults. When carrying out trials in Holy Loch, he rammed the tanker *Vancouver* but managed to get away without any comment from his superiors.

On 6 March 1941, *Torbay* was ordered to sail to Halifax, Nova Scotia, but five days into the voyage she was ordered to return. Almost immediately she was detailed to join other submarines in the Bay of

Biscay, where the German battlecruisers *Scharnhorst* and *Gneisenau* had arrived in Brest. The submarine patrol had been hastily organised but after nearly three weeks of fruitless watching, *Torbay* was ordered on to Gibraltar.

Miers left Gibraltar on 23 April with orders to patrol of the east coast of Sardinia and the north-west coast of Sicily. On the 27th she spotted and attacked a 4,000-ton merchant ship with two torpedoes, both of which missed. As he prepared to surface and fire his deck gun, a plane was spotted and Miers took his submarine deep to avoid any attack. On 13 May, HMS *Torbay* reached Alexandria and joined the 1st Submarine Flotilla.

Leaving Alexandria on 28 May for what was the third patrol, Miers headed for the northern Aegean Sea. On 1 June, it spotted a fully laden German-controlled Greek *caique* (fishing vessel) in the Doro Channel of Greece. In his report, Miers wrote:

> The vessel was sighted at 0745 hours. At 0936 hours it was noticed that the vessel was wearing the German flag so *Torbay* surfaced and sank the vessel with five rounds of gunfire ... The second round was a hit aft and was followed by a violent explosion which blew the stern off and a cloud of yellow smoke enveloped the target.

Two days later *Torbay* surfaced off the island of Lemnos and sank another fully laden *caique* named the *Menelaos*. On 6 June *Torbay* began a four-day attack of the Vichy French tanker, *Alberta*, off Cape Hellas. Miers' report describes the protracted attack:

> At 1242 hours a 3000 ton merchant was sighted. *Torbay* struggled with the strong current to get into an attack position but at 1415 hours a torpedo was fired, that hit the target aft. The ship appeared to be sinking so *Torbay* left the area to the north-west.
>
> Later *Torbay* closed in again to finish off the ship. At 1545 hours another torpedo was fired. The target was again hit but as the ship was already flooded in that part not much more damage was done. After firing this torpedo *Torbay* once again left the area to the north-west ...
>
> At 0448 hours (7 June) *Torbay* submerged and closed the entrance to the Dardanelles once again from the west. At 0600 hours *Alberta* was sighted still afloat and at anchor. The ship was just within Turkish territorial waters and not aground.
>
> At 0751 hours *Torbay* spotted a merchant of about 1500 tons coming from the entrance of the Dardanelles and gave chase. The ship was later identified as Turkish so it was not attacked.

At 1130 hours *Torbay* was back at the position where *Alberta* was anchored. The ship appeared deserted. Miers decided not to fire another torpedo but to board the ship after dark to search for valuable documents and to scuttle the ship.

At 1515 hours a small Turkish vessel emerged from the Dardanelles and went alongside *Alberta* but continued south. At 1600 hours a merchant of 4000 tons was sighted approaching from the south and identified as the Turkish ship *Refah* and not attacked.

At 2305 *Torbay* surfaced alongside *Alberta*. It proved however impossible to scuttle the ship as the engine room was completely flooded. At 2344 hours *Torbay* slipped and proceeded back out to sea. At 2359 an explosion was observed aboard the *Alberta* but this failed to sink the ship …

At 0545 hours (8 June) *Alberta* was observed shattered by fire and aground on the shoal to the north of Rabbit Island. It was decided to leave the ship there in the hope that she would break up in the next gale.

At 0900 hours (9 June) a 3000 ton merchant was sighted coming out of the Dardanelles. The ship was identified as the Turkish *Tirhan*. The ship proceeded towards the *Alberta* and attempted to tow her off … At 1700 hours it was observed that *Tirhan* had succeeded in towing off the vessel and was heading towards the straight with the *Alberta* in tow. Lt. Cdr Miers decided that *Alberta* was not to be allowed to escape and that he had to attack again.

At 1742 hours … *Torbay* fired a torpedo that missed the target. The Turks slipped the tow and the *Tirhan* fled at high speed into the straights … At 1830 hours, Lt. Cdr. Miers intended to surface and finish off the *Alberta* with gunfire when an Italian torpedo boat of the Spica class was sighted only 2.5 nautical miles away. *Torbay* went deep and retreated to the north towards Lemnos.

Finally, on 10 June at 0242 hours, Miers and *Torbay* finished off the deserted hulk of the *Alberta*. It took forty 4in shells to set this seemingly unsinkable vessel ablaze before she slipped beneath the waves. This illustrates Miers's determination to see a problem through. Some would have assumed a semi-wrecked hulk would be of no further use to the enemy but Miers wanted a confirmed 'kill' to put on the ship's Jolly Roger trophy flag listing their successes.

Later that day *Torbay* attacked the Italian tanker *Utilitas* and a Romanian merchant ship, *Alba Julia*. Frustratingly, both torpedoes failed to explode. They had better luck later when the Italian tanker *Giuseppina Ghiradi* was sunk.

The following day, 11 June, *Torbay* rammed and sank a small Greek *caique* south of Lesbos. He allowed the crew to escape before finally destroying the vessel. On 12th, *Torbay* chased and sank the Italian schooner *Gesu E Maria* with twenty-five rounds of gunfire. With his patrol period completed, Miers returned to Alexandria. When Captain 'Sammy' Raw, the flotilla's commander and learned of the *Torbay*'s exploits, he sent a message congratulating Miers and his crew on a patrol that had been 'brilliantly conducted'. In a short time, Miers had already made his mark.

The *Torbay*'s third Mediterranean patrol brought further plaudits. Departing on 28 June with orders to patrol the Aegean Sea, the ship did not have to wait long before chalking up another victim. This was a small Greek *caique* named *Issodia Theotokou*, which was sunk by gunfire on 30 June.

In the early morning of 2 July, two merchant ships were sighted escorted by an Italian torpedo boat and with an aircraft circling overhead. Miers had to be cautious in his approach and took up a position where he fired off a spread of three torpedoes at the leading ship. Two minutes later he fired off another spread of three at the ship bringing up the rear. A minute later, one of the torpedoes struck the first ship, *Citte di Tripoli*. The German aircraft escorting the convoy spotted the torpedo tracks but his warning came too late.

Two days later in the Doro Channel, *Torbay* spotted a large *caique* carrying troops and equipment. Surfacing at 0700 hours, she sprayed the sailing vessel with machine gun fire and rounds from her deck gun until the enemy ship sank just three hours later. That afternoon a schooner displaying the swastika flag laden with troops and stores was also sunk by gunfire.

Miers had no compunction in machine-gunning the German troops floundering in the water as these were the enemy. These episodes would come back to haunt the memory of this VC long after he had died. The writer and broadcaster Ludovic Kennedy wrote in his own autobiography that what Miers did in on patrol in July amounted to a war crime. He accused the *Torbay*'s commander of shooting unarmed men in the water after he had sunk their ships. These incidents took place in the waters around Crete soon after the battle and evacuation. In probably what was the only incidence of acts of atrocity in the African campaigns, Crete became a byword for barbarous conduct. The German pilots machine-gunned helpless seaman as they escaped their sinking ships. They also attacked Red Cross hospital ships taking the sick and wounded from the island and, after the fall of Crete, they executed 900 civilians as reprisals and destroyed entire villages.

This became a long-running dispute between those who believed what Kennedy wrote was correct and those, some of them witnesses, who said the allegations were distorted and wrong. (For more details see Brian Izzard's book, *Gamp VC*).

On 5 July, Miers pulled off a rare sinking; the destruction of an enemy submarine. In his patrol report, he wrote:

> At 1946 hours off Stapodia Island, a submarine was sighted bearing 080 degrees four nautical miles away. *Torbay* at once turned to engage the target.
>
> At 2016 hours, six torpedoes were fired from 1500 yards. One minute later an explosion was heard followed by a tremendous double explosion 10 seconds later. The explosion shook the *Torbay* violently causing some light damage.

Miers had sunk the 600-ton Italian minelayer submarine *Jantina*, whose lookouts failed in their duty. The huge double explosion was caused by mines on board, which blew the *Jantina* to smithereens. Even at a distance of 1,500 yards the force was enough to shatter the glass in *Torbay's* navigation lights.

Miers moved just east of Kytheria and on 8 July, surfaced and opened fire on a 200-ton swastika-flying schooner full of German troops. Before being able to bring his deck gun into action, a German plane appeared and the sub dived deep. Miers resumed the pursuit and later that morning he surfaced and sank the vessel with his 4in gun.

In the early hours of 9 July another target was spotted. Lieutenant Commander Miers wrote:

> At 0220 hours, while *Torbay* was off Cape Malea, a *caique* was seen on the horizon in very good visibility. *Torbay* turned to close. While doing so three more *caiques* were seen about two nautical miles apart steering the same course. As *Torbay* had not much ammo left for the deck gun it was decided that they were to be stopped with one well aimed round of the deck gun, then clear the decks with a Lewis gun and then scuttle them with demolition charges.
>
> At 0320 hours … fire was opened on the first *caique* with the Lewis gun and the four inch gun. Such a blazing fire was started in the *caique* that it was not possible to go alongside. Lewis gunfire was continued with until all the occupants were either killed or forced to abandon ship. The *caique* of about 100 tons was left to burn.

At 0327 hours *Torbay* set course to engage the second *caique*, At 0357 hours fire was opened on the second *caique*. Most of the crew took to the water and those who remained on board made signals as if to surrender shouting 'captain is Greek'.

Miers formed the opinion that the voice did not sound Greek and cautiously pulled alongside. Corporal Bremner of the SBS spotted one of the crew in the act of throwing a grenade and promptly shot him:

> The whole crew turned out to be Germans and they were forced to launch their rubber boat and jump into it. Another German was shot by the navigating officer when he tried to shoot this officer with a rifle from point blank range.
>
> The 100 ton *caique* had LV painted on her side and was carrying troops, ammo and petrol. The boarding party fitted with demolition charges and prepared to leave. Miers ordered the Lewis gun to open up on the German soldiers in the rubber boat to prevent them from returning to their ship. At 0435 hours the demolition charges exploded and the *caique* was sunk.
>
> At 0445 hours, a third sailing vessel was sighted, a large auxiliary schooner of about 300 tons making for Anti-Kythera. *Torbay* chased at full speed but as the target was making a good 10 knots it was not until 0530 that *Torbay* was close to the target. By that time it was daylight and boarding was out of the question.
>
> At 0530 hours … fire was opened. The schooner was filled with petrol and explosive and was quickly ablaze from stem to stern. *Torbay* dived soon after. This schooner was seen to sink at 0900 hours. The fourth *caique* escaped due to the arrival of an aircraft.

On the last day of *Torbay*'s patrol, she torpedoed and damaged the Italian tanker *Strombo* off Zea Island. Miers reported that he had sunk her but the Italians' official history states that she was taken in tow and taken to Salamis. Now with all torpedoes expended and a few rounds left for the deck gun, Miers returned to Alexandria. He arrived on 15 July to the sounds of cheering from the battleship *Queen Elizabeth* in respect of the submarine's exceptional patrol in which a submarine, a merchant ship, a tanker, three schooners and five *caiques* had been sunk.

On 2 August, *Torbay* left for the Gulf of Sirte off the Libyan coast and had a lucky escape. An Albacore torpedo-bomber of 826 Squadron attacked what it thought was an Italian 'Argo' class submarine. The aircraft dropped its torpedo but it sank after a run of 100 yards.

Miers was unaware of this as he had spotted what he thought was an enemy aircraft and was in the process of crash-diving. Through lack of intelligence, 826 Squadron had not been informed that a British submarine was in the area and fortune favoured the *Torbay*.

The targets around Benghazi were too well guarded and Miers had no luck. He then went to his next position off Crete, where he pulled off a great feat of rescue. Despite high-running seas, he managed to land an SBC soldier to liaise with a naval officer, Lieutenant Commander Francis Pool, who was part of a secret mission to organise escape routes for the many Allied soldiers still on the island. After a fraught night when hundreds of Greeks, including children and dogs, filled the rendezvous beach, many of whom wanted passage on the submarine, it was a small wonder that the Germans were unaware of this chaotic scene. It was finally was sorted out and *Torbay* departed with sixty-two New Zealanders, forty-two Australians, eleven British soldiers, one RAF serviceman, five Cypriot troops, three genuine Greek guides and a Yugoslav. The return to Alexandria proved to be very uncomfortable but at least the rescued men were now safe.

Miers' experience in the rescue of Allied soldiers just off the enemy-held island of Crete involved him in another special forces mission, (see 'Geoffrey Keyes VC'). *Torbay* left Alexandria on her sixth patrol on 7 October with an intelligence officer, Captain John Haseldon, and an Arab guide. They were dropped off at a small beach surrounded by rocks, at which Miers had to carefully manoeuvre to within 300 yards of the shore. The two agents managed to reach the beach with their folboat (a collapsible canoe) and eventually arrived back in Cairo – mission accomplished.

Miers would meet indirectly with Haseldon again on 14 November when *Torbay* and *Talisman* dropped the members of Operation *Flipper* at the beach at Zaviet el Hamama. Haseldon had kept his promise to be at the beach to meet the Commandos. The disembarkation from the submarines in heavy swell did not go well. Most of the folboats were swept from the submarine's casing and much of the equipment was lost. The number of Commandos that could be landed was drastically cut and already the operation had the look of failure. Lieutenant Colonel Laycock, with a few Commandos from *Talisman*, stayed on the beach while Keyes' diminished party headed the 18 miles inland for their attack.

Miers headed away from the shore but kept in the vicinity. On 20 November, he returned to search the beaches for activity but could not see any. Laycock and his party had been discovered earlier and scattered. Miers had two SBS men on board who paddled ashore but could not find any of the party. On their return, Miers decided to give Laycock another day before returning to Alexandria.

Torbay was involved in several more covert operations involving the now notorious folboat. Finally Miers complained that these operations were preventing his submarine from carrying out its sole purpose – sinking enemy shipping. He was supported by Captain Raw and Admiral Cunningham and Miers was never again involved in these undercover operations.

On 31 December 1941, Miers was promoted to commander and received the DSO. It was on his tenth patrol started on 20 February 1942 that the events took place that led to the awarding of his Victoria Cross and many gallantry awards for his crew.

It was now midwinter in the Mediterranean with high seas and poor visibility. While stalking a tanker on the 27th, *Torbay* was spotted by a destroyer and had to quickly dive. Miers was the last to descend down the conning tower but could not close the top hatch. Scampering down the ladder, he managed to slam close the second hatch as the conning tower flooded, short-circuiting the klaxon, which filled the submarine with its rasping din until someone pulled out the fuse and silence returned. The submarine was then treated to one of the worst depth-chargings so far experienced. Miers was furious and publically upbraided the engineer officer for poor maintenance. When it was safe to surface, Miers had to eat his words and apologise for it was his cushion that he used to snatch some sleep on the tower that had fouled the upper hatch.

The patrol was initially frustrating with near misses and ships too distant to attack. The area to the west of Greece seemed to be full of anti-submarine vessels and *Torbay* spent much time dodging them. Then on 4 March a convoy of four large troop ships and three destroyers was spotted heading north towards the Corfu Channel. Frustratingly, *Torbay* needed to recharge her batteries but Miers took a chance that the convoy would lay up at Corfu Roads, the anchorage off Corfu harbour.

This was a hazardous undertaking as the waters between Corfu and the Greek–Albanian mainland were quite confined and well-protected, and escape would be a difficult. For Miers the possibility of attacking such an irresistible target outweighed the dangers. Having recharged the batteries, *Torbay* sailed up the centre of the channel until she reached a point off Corfu harbour. The sea was calm and there was a moon but not enough to shed light on any ships at anchor. Miers decided to wait four hours until just before dawn to launch an attack. This would mean he would have to escape south in daylight through the narrow South Channel. During these four hours they had to be wary of the anti-submarine patrols that constantly appeared out of the darkness.

By the time *Torbay* approached the Corfu Roads it was light and to Miers disappointment, the large convoy had sailed. The Roads were not empty for there were two merchant ships, the *Maddalena G* (5,000 tons) and an unidentified 8,000-ton vessel and a destroyer. Despite the calm surface and the good visibility, Miers fired off two torpedoes at the smaller ship and two minutes later fired another two at the larger vessel. He also fired at the destroyer but missed. Diving deep, Miers set a course to speed for the South Channel before the anti-submarine defences could organise themselves. As they moved away they heard the satisfying sound of distant explosions, signifying hits.

After four hours they cleared the South Channel safely and, hoping to return to Alexandria, they received orders to head for the Gulf of Taranto and attack any ships of the Italian Fleet. After days of fruitless search, they reached their home port on 18 March.

There was a final patrol before *Torbay* sailed for England for a refit, and it was quite a fruitful one; she sank a minesweeper, a laden schooner, a 5,000-ton merchantman and 1,400-ton petrol carrier. Miers then left Alexandria and sailed his submarine back to England. On 7 July 1942, *The London Gazette* published his Victoria Cross citation for his attack on Corfu Roads.

On 28 July 1942, Commander Anthony Miers received his VC from the King at Buckingham Palace. Even then he managed to overturn protocol when he said he would not attend unless all his crew who had received gallantry awards were honoured with him. In the end the Lord Chamberlain's Office gave way and three of his officers received DSOs and DSCs and twenty-four ratings received their DSMs (Distinguished Service Medals). After the investiture, Miers took his crew for lunch at the Connaught Rooms.

Now promoted to captain, Anthony Miers VC, DSO was sent by the Admiralty on a world tour that lasted the rest of the war. He departed in late 1942 as commander of a naval draft of more than 2,000 officers and men sailing to Canada on the world's largest ship, the 83,673-ton *Queen Elizabeth*. From Canada he was part of an Admiralty delegation that visited Washington. During which time he had Christmas dinner with President and Mrs Franklin D. Roosevelt at the White House.

He then was sent to Pearl Harbour as submarine staff liaison officer to Admiral Chester Nimitz, Commander in Chief of the United States Pacific Fleet. Eager to get back into submarines, Miers persuaded the Americans to let him sail on the newly launched 1,526-ton US Navy submarine. USS *Cabrilla*. It was commanded by the inexperienced Lieutenant Commander Douglas Hammond, someone with whom Miers would soon fall out and all but accuse of cowardice.

The Americans had broken the Japanese naval codes and were aware that four large ships had sailed from their base at Truk in the Caroline Islands. At 0700 hours on 24 September 1943, Miers was taking turns on the periscope when he spotted the convoy and was thrilled to see that there were two Japanese aircraft carriers each about 17,500 tons escorted by just a single destroyer.

Lieutenant Commander Hammond was late with his manoeuvre and was too late to attack the leading carrier. His more experienced executive officer, Lieutenant Commander Henderson, insisted they attack the second carrier and fired off six torpedoes. A loud explosion was heard and Miers knew they had hit their target. Hammond, on the other hand, was convinced they were being depth-charged and dived deep rather than check the result through the periscope. There was some depth-charging but it was not near. The cautious US commander continued to creep away from the area until hours later they rose to periscope depth and saw that the aircraft carrier had been hit in the stern and was crippled. The first carrier had returned and was preparing to tow her sister ship to port. Miers was beside himself with frustration and impatience. This was a wonderful opportunity to sink two aircraft carriers that were stationary but still Hammond did little except watch the targets move away over the horizon.

Miers prepared a report of the day's activities, mentioning that a great opportunity had been wasted due to timidity on Hammond's part. Naturally Hammond objected and instead sent a watered down and ambiguous report to Pearl Harbour. The voyage would last for fifty-six days without having to refuel. For Miers it was one of increasing frustration with Hammond being over-cautious and missing obvious targets.

USS *Cabrilla* completed her long patrol when she reached Fremantle in Western Australia. One of Hammond's excuses for cutting down the submarine's speed and missing potential targets was that he was running low on fuel. Once they arrived in Fremantle it was shown that

Cabrilla carried 14,000 gallons of fuel and still carried twelve torpedoes. Despite his criticisms of the patrol, Miers was impressed by the US submarines over current Royal Navy classes and recommended that the Royal Navy implement similar improvements. The response he received from the Admiralty was predictably frosty and implied that Miers should keep his opinions to himself.

Commander Miers then went on an extended tour of New Guinea and the Solomon Islands before returning to Pearl Harbour. On 13 May 1944, he departed to Trincomalee, Ceylon, to take up command of the 8th Submarine Flotilla with HMS *Medway* as the depot ship. When the European War ended, the Allies made an all-out effort in defeating the Japanese. The 8th Submarine Flotilla was transferred to Fremantle. At nearby Perth, Anthony Miers rekindled his friendship with an eighteen year old student named Pat Miller and in January 1945 they were married. Soon they had a daughter.

The Miers family returned to England, where he took up command of HMS *Vernon II*, and on the last day of 1946 he was promoted to captain. The Americans presented him with their US Legion of Merit for his liaison duties on Admiral Nimitz's Staff. In 1948 he passed his 'A' pilot's licence and assumed command of the Royal Naval Air Station at Stretton. In 1950, he was appointed to command the depot ship HMS *Forth* and the 1st Submarine Flotilla Mediterranean Fleet. Two years later he was made captain of the Royal Naval College in Greenwich and in 1954 was in command of the aircraft carrier HMS *Theseus*. This was followed by promotion to Rear Admiral and Flag Officer, Middle East, in 1956 at the time of the Cyprus Emergency. On 4 August 1959, Miers retired from the Royal Navy.

For Miers, retirement was anything but humdrum; he was out of work for six months with little money behind him. He then received a knighthood and a job with a Birmingham button factory. The following year he took up a position with London and Provincial Poster Group and moved to a house in Roehampton. From 1971 he worked as a director for National Car Parks.

Miers also was involved in several associations including being national president of the Submarine Old Comrades Association, a member of the Worshipful Company of Tin Plate Workers, president of both RN Tennis and Squash Associations and a member of the MCC, Royal Highland Society and London Scottish RFC.

In 1970, he and Lady Miers joined nine other VC recipients for a tour of East Africa under the banner of '10 VCs in a VC10'. This was a publicity launch of the new extended version of the Vickers VC10 airliner, which was being introduced to BOAC's East African route. The Victoria Cross and George Cross Association had been asked to pick ten VCs at random, which included William White, Tom Adlam, Donald Dean, Arthur Proctor, Vic Turner, Philip Gardner, Bill Reid, Norman Jackson and Richard Annand. The only one who insisted on bringing his wife was retired Admiral, Sir Anthony Miers.

On 30 June 1985, this extraordinary force of nature died at his home in Roehampton. At his instruction, his body was taken back to Scotland and he was buried in the Roman Catholic section of Tomnahurich Cemetery in Inverness. His medals are on display at the Lord Ashcroft Gallery, Imperial War Museum.

John Linton VC

John Wallace Linton was born in Malpas near Newport, Monmouthshire, on 15 October 1905. He was the son of Edward, a local architect, and Margaret (née Wallace). Although there were no naval connections in the family, John Linton was keen to make the Royal Navy his career. In 1919, after preliminary training at Osbourne College on the Isle of Wight, he became a cadet at the Royal Naval College at Dartmouth. Although he was academically average, he was outstanding at mathematics, collecting the second prize in his term.

He served at Midshipman in HMS *Dauntless* and *Royal Oak* until 1927, when he joined the Submarine Service. He was a talented sportsman and, even though he was Welsh, he was given a trial game for England in 1927. He represented the rugby XVs of the Royal Navy, Hampshire and United Services. Along the way, he played with Anthony Miers, who described him as 'a most fearsome man with a heavy black beard'. When he gave up rugby in 1937, he began to put on weight to the extent that he was forever known as 'Tubby' Linton.

During the 1930s he served on the submarines *L.22*, *Oberon*, *H.43* and *Oswald*. He was given command of *L.21* and *Snapper*. When war broke out in 1939, he was serving on China Station, commanding the 2,000-ton *Pandora*, a large ocean-going vessel not well-suited for the Mediterranean Sea. In 1940, despite its unsuitability, *Pandora* was sent with other subs from the China Station to join 1st Flotilla in Alexandria. Linton carried out patrols around Crete and Greece without much success.

On 28 June he was ordered to Malta to conduct patrols off the Algerian coast in what became a notorious and regrettable episode in

Anglo–French relations. With France's surrender and the installation of the puppet Vichy government, Britain was bracing herself for a German invasion supported, it believed, by the might of the French fleet. Those French ships in British ports were seized with little resistance but those in French ports were regarded with alarm, especially the large French Mediterranean Fleet. The British government gave the Vichy French four options to avoid the Germans taking their ships into the *Kriegsmarine,* all of which were rejected.

The British then set in motion Operation *Catapult*; the naval bombardment of the French fleet at Mers-el-Kébir at Oran, Algeria. A last rejected call to surrender was followed by a bombardment on 3 July 1940, resulting in the deaths of 1,297 French servicemen and the sinking and damaging of six ships; French grievances over what they considered a betrayal by their former ally has festered for generations.

The following afternoon, 4 July, the *Pandora* spotted what she thought was a *La Galissioniere*-class light cruiser en route from Algiers to Bizerte. Linton fired four torpedoes, three of which struck home and caused a heavy blaze. An hour later it was seen to sink stern first, followed by a terrific explosion as its mines blew up. *Pandora* was subjected to depth-charging by a French minesweeper and bombs from three French aircraft.

The victim had been misidentified as a light cruiser when she was, in fact, the minelaying sloop *Rigault de Genouilly,* and not regarded as one of the objectives of Operation *Catapult*. Rather bizarrely in the light of the earlier bombardment, the British Admiralty apologised to the French legation.

Pandora's year in the Mediterranean was not fruitful. A couple of small vessels had been sunk and there were several near misses. On her ninth patrol she had better luck. On 9 January 1941, while searching off the north-east coast of Sardinia, she spotted two merchant ships, the 5,400-ton *Valdivagna* and the 2,715-ton *Palma,* both of which she torpedoed and sank.

There followed a period of routine patrolling and escorting in the Atlantic until in June *Pandora* was sent to the American shipyard of New London, Connecticut, for a refit. At this point, newly promoted Commander 'Tubby' Linton was given command of the new T-class submarine *Turbulent* on 18 November 1941. After trials, she sailed for Alexandria on 3 January 1942.

There followed a lengthy period of patrols that bore little fruit. Then, on the fifth patrol in the Gulf of Sirte, *Turbulent*'s luck changed.

On 14 May 1942, she surfaced and sank with gunfire the *San Giusto* carrying 160 tons of gasoline. On 18 May *Turbulent* fired three torpedoes at the 2,384-ton Italian merchant ship *Bolsena,* two of which hit home.

On 29 May, in poor weather, a convoy was spotted. Linton pursued it for four hours to get in a favourable position. He reported:

> 0401 hours – Sighted the convoy a little closer than expected. The escorting destroyer on this side could not be seen or heard.
>
> 0405 hours – Sighted the destroyer, it was much closer than anticipated. *Turbulent* was right ahead. The destroyer was seen to be on a steady bearing.
>
> 0407 hours – Fired four torpedoes at one of the merchant vessels. The destroyer was very near now. *Turbulent* went deep upon firing. 1min. 13secs after firing the first torpedo an explosion was heard. Shortly afterwards one of the torpedoes passed over the conning tower. Two further explosions were heard after firing the first torpedo. The torpedo that ran overhead had a gyro failure and with a great deal of luck had hit the destroyer that was so near to *Turbulent.*
>
> 0610 hours – Came to periscope depth and found one destroyer about 3 nautical miles away moving slowly around the position of attack. Nothing else in sight.

Linton had sunk the 3,172-ton *Capo Armo*, the 3,289-ton *Anna Maria Gualdi,* together with the 2,000-ton destroyer *Emanuele Pessagno.* On 2 June, he attacked the German submarine *U-81*, firing off five torpedoes. He heard two explosions and was certain he had destroyed the enemy sub, but on reaching the area could find no trace of it. In recognition of his service between 23 February and 4 June, Linton was awarded the DSO.

On his seventh patrol from 22 September to 14 October off Benghazi and Tobruk he did not net any targets but brought down several severe depth charge attacks, which even disturbed some rats living behind Tubby's partition in his cabin. In early November, *Turbulent* was part of a submarine cover for Operation *Torch;* the invasion of French North Africa.

On 11 November, off Sardinia, Linton torpedoed and sank the German auxiliary submarine tender *Benghasi.* Returning to the Gulf of Sirte, he surfaced and bombarded parked military transports at Sirte until coastal guns began returning fire. On his tenth patrol, near Sardinia, *Turbulent* torpedoed the 5,290-ton merchant ship *Marte.* On

11 January 1943, she sank the *Vittoria Beraldo* off Calabria after several attempts with torpedo and gunfire. Eventually the vessel ran aground and was seen to break in two. Just down the coast, *Turbulent* surfaced to bombard a goods train near San Lucido.

Sailing to the coast of Sicily, Linton torpedoed the 5,345-ton *Pozzuoli*. Five days later, she sank the 5,342-ton tanker *Utilitas* from a distance 4,500 yards. On 7 February, *Turbulent* spotted a train at Sant'Ambrogio station, surfaced and destroyed the engine and six wagons. With that, Linton returned to Algiers.

On 24 February, *Turbulent* departed on her twelfth and final Mediterranean patrol as she was to return to England for a refit. It was also the last time anyone saw her for she disappeared after heading for the Tyrrhenian Sea. She reported sinking a ship off Bonifacio on 1 March and is likely to have sunk three Italian sailing vessels with gunfire off Sicily. Her last sighting was on 14 March near Corsica, after which – silence. The probability was that *Turbulent* struck a mine near Maddalena off northern Sardinia and was sunk.

Turbulent, under the skilful command of Tubby Linton, was a highly successful submarine and its commander was the Royal Navy's second most successful submarine commander after David Wanklyn VC. In a similar way that Group Captain Leonard Cheshire was awarded the Victoria Cross for long and conspicuous gallantry rather than referring to a single event, so Commander John Linton received his posthumous award with the following citation:

> Commander Linton has been in command of submarines throughout the War. He has been responsible for the destruction of 1 cruiser, 1 destroyer, 20 merchant vessels, 6 schooners and 2 trains. A total of 81,000 tons of enemy shipping sunk. From 1st January 1942 to 1st January 1943 he spent 254 days at sea, including 2,970 hours diving. During this period he was hunted 13 times and had 250 depth charges dropped on him. His career has been one of conspicuous gallantry and extreme devotion to duty in the presence of the enemy.

His Victoria Cross was presented to his widow on 23 February 1944 and sixteen decorations were presented to the families of other members of the crew of HMS *Turbulent*.

With awards for prolonged periods of gallantry there are always those who question the awarding of the Victoria Cross for such apparently less prestigious or eye-catching acts. One recipient who questioned Linton's award many years later was the outspoken Anthony Miers VC, who reportedly said: 'I can't understand why that chap Tubby Linton was awarded the Victoria Cross.'

A tragic postscript occurred when Linton's son, William, joined the Royal Navy and volunteered for submarines. On 17 April 1951, he was aboard HMS *Affray*, which failed to surface while on exercise in the English Channel with the loss of seventy-five lives.

Chapter 10

Gazala Aftermath

On 14 June 1942, General Ritchie ordered the evacuation of the Gazala Line, which was initially successful. He wanted to fall back on the Egyptian border but General Auchinleck did not want another siege of Tobruk and ordered that a line should be held from Acroma, just west of Tobruk, to Bir el Gubi. The following day the 1st South African Division had pulled back around Tobruk. The 50th (Northumbrian) Division pulled off a dramatic move of which Rommel would have been proud. Finding the German had blocked their passage to the east, General Ramsden ordered an about-face and attacked his Italian pursuers. Taken by surprise, the Italians gave way and the Northumbrian Division swung south of Bir Hakeim and headed east across the desert. They managed to reach the Egyptian border safely and were in position to face the next stage of the fighting.

The new line Auchinleck had ordered was abandoned on the night of 16–17 June and the retreat continued. Tobruk was once again under siege, this time under the command of the inexperienced General Klopper. Much to the defenders' disgust, Klopper surrendered on 21 June and 32,000 Allied troops went into captivity.

Ritchie became the latest commander who fell victim to the axe and Auchinleck took charge. Rommel continued his pursuit into Egypt. There was resistance on 26–28 June at a piecemeal line that stretched from Marsa Matruh south to a rocky escarpment known as Minqar Qaim. It was midway between the two positions on some slightly elevated ground some 16 miles south of Marsa Matruh that a remarkable Victoria Cross was won by a Geordie squaddie.

111

Adam Wakenshaw VC

Adam Herbert Wakenshaw was born in Newcastle upon Tyne on 9 June 1914, one of six children to survive (seven died in infancy). His parents were Thomas, a labourer, and Mary and the family were brought up in abject poverty in industrial Gateshead. He left St Aloysius's Roman Catholic Boys School when he was fourteen and worked as a newsboy, briefly in a tripe factory, at the Elswick Colliery and as a builder's labourer. When he was sixteen he tried to enlist in the Army but his mother learned of this and promptly brought him home. When he was eighteen, he married Dorothy Ann Douglass and soon had three children. At that time the family was living at Duke Street, Newcastle.

Wakenshaw realised his ambition to join the Army by volunteering for the 9th (Territorial) Durham Light Infantry. When the Second World War broke out, many of the Territorial battalions were sent to France with the British Expeditionary Force. The 9th Battalion formed part of the 151st (Durham) Brigade and saw action in the retreat from Belgium in mid-May 1940.

On 20 May, the 151st Brigade was chosen as part of the Arras counter-attack. After initial success, the Germans counter-attacked and the British retreated to Vimy Ridge. The 151st Brigade was then ordered to move north to plug the gap brought about by the Belgian surrender. During the fighting, Wakenshaw was wounded. After a fighting retreat from Le Bassee Canal, the brigade fell back to Dunkirk, from where they were evacuated on 1 June. Private Wakenshaw has been described by his comrades as a keen if scruffy soldier, quiet and kind but one who knew how to look after himself. In February 1941, a tragedy hit the Wakenshaw family; his seven year old son, John, was killed in a road accident near his home. Wakenshaw was given compassionate leave and it was to be the last time his family saw him for he and the 9th Battalion were ordered to North Africa as part of the 50th (Northumbrian) Division.

The retreat from Gazala halted at Marsa Matruh, where the Eighth Army attempted to fight a rearguard action while further behind them a defensive position was being formed at El Alamein. The 151st Durham Brigade had been positioned on a flat and rocky plateau called Point 174, where it was impossible to dig in. Instead, the troops sheltered behind boulders and rock-built sangers while they waited for the appearance of the Afrika Korps.

Totally exposed in front of the infantry were placed the nine 2-pounder guns of the anti-tank platoon, of which Wakenshaw was a crew member. About 0515 hours on 27 June 1941, the German 90th Light Division approached supported by tanks and artillery. As they advanced, a tracked vehicle towing a light gun came within range of Wakenshaw's gun. The 2-pounder opened fire and scored a direct hit on the engine, which stopped dead. Another mobile gun opened fire and killed or badly wounded the crews of the little anti-tank guns. With the guns silenced, heavy mortars and artillery opened fire as the Germans moved towards the damaged tracked vehicle and the light artillery piece. If the Germans reached it they would only be 200 yards from the battalion. This was spotted by Wakenshaw, who was lying beside his gun but cruelly wounded – his left arm had been blown off above the elbow. As Wakenshaw raised himself to a kneeling position, a sergeant major repeatedly called to him from behind a boulder to retreat. Either he did not hear him or he was determined to do damage while he was still alive.

With the help of Private Eric Mohn, the wounded gun-layer, he managed to load five shells with one arm. A direct hit and the tracked vehicle burst into flames and the gun was damaged. Then a German round exploded close by, killing Mohn and further wounding Wakenshaw as he was thrown from the gun by the blast.

Painfully, he dragged himself back to his gun and loaded another round, but before he could fire a German round hit his gun and exploded the ammunition, killing him. With no anti-tank guns, the position was soon overrun. The Durhams lost twenty dead and 300 were taken prisoner. The Germans had also suffered and pulled back some miles to lick their wounds.

After the Germans had withdrawn, members of the 8th Battalion searched the defensive area and found Wakenshaw slumped over the breech-block. He was buried in the hard ground where he had fallen. In 1943, his body was reinterred at the El Alamein Cemetery.

His citation appeared in *The London Gazette* on 11 September 1942 and his widow and son, Thomas, received his VC on 3 March 1943 from the King at Buckingham Palace. Wakenshaw's anti-tank gun and Victoria Cross are now displayed at the DLI Museum in Durham.

On 28 June, the Allies made a second delaying attempt 30 miles to the east of Mersa Matruh at the coastal village of Fouka (Fuka). Unfortunately there was confusion in communication that left X Corps out of touch with the rest of the Eighth Army, which had moved back to El Alamein. Ordered to retreat from Mersa Matruh, X Corps found that the coastal road had been blocked by the Axis and they were forced south into the desert and to make their way to El Alamein the best way they could. In the night-time confusion, 5th Indian Division blundered into the enemy and sustained heavy casualties. The 29th Indian Infantry Brigade at Fouka was all but destroyed and the Axis took more than 6,000 prisoners and captured forty tanks and an enormous amount of supplies.

This poorly organised withdrawal and the subsequent battle at Ruweisat put pressure on General Auchinleck and his days were numbered as commander in chief. For the New Zealand 2nd Division the Battle of Ruweisat was a disaster but one that resulted in two exceptional Victoria Crosses.

Charles Upham VC and Bar

Charles Upham had returned from Crete a sick man and fortuitously missed Operation *Crusader,* as the entire 20th Battalion had been overrun at Belhamed Ridge. When the battalion was reformed, Upham was promoted to captain and placed in command of C Company. When Rommel broke through the Gazala Line, the 2nd New Zealand Division under the command of General Bernard Freyberg was recalled from Syria to help shore up the defence at Mersa Matruh. They were sent to a steep cliff-like escarpment known as Minqar Qaim about 10 miles south of the Durham's position at Point 174.

The division was motorised and some of the transport was parked below the escarpment on its right flank. On 27 June, the 21st Panzer with some of the 90th Light Division under the command of Major General Georg von Bismarck, and accompanied by Rommel, had swung south and unexpectedly come upon the New Zealanders.

At the height of the sun, the Germans began to shell the Kiwis while the tanks and infantry began to encircle around Freyberg's eastern flank, cutting off his retreat. The barrage continued until nightfall as the infantry made advances on the New Zealand positions.

Once again Captain Charles Upham, now commanding C Company, displayed contempt for the Germans and constantly exposed himself to incoming fire as he positioned his men. One of his platoons was being harassed by a mortar they could not locate. Upham leapt up on the roof of his cab and scanned the enemy lines with his binoculars, all the time drawing fire. Finally locating it, he passed the information to his platoon.

Ammunition was running dangerously low and Freyberg had been badly wounded in the neck. The command devolved on Brigadier Lindsay Inglis, who decided that come nightfall he would gather the division, punch a hole in the German line and breakout to the east. Forming up the three infantry battalions of 4th Brigade into an arrow formation, followed by the transport, with the artillery and anti-tank guns on the flanks, the unwieldy division got under way and moved east. When they neared the 104th Panzer Grenadiers, they came under heavy fire. Spontaneously, the Kiwis charged, causing great mayhem in a savage assault as the division pushed its way through; one soldier described it like a charge of the All Blacks.

Naturally Upham was in the thick of the action. Armed with a revolver and a bag full of grenades, he ran at the German transport as they tried to drive away. From the back of one vehicle, a machine gun opened up. Upham raced after it and hurled a grenade, killing all in the truck. A crowded staff car tried to pass but he pulled open the door and threw in a grenade, then shut the door again. In the process of the running fight, he was wounded in both arms but paid them no heed as he continued to attack the enemy. Upham was somewhat derisive about the German troops, many who had literally been caught with their pants down:

> In the advance the enemy were completely taken by surprise and many were killed at point-blank range without trousers or boots on. I have never seen trained soldiers so bewildered or 'flap' so much.

The charge continued for 5 miles before the New Zealanders finally halted to reorganise and head for the comparative safety of the defence line at El Alamein. The breakout saved the division from certain captivity and disrupted the Germans, who delayed their advance for three days. Later, Brigadier Jim Burrow, commanding 4th Brigade, recommended Upham for another VC. Charles Upham's aggression at Minqar Qaim was soon to be repeated at the battle of Ruweisat and he was destined to be the only combat soldier to be awarded a bar to his Cross.

They reached the El Alamein Line, which was more a series of defensive boxes running 30 miles north to south than a continuous line. El Alamein was little more than a small station on the coastal railway line and chosen because 34 miles south was the deep sand and salt marshes of the Qattara Depression. It was a position that afforded the shortest defensive line and acted as a bulwark against any flanking movement by Rommel. It was also the last possible defence before reaching Alexandria, just 50 miles away. The New Zealanders and the 5th Indian Brigade were given the task of taking Ruweisat Ridge, a long, low feature ranging from 150 to 200ft in height and 5 miles south of El Alamein. It was important to capture as it was the only high point and dominated the whole area. Unfortunately, the planning was almost non-existent and there was little co-ordination between the brigades; the New Zealanders narrowly avoided firing on a British column and were themselves shelled by British artillery. The lack of communication would later prove a disaster in the Battle of Ruweisat Ridge.

Facing the New Zealanders was the Italian Ariete Armoured Division. In the opening artillery duel, the Kiwis destroyed the enemy's guns and it appeared that a swift victory would be theirs. It developed into a battle that was difficult for the ordinary soldier to understand as the enemy appeared to be coming at him from all directions. It was not much clearer for the senior officers. Brigadier James Burrows asked Major Ian Manson the CO of 20th Battalion, which was held in reserve, to send an officer forward to find the 19th Battalion as all contact had been lost. He chose Captain Charles Upham, who went in search in a jeep and returned with the disturbing news:

> I could not find 19th Battalion when going forward and 18th and 19th were in confusion. So were the Germans. They were getting trucks out and pulling guns back by hand and ropes. All this went on under cover of fire from tanks, in groups of three, which were covering the withdrawal. It was a very colourful show with flares going up, tanks firing and red tracer bullets from machine-guns. Two German tanks were put out with sticky bombs: they went up quite close to us ... The German troops were being badly cut up while the Italians were surrendering in hundreds. They were out of all proportion to our people and really broke up the attack with their crowds ... All the time this was going on and even before, there was a rumble of tanks on our exposed left flank ... I returned to Brigadier Burrows and reported that there appeared to be confusion on our right flank, 19 Bn had gone through its objective and 18 Bn was not so far forward. The enemy line appeared to have collapsed but there were a lot of tanks holding out in groups of three.

Upham omitted to mention that he found himself in the half-light between night and day in a very confused situation and felt himself inadequately armed. He found a German machine gun, with which he cleared his path. He found a lone artillery officer and together they went in search of the missing battalions. On one occasion they ran into a sandy trench and, with the help of some Italians who wished to surrender, managed to extricate their vehicle. After an hour Upham returned with his report.

Burrows then ordered Manson to attack and occupy the western end of Ruweisat Ridge and take a rocky prominence called Point 63. By that time it was expected that the tank support would arrive and continue to sweep the enemy from the ridge. The attack on Point 63 went in, while Upham's C Company dealt with the heavy fire coming from their left flank.

Moving to a slight ridge, Upham looked down on a shallow depression in which there were about 400 trucks and infantry firing machine guns at the attacking Kiwis on the ridge. From a distance of 400 yards, Upham led his men in a charge in the face of severe fire across the depression. Gaps soon appeared and all three platoon leaders were killed. Upham was also hit painfully in the elbow but still kept going, urging his men on. The survivors closed with the enemy and with grenade and bayonet they cleared the machine gun nests and pursued the fleeing Germans and Italians. As the fight quietened down, the 20th found that they had captured forty-two Germans and 100 Italians despite their number reduced to fifty men.

Upham was driven back to the regimental aid post to have his wound dressed and, after taking a rest, he re-joined his men and they waited for the anticipated enemy counter-attack. The British armour support had not materialised due to one of the many communications failures. This left the New Zealanders in a very vulnerable position on a rocky ridge where digging foxholes was an impossibility.

The Axis forces did not immediately counter-attack but spent the day shelling the exposed Kiwis, who suffered from the shells exploding on the hard rock of the ridge. In the late afternoon, the Panzers advanced and soon wiped out the anti-tank guns mounted on flatbed trucks. The New Zealand infantry suffered severely from the relentless sun, thirst and the clouds of flies that infested the insanitary positions left by the Italians. Facing the sinking sun and the huge clouds of dust thrown up by the advancing Axis armour, the enemy was able to get within 250 yards of the defences. The outcome was almost inevitable.

Upham was with his men when a mortar bomb exploded close by and he was wounded in the leg. Unable to walk, he waited with the six survivors of his company as the Germans arrived to take them prisoners of war. The Battle of Ruweisat Ridge had been a disaster for the 2nd New Zealand Division, which suffered 1,405 casualties.

From Ruweisat, Upham was taken to a cellar of an ill-equipped hospital where terminally wounded officers were collected. It was recommended that he have his arm amputated as the hospital did not have sufficient medication to treat gangrene or, for that matter, anaesthetic; Upham vehemently refused to lose his arm. After a while in this wretched hospital he recovered sufficiently for him to move to Italy and a POW camp. When the Italians surrendered he obeyed the senior officer's order to stay put having been told that arrangements were being made to return him to the Allies. Unfortunately the Germans took control and shipped the prisoners back to Germany. Upham decided that if he could not fight the Germans, he would set about making life uncomfortable for his captors by persistently trying to escape. In one attempt, he jumped from an open truck but was soon captured, having sustained a broken ankle.

He tried again by leaping from a speeding train but knocked himself unconscious. When he reached the POW camp in Germany, he attempted to climb the barbed wire fence in broad daylight but fell between the two barriers and became entangled in barbed wire. A furious prison guard pointed his gun at Upham and threatened to shoot but the trapped prisoner calmly ignored him and lit a cigarette.

Upham was considered a great risk and put in solitary confinement. He exercised alone in a small yard accompanied by two guards and covered by a machine gun in a guard tower. One day he broke away from his exercise yard, sprinted through the guard's barracks and out of the front gate but ran into some soldiers on the road to the camp. On 14 October 1944, tiring of his many fruitless attempts to escape, the Germans sent Upham to the infamous Oflag IV-C (Colditz Castle), where persistent officer escapees were incarcerated.

On 15 April 1945, the US Army liberated Colditz and the freed prisoners made their way to their own lines. Upham elected to join an American unit to continue the fight against the Germans. This extra service with a foreign army was short-lived as American senior officers discovered Upham serving unofficially in their ranks. Returning to England, he and fellow 20th Battalion comrade, Jack Hinton, attended their investiture at Buckingham Palace. On 11 May 1945, Upham belatedly received his Victoria Cross for his exploits in Crete. He was also reunited with his fiancée, Molly McLane, whom he married at New Milton, Hampshire, on 20 June 1945.

Upham further received a mention in despatches for his many escape attempts. When he returned home he learned that he was to receive the Distinguished Service Order for his gallantry at Ruweisat Ridge. This was soon changed by Major General Kippenberger, who felt the award should be a second VC. The King was won over by Kippenberger's advice that Upham had won the VC several times over, and so became the only combat soldier to receive a bar to affix to his Cross. Hancocks, the maker and supplier of the VCs, had a dilemma. The date of the action was engraved in the centre of the reverse of the Cross and there was no room to add the second date. Instead, they said they would engrave it on the reverse of the bar, as had been done to the two medical VCs of the First World War. It was suggested that Upham return his VC to London so that Hancocks could fit the bar to the ribbon. An alternative was that a duplicate VC with bar be made by Hancocks and sent to New Zealand, where it could be presented to Upham. In the event, Upham received the duplicate Cross, removed the bar and had it fixed to the Cross he had presented to him by the King. The duplicate, minus bar, was then returned to Hancocks.

After the trials he had endured during the war, it would have been natural that he would accept the help that was offered him by a grateful nation. Instead, he refused to accept the money that had been allocated to him and used it to set up a scholarship fund for the children of returning servicemen. The ever-retiring Upham won a returned servicemen's ballot and was donated a farm on the remote Conway Flats in North Canterbury. Without roads, water or electricity, he and his wife endured hardship in the first years but established a home in the wilderness. He relished working this farm with a land that was wild and unproductive. Satisfyingly, he used his agricultural skills and turned it into a productive farm running some 1,600 sheep, fifty Hereford cattle and nine horses. His dislike of anything German stayed with him and this included refusing any German-made car entry to his land.

He retired in January 1994 and moved into a residential home at Bishopspark, Christchurch. By this time, his health was deteriorating and he knew the end could not be far away. When it was suggested that he might have a state funeral, he replied simply that, 'A bugle will do.'

Charles Upham died on 22 November 1994. He was cremated and his ashes placed in the family plot at St Paul's Anglican Church, Christchurch. The people of New Zealand were not to be deprived of the opportunity to pay their respects to their most famous soldier and plans for a state event were already in place when he died. On 25 November 1994, thousands lined the streets of the provincial capital to say their farewell, among them the Prime Minister, the Minister for Defence, the Chief of the Defence Force, numerous politicians and thousands of ex-servicemen, some of whom had been with Upham in Crete and North Africa.

The New Zealand nation's efforts to remember its hero are unsurpassed. Some, like the educational foundation named after him, and the Charles Upham Bravery Award, have existed for many years. Others came thick and fast, including the following:

> A troop transport ship was renamed the RNZS *Charles Upham.*
> An 80c postage stamp issued by the NZ Post Office.
> The *Charles Upham Story* was broadcast by TVNZ.
> *Mark of the Lion* by Kenneth Sandford, published in 1962, is still in print.
> Upham House at Macleans College, Auckland.
> The *Charles Upham March,* composed as the regimental march of the 2nd Bn Royal NZ Regt.
> A bronze sculpture at his old school, Christ College.
> Streets named after him.
> A statue by Mark Wyte at Amberley North.

His unique medal group went through a period of controversy that has been resolved to the satisfaction of all parties. Upham's daughters wished to sell the group for £1.17 million. The group was offered to the New Zealand government for the same price that was offered the previous year by a private collector. The government was not willing to offer this sum but stressed how important it was that the country should retain such a treasure. In September 2006 the Imperial War Museum in London agreed to purchase the group, made possible by the generosity of the Garfield Weston Foundation based in the UK. The proviso was that it would be loaned to New Zealand for a period of 999 years and would remain in that country.

Keith Elliott VC

Keith Elliott was born in the small settlement of Apiti near Feilding on North Island on Anzac Day (25 April 1916). He was the eighth of nine children born to Frank Capper Elliott and his wife, Ethel Marie (née Knyvett). His formative years were spent at Apiti before the family moved to Feilding, where they ran a succession of poor farms in the area.

Elliott attended the Feilding Agricultural High School, where the headmaster made a great impression on him. Unfortunately, at the age of seventeen he was forced to leave to work on the farm because his eldest brother fell ill. He spent four rough years scraping out a living on the family 96-acre farm before the beginning of the Second World War. He was often tempted to walk away from this grinding life but his mother persuaded him to stay. News of the outbreak of war gave him the excuse to enlist, which he did in 1939. Although he was a fit rugby-playing volunteer, he was rejected because of his bad teeth. He persisted and was eventually accepted in January 1940, joining the 22nd Battalion. His commanding officer was the First World War VC, Leslie Andrew, a strict disciplinarian.

Unlike the first troops sent to the Middle East, the 22nd Battalion was sent to a camp near Aldershot in England, where it arrived on 16 June 1940. The battalion was inspected by an array of important dignitaries including King George VI and Winston Churchill. On 4 January 1941, it sailed to Egypt and almost immediately to Greece. Lance Corporal Elliott saw his first action against the Germans at Mount Olympus. Despite putting up a resistance, the 22nd was forced to retreat at night after just one day's fighting. They travelled for two days until they reached Porto Rafti, where they were evacuated to Crete, arriving on 25 April, Elliott's birthday.

The 22nd Battalion was given the task of defending the crucial airfield at Maleme, which bordered the coast on north-west Crete. The battalion occupied positions on a hill known as Point 107 and along the western edges of the airfield. On the clear sunny morning of 20 May, the German invasion began. Hundreds of three-engine Junkers Ju 52 transports disgorged the elite German paratroopers. Elliott recalled:

> My most vivid impress is that the invaders were squealing like pigs as they drifted down, which is understandable, because they must have seen the grim-faced Kiwis below them waiting with their weapons. And we had to deal with them like pigs, charging with our bayonets. It was horrible putting our training into first practice.

The New Zealanders were joined by the Cretans, who attacked the Germans with an assortment of agricultural implements. By the afternoon, the Germans had managed to land some of their gliders with artillery and the battle began to swing in favour of the enemy. The battalion's commander, Lieutenant Colonel Leslie Andrew, requested support from 23rd Battalion in the east. This was turned down as it was erroneously thought that they were tied up fighting paratroopers in the area. In desperation, Andrew used his meagre reserve – two tanks and an infantry platoon – to drive back the Germans from the edge of the airfield. The tanks soon broke down and Andrew was unable to contact his forward companies. Another communications lapse forced Andrew to order his battalion to pull back and join 21st Battalion to the east.

Elliott and his platoon was part of B Company and did not receive the order to withdraw. That evening when his company's commander, Major Leggitt, belatedly discovered that the battalion had pulled back, Elliott was furious for he felt the Germans had suffered a defeat at the hands of the New Zealanders. As a consequence, Andrew, a brave man who had won the VC in 1917, was heavily criticised for his abandonment of Maleme airfield and later lost the command of his battalion.

The rest of the battle for Crete was one of retreat. Elliott and his platoon fought a brief skirmish at Pirgos, where he was wounded in the arm. There followed a grim retreat over the mountains to Sphakia on the south of the island, where he was again evacuated for the second time in a month.

When he reached Egypt, Elliott was promoted to platoon sergeant. In November the 2/New Zealand Division took part in Operation *Crusader* with the aim of linking up with the 70th Division breaking out of Tobruk. The 22nd Battalion was allocated to protect 5th Brigade HQ at Sidi Azeiz near the Egyptian border on the British right flank. Towards the end of *Crusader*, Rommel ordered 15th Panzer to attack any forces besieging the border positions between Fort Capuzzo and Sidi Omar. In order to do this 15th Panzer would first have to capture Sidi Azeiz, where it expected to find a large supply dump. Instead, it found B Company 22nd Battalion, plus some armoured cars, field artillery and anti-tank units. Holding out for two days, the New Zealanders were overrun and 700 prisoners were taken, including Elliott.

There followed two months of captivity in Bardia in an overcrowded POW pen with no sanitation and a near-starvation diet. They were liberated by the South Africans on 2 January 1942. Elliott went in weighing 12 stone and when he was released he was down to 7 stone. When he had regained weight he joined the 2/New Zealand Division, which had been moved from the Western Desert to Syria to re-equip and replace its losses. It was during his stay in Syria that Elliott contracted malaria and was hospitalised in Nazareth, missing the breakout at Minqar Qaim.

He re-joined his platoon on 13 July 1942 in time for the attack on Ruweisat Ridge. Due to sickness and a shortage of commissioned officers, Elliott was elevated to commander of 11 Platoon. They set off on the morning of 14 July; the 4th Brigade was on the left and Elliott's 5th Brigade alongside on the right. Advancing 6 miles in a north-westerly direction from south, the two brigades attacked the Axis holding the western end of the low ridge.

By midnight the 22nd Battalion had hit serious resistance and fought for the next four hours before it reached the ridge. As dawn broke, the New Zealanders were confronted by ten tanks of the 8th Panzer Regiment, which unbeknown to them had been laagered in the middle of their position. Without their own armour, the 22nd Battalion stood little chance of resisting the Germans and soon they were overwhelmed and captured. The exception was Sergeant Elliott's 11 Platoon on the extreme right flank.

Elliott was up before daybreak and in the grey light saw tanks approaching from the south-west. He quickly noticed that they displayed black crosses on their turrets. Hurrying to the commanders of 10 and 12 Platoons, he reported what he had seen but was reassured by the inexperienced junior officers that these were the British tanks that had been promised. Unconvinced, he returned to his platoon and, taking a chance that he was disobeying orders, led his men forward and away from the approaching tanks. An eyewitness later recorded:

> It was all very bewildering to have tanks coming in from the front and the rear and they now had their machine-guns going all the time to keep us down … One platoon on our right that was near a bit of a ridge made a run for it, they had of course to run a gauntlet of machine-gun bullets, and it was pretty grim to see these men running with dust being kicked up all round them as they fell or dived to the ground and then up and on again …

As they headed for a slight rise 300 yards away, one of the tanks' machine guns opened fire. One of the bullets fired across Elliott's chest was fortuitously diverted, hitting his pay book in his breast pocket before grazing his breast but not incapacitating him. The entire platoon made it to the rise but noticed that they were in the line of fire from their anti-tank guns. Spotting another ridge 400 yards further on, Elliott's small party ran to the meagre cover it gave and looked back at the fight that was going on behind them. They were in time see the rest of their battalion being marched into captivity.

Elliott had his chest wound dressed and was able to link up with two platoons of 21st Battalion. Later that morning it was learned that a badly wounded officer from the 21st was lying out close to the enemy. Elliott volunteered to go and look for him. Taking eight men, they went forward until they came under fire from a machine gun hidden in a slight depression some 500 yards away and another nest 250 yards distant. Elliott ordered five men to take care of the nearer machine gun nest while he led a bayonet charge across the open 500 yards to take out the further enemy post. With no cover to help them, Elliott and his three men got to within 50 yards of the enemy position before eleven pairs of Italian hands shot up in surrender.

Elliott found there was an anti-tank gun and four machine guns in the post, which he set about destroying. As he did so, another two enemy positions started firing at the Kiwis from about 100 yards. Sending one of his men back for reinforcements, Elliott and his two companions herded the prisoners and, taking them with them, captured the other two positions easily. Elliott and his men now had fifty Italian prisoners, albeit willing captives, when they again came under fire. Elliott let his two men look after the prisoners while he took on the new threat.

Bent double, he ran across 200 yards of open ground under heavy fire and found shelter behind an abandoned water truck close to an enemy machine gun nest. A burst of machine gun fire punctured the tank, which gave Elliott a welcome shower of cool water. Another burst hit him in the thigh and he rolled over. In doing so, he saw a sniper firing at his two companions. Taking aim, he saw the sniper fall.

He recommenced the charge and hurled a grenade into the machine gun post, at the same time receiving a wound in his knee. Entering the post, he found the machine-gunner and some others dead but took fifteen more German prisoners. With the immediate area neutralised, Elliott returned to his men and helped them overcome any last resistance.

They were now able to shepherd their prisoners back to 21st Battalion, where it was found that Elliott and his small party had killed thirty and captured 142 prisoners. The platoon had suffered just two casualties, including Elliott, whose wounds were the most serious. The injured officer, who had been the main focus of Elliott's foray, was found and later recovered.

Elliott's incredible exploit in subduing five enemy posts, one of which he attacked single-handedly, was one of the outstanding actions in the North African campaign and richly deserved the awarding of the Victoria Cross. He was gazetted on 24 September 1942. General Freyberg gave Elliott a field commission and the new Eighth Army commander, Lieutenant General Bernard Montgomery, presented him with his VC ribbon. According to Harper and Richardson's book *In the Face of the Enemy*, a note in Elliott's personal file states:

> In a private latter to me (Brigadier Conway – Adjutant General) dated 12 June, Brigadier W.G. Stevens explains that in May 1943, the proposal to commission Sgt. Elliott was submitted to GOC (Freyberg) and it was decided that Sgt. Elliott was to be sent home as not being really fit for a commission.

It would seem that General Freyberg had been swept along by the outstanding leadership of Sergeant Elliott and that he gave him a field commission without pondering about his suitability as an officer. In the event, and much to Elliott's chagrin, he was ordered to return to New Zealand, probably to keep him safe as fellow VC Charles Upham had been captured. He arrived back in New Zealand on 12 July 1943 and in September received his Cross from the Governor-General. In December 1943, he left the Army with the rank of second lieutenant and returned to farming.

In February 1944, he married Margaret Markham and together they produced five children. Encouraged by a friend who had been a military padre, Elliott began training for the priesthood. In 1948, he became a priest and took up a curate in Palmerston North before becoming chaplain at Linton Military Camp. For the next few years he served in several parishes in the North Island. In 1954, he attended the unveiling of the Alamein Memorial and in 1956 came to London for the centenary of the Victoria Cross. In 1977, he walked 3,400km, the entire length of New Zealand, to raised money for a new church. In 1981, he retired from the priesthood, moving to Raumati.

The Reverend Keith Elliott VC died on 17 October 1989 after a long battle with cancer. He was buried with full military honours at Paraparaumu Cemetery.

Arthur Stanley Gurney VC

Arthur Stanley Gurney was the fourth of five children born to George Gurney, a miner, and his wife, Jane (née Roberts). Stan, as he was commonly known, was born at Day Dawn, on the Murchison goldfields in Western Australia. He was educated at the local state school and at Stott's Business College in Perth. Starting work as a real estate agent, he then joined the City of Perth Electricity and Gas Department in 1927 as a clerk and meter engineer. He was an enthusiastic cyclist, winning many road-races, and he was well-known locally as a successful amateur and professional cyclist.

When war broke out, he enlisted into the Australian Imperial Force on 6 December 1940 and eight months later embarked for the Middle East. On 12 September he joined the 2/48th Battalion at Tobruk, before being relieved and moving to Palestine in October and Syria in January 1942.

As part of the 26th Brigade, 9th Division, the 2/48th was deployed to Egypt in June to meet the advance of the Axis forces after their victory at Gazala. The commander of the 9th Division, General Leslie Morshead, was ordered forward 10 miles west of the Alamein box to the small railway station of Tel el Eisa. The coastal road ran parallel with the narrow-gauge single track railway wedged between the salt marshes that bordered the coastal beaches and the series of small hills and outcrops to the south. The most significant of these was the twin 75ft-high humps of a mound known as Point 24 East and Point 24 West. In what became known as the Second Battle of Ruweisat, its outcome was as disastrous as the first. General Morshead protested to Auchinleck that the plan was ill-conceived with inadequate support. Because the 26th Brigade had to hold its existing ground, the 2/23rd and 2/48th battalions could each spare only two companies for the assault and these would lack reinforcements. Nevertheless, the assault had to go in.

On the night of 22–23 July 1942, the 2/23 Battalion attacked Point 24 East supported by artillery and was successful in occupying the feature. This was a signal for B and D Companies to launch their attack on Point 24 West. D Company made straight for the objective while B Company swung to the far left to attack from the south. Almost immediately they came under heavy artillery and mortar fire that brought many casualties. D Company lost all its officers and became pinned down 100 yards from the summit. Adding to their discomfort, several machine guns on the left flank opened up on the prone infantrymen.

Private Stan Gurney carried 11 Platoon's cumbersome Boyes anti-tank rifle until his platoon commander told him to replace it with a rifle and bayonet. Shortly after, both officer and the platoon sergeant were dead. Unable to move, D Company was in crisis. Taking the initiative, Gurney stood up and rushed towards the nearest enemy weapon pit followed by another private. Within a few yards of the enemy position, he pulled the pin from his grenade and threw it. As he did, a German leapt out at him but Gurney turned quickly and used his bayonet to good use. The two Aussies dashed into the trench and despatched two more Germans.

Leaving his mate, Gurney jumped out of the trench and raced towards another machine gun nest 30 yards away. Despite a hail of fire, he reached it, bayoneted two more Germans and sent the third back as a prisoner. As he accomplished this, another machine gun opened up on him and, just as he approached the nest, a grenade exploded at his feet, throwing him to the ground but not wounding him. Recovering his rifle, he completed his charge and was seen wielding his bayonet 'with great vigour'. It was the last to be seen of him until later when his body was recovered. The effect on the rest of D Company was inspirational and they rose to take Point 24 West.

B Company on the left was successful in its advance and soon joined B Company on Point 24 West. Unfortunately, both companies had taken heavy casualties and were unable to withstand the enemy's counter-attack that evening.

Gurney's body was found and taken to be buried in El Alamein's war cemetery. His outstanding feat of bravery in the face of overwhelming odds was soon recognised with the awarding of the Victoria Cross. It was given to his family by the Lieutenant Governor of Western Australia and is now displayed at the Australian War Memorial, Canberra. It is of note that the 2/48th Battalion set a record for the Second World War. Gurney was one of four VCs awarded to the battalion; the others were William Kibby, Percy Gratwick and Tom Derrick. Stan is still remembered for his cycling skills and the Stan Gurney (VC) Memorial Race is held every Anzac Day.

Chapter 11

El Alamein

The battles for Rusweisat and Tel el Eisa, sometimes called the First Battle of El Alamein, ended in stalemate but halted the Axis advance on Alexandria, Cairo and, ultimately the Suez Canal. To the Axis troops these objectives seemed as close as a mirage, yet so far away. The Eighth Army had suffered more than 13,000 casualties in July, the bulk of which included 4,000 in the New Zealand Division, 3,000 in the 5th Indian Infantry Division and 2,552 in the 9th Australian Division. The Axis forces had also received considerable damage, with 7,000 men taken as prisoners and heavy injuries to troops and damage to equipment. Both sides needed a period to recover; replace munitions and men before re-joining the battle. In spite of the enormous distance the Eighth Army had retreated, it was now in a much stronger position with supplies and men arriving daily. Despite this, there still pervaded an atmosphere that the force was second best to Rommel's Panzers and morale was low.

General Auchinleck was confident that the Eighth Army would be ready to take the field against by mid-September in a defensive role but he did not get the chance to put this to the test. In early August, Winston Churchill and General Sir Alan Brooke, the Chief of the Imperial General Staff (CIGS), visited Cairo on their way to meet Joseph Stalin in Moscow. The Eighth Army's defensive position so close to Egypt's major cities and the lack of fighting spirit made up their minds to replace Auchinleck with the XIII Corps commander, Lieutenant General William Gott, as Eighth Army commander and General Sir Harold Alexander as Commander in Chief Middle East Command. Before this could be put into effect, Gott was killed when his aircraft was shot down while on the way to take up his command.

General Brooke persuaded Churchill to appoint Lieutenant General Bernard Montgomery, who was about to assume command of the First Army, which was assigned to the Anglo–American Operation *Torch* landings in French North Africa. Montgomery had commanded the 3rd Division of the BEF in the retreat from Dunkirk and had impressed his Corps commander, Brooke, in the handling of his men. It turned out to be an appointment of mixed blessings. Montgomery lacked social skills, was supremely confident in his own ability and opinions and rudely intolerant of those of others. However, he did have a knack of communicating with the ordinary soldier and was what was needed for the Eighth Army, which had suffered a succession of defeats mainly due to lack of communication and poor planning.

Montgomery took command on 13 August and immediately made an impact. He was determined that the Army, Navy and Air Force should coordinate their battles in a unified manner according to a detailed plan. At his first meeting with his senior officers he ordered all contingency plans for retreat to be destroyed, even though Auchinleck had never contemplated this. Montgomery made himself visible to the troops and visited the various units, where he engendered a spirit of optimism. He took to wearing unconventional headgear that endeared him to the men and settled on the black beret of the Royal Tank Regiment, displaying the badges of the regiment next to the General Officer's badge. When Generals Brooke and Alexander visited the El Alamein front they were amazed at the transformation that Montgomery had brought about.

Tactically, Montgomery scrapped Auchinleck's orders for a 'mobile defence', replacing it with a continuous front 20 miles long held by four infantry divisions: from north to south: 9th Australian, 1st South African, 5th Indian and 2nd New Zealand. He was also enormously helped by Ultra intelligence intercepts from the Government Code and Cypher School (GC&CS) at Bletchley Park giving him knowledge of Rommel's intentions. This was illustrated when the Allies got intelligence that Rommel had decided to strike before the Allied build-up was complete.

Two Panzer armoured divisions led an attack on 30 August that was stopped by the Allies at Alam el Halfa Ridge. With a continuous night-time bombardment by the RAF the Germans were forced to pull back but Montgomery did not follow up, preferring to wait until all his forces were prepared.

Rommel, with his problematic supply line, sowed his 'Devil's Garden', the defensive entanglements of land mines and barbed wire protecting his positions about 12 miles west of El Alamein. His defensive line ran from Tel el Elsa on the coast to the Qattara Depression in the south. During the weeks before Montgomery planned his attack, a mine clearance school was organised to train Royal Engineers on the use of a new mine detector developed by a Polish officer. The limited number of Scorpion tanks fitted with rotating flails was not a great success so the sappers had to do this dangerous work manually. In what has been described as the world's largest minefield, an estimated 3 million mines were laid along the 30-mile front.

By October, the Eighth Army was ready with 195,000 men and 1,029 tanks, including the new American M3 Sherman tank that now gave the Allies superiority over the Panzers. Facing them was a well-entrenched Axis army of 116,000 men and 547 tanks.

At 2130 hours on 23 October 1942, Montgomery unleashed XXX Corps (9th Australian, 51st Highland, 2nd New Zealand and 1st South African) from his rejuvenated Eighth Army against the Italian-held positions in the north. Supported with 426 field and forty-eight medium guns, the bombardment could be heard in Alexandria. Taken by surprise, Rommel's temporary replacement, General Stumme, drove to the front line to find out what was happening and died of a heart attack. Fortunately for the Afrika Korps, Rommel returned from sick leave on 25 October.

The initial hoped for breakthrough did not materialise. Although a 6 mile-deep hole was punched in the Axis defence it was not enough to enable the British armour to break out.

The battle had been in progress for about two days when Montgomery switched the emphasis on the 9th Australian Division, which had made progress on Miteirya Ridge, held by the Trento Division. It was here that two El Alamein Victoria Crosses were earned by members of the same regiment.

Percy Gratwick VC

Percival Eric was born on 19 October 1902 at Katanning, Western Australia, the fifth son of Ernest Albert Gratwick, a postmaster, and his wife, Eva Mary (née Pether). When his father died when Percy was aged nine the family struggled to make ends meet. Percy was educated at state schools in Katanning, Boulder and Perth before leaving at the age of sixteen. He worked as a messenger at Parliament House, Perth, before he left in 1922 and went north to work at Indee Station as a drover and blacksmith.

He then moved south to Yandeyarra as a station-hand. He gradually built up a droving business, employing mostly Aboriginal stockmen. This came to an end in 1931 when a drought hit the area and he was forced to work part-time on White Springs Station. In about 1936, he prospected at a tantalite mine (used in alloys) at nearby Wodgina, where he was a blacksmith and worked with cattle at White Springs.

Like many men scraping a living at that time, the outbreak of war gave Gratwick a chance of some stability. Unfortunately he was rejected because his nose had been broken some years before. Determined to be accepted, he paid to have it fixed and on 20 December 1940 joined the AIF. After training, he sailed from Perth on 5 July 1940 and joined the 2/48th Battalion at Tobruk.

After a spell in Palestine, the regiment was sent to Egypt and fought at Tel el Eisa in July 1942. Gratwick was held in reserve so did not take part in the fighting but would soon get his chance in October. A quiet, self-contained man, he had never been in action before but his subsequent act of outstanding gallantry saved his mates and gained a significant victory.

On the night of 25–26 October, the 2/48th was ordered to attack a point known as Trig 29 on Miteiriya, or Ruin, Ridge. This was a flattened spur south-west of Tel el Eisa, an undistinguished feature that was no more than 20ft above the flat desert. This made Trig 29 tactically vital as it commanded the surrounding area, including the coastal railway line. Setting off at midnight on the 25th, the 2/48th was supported by artillery but soon ran into a situation from which there appeared no escape. The ground ahead sloped down, then up, and both slopes were dotted with mortar and machine gun posts. Kenneth Slessor, an Australian official war reporter, interviewed some of the men who took part in this fight:

> A Company got the job and in the final phase Percy Gratwick was out in front on his own. Already on their way and 800 yards from their starting line they came to a rise on the other side, a little to the south, which was their objective. But once over that rise they were barred by a strongpost on the slopes below, from which Spandau machine-guns and mortars swept all the high ground above. The strongpost had to be eliminated before Trig 29 could be reached.
>
> No.7 Platoon with 20 men under Lieutenant Colin Taggart was given the job. They set off in three sections, Corporal Bart Lindsey in charge of number one on the left; Corporal Mick Cleave in charge

of number two on the right; Colin Taggart between the two sections with Sergeants Lock and Meyer bringing up the rear.

Corporal Frank Dillon recalled, 'The moment we crossed the skyline we got belted with everything – mortars, Spandau's and later on, grenades. Bill Perce was one of the first to be hit, We reached a point where we had to swing south and there Colin Taggart was killed by a burst from a machine-gun nest about 50 yards ahead. We could see other nests further forward down the slope. They seemed to be spread everywhere. We went to ground in a hurry. Sergeant Alf Meyer took over command and Harry Lock brought his section forward and we went on again. Almost at once there were two more casualties. Alf Meyer was killed by a burst similar to that which got Colin Taggart.'

Algy Walker continued the story at this point.

'Not many of us left. I remember Percy Gratwick and a few others. That machine-gun post in front had us pinned to earth and we couldn't move. If they'd started with their mortars it would have been the end for us. Every move we made on that slope could be seen from below.

Then suddenly, without saying a word, Percy Gratwick takes out a grenade, climbs to his feet and gallops forward, holding his rifle in his left hand. It was so crazy, and he was so quick that the Jerries didn't realise what was happening. Some of them never did. Percy gave them the grenade, dropped down on one knee, got out another and let fly with that. Next instant, he had scrambled forward and dropped into their pit.

Another Jerry about 20 yards further down the slope was trying to finish him off with a Tommy-gun. There were two other Germans in another post with a mortar between them. Percy must have seen them at the same time as we did, but apparently he had no more grenades. We ducked, and next time we looked Percy was up on his feet charging with fixed bayonet – and the Jerry was still trying to spray him with his Tommy-gun. It was all over in a few seconds. Percy only had 20 yards to go, and you don't miss much with a Tommy-gun at that distance. But we saw him make it and then he disappeared. But he got the Jerry first. We didn't hear that Tommy-gun again, nor the mortar.

Inspired by his action, A Company moved forward against a now unnerved enemy, who fell back and the ground was captured. Gratwick's body was found and interred at the Tel el Eisa cemetery on 27 October and later reinterred in the war cemetery at El Alamein. He was quickly recommended for the Victoria Cross, which was published in *The London Gazette* on 28 January 1943. His Victoria Cross was presented to his family by the Lieutenant Governor of Western Australia on 21 November 1943 and donated to the Army Museum of Western Australia in Fremantle.

William Kibby VC

Born at Winlaton, County Durham, on 15 April 1903, William (Bill) Henry was the second of three children of John Robert Kibby, a draper's assistant, and his wife, Mary Isabella (née Birnie). In 1914, the family emigrated to Australia and settled in Adelaide, where Bill attended Mitcham Public School. He had several jobs when he left school but settled on working for the Perfection Fibrous Plaster Company to design and fix plaster decorations. In 1926, he married Mabel Morgan and together they had two daughters.

Physically he was short – 5ft 6in – but very fit. Enjoying hikes and sailing, he became assistant scoutmaster of the Sea Scouts and in 1936 joined the 48th Field Battery, Royal Australian Artillery (Militia). He had an artistic bent and, besides working as a designer, he painted and sketched. He was friendly with the watercolourist and art critic, Esmond George, and accompanied him on sketching trips.

When war broke out, he joined the Australian Imperial Force on 29 June 1940 and was posted to the 2/48th Battalion. He was quickly promoted to sergeant and sailed for Palestine in December. On New Year's Eve, he fell into a slit trench and badly fractured his leg, which hospitalised him for a year and he was medically downgraded to B Class. The accident had left him with one leg shorter than the other and he appeared destined to serve in a training battalion. After much lobbying, he managed to be included in reinforcements for the 2/48th Battalion and in June 1942 moved with the regiment to Egypt.

He was involved in the July fighting at Tel el Eisa and was part of the 9th Australian Division that advanced from El Alamein to once again fight on its old battleground. The Second Battle of El Alamein began at 2350 hours on 23 October with the 2/48th Battalion on the right-hand side of the Eighth Army's front near Tel el Eisa. Sergeant Kibby took command of 17 Platoon, after his platoon officer was badly wounded, with orders to eliminate the machine gun nest on his right. He leapt up calling, 'Follow me!' but the noise of the battle drowned his voice and nobody reacted. Whether he knew his platoon was following or not, he charged forward firing his Tommy gun and, in five minutes, killed the machine gun crew and captured twelve prisoners.

Kibby continued to perform gallant acts during the week-long battle. On the night of the 26th, he went out on a least five occasions through a murderous fire to mend signal wires connecting the platoon with the company HQ. The next night, under heavy artillery fire and repeated attacks by tanks and infantry at Trip 29, he moved around the perimeter directing and inspiring his men.

Kenneth Slessor, the official war correspondent, interviewed some of the members of Kibby's platoon including Tom Martin, who recalled:

> Our job was to cut across Thompson's Post, take the railway, straddle the coast road and then work back cleaning up enemy pockets and strongposts. We straddled the road all right and then started to work back east, D Company cleaning up between the road and the sea. It was easy at first, but then we ran into real opposition. We saw a couple of lights shoot up from a ridge – actually there were two humps, one of the left and one on the right, with a saddle between. We got within 50 yards and then they opened fire – and how!
>
> Three Spandaus started shooting from the hump on the left and two more and a couple of three inch mortars from the right. At first it came waist-high, but when we went down like wet sacks, they sent the stuff skimming just over the top of the ground. We got most of our casualties there.
>
> Captain Robbins hadn't made a mistake to that stage, refusing to be bluffed. A burst from a Spandau killed him and another got his batman and several others. We were all over the show and badly cut up. Unless we could be got together to wipe those Jerries off the ridge they were certain to wipe us out. That's when Kibby got going, yelling orders and reorganising, and in no time we were ready for a crack at that ridge.
>
> We split into two sections. There were a few from Company Headquarters with us and they were in section with myself and Len Steike, detailed to clean up the Jerries on the left. Kibby was with the others. Well we cleaned up the Jerries on the left, but that didn't help. Kibby's section had been driven to earth scarcely 20 yards in front of a Spandau which was ripping them to pieces.
>
> We seemed to be in a worse position than before, being nearer and more exposed. Kibby saved the bunch of us. We saw him run forward with a grenade in his hand and throw it. Then he disappeared, but after that grenade exploded there wasn't any more firing from that quarter.

We stayed quiet for a while and then looked at the shambles around us. There were dead and wounded everywhere. On the way east we had captured a German Regimental Aid Post and we set about getting our wounded back there. We were dog-tired by daylight when we retired a couple of hundred yards and dug in. It wasn't until two days later that we had the opportunity to go out and look for our dead.

When we got to the place, they had disappeared. We guessed that Jerry had dropped them in a shallow trench and covered them over, so we started searching below every freshly turned patch of sand. We spent ten days searching before we found them. They were all lying together in one grave. We did the job properly, burying them in a row. We couldn't say much but I guess we all knew, every man of us, that if it hadn't been for Bill Kibby we might have been lying there with them.

When Captain Robbins body was searched, they found a note on which he had written, 'And if I am killed tonight recommend Bill Kibby for the DCM for what he did on the 25th.' Kibby was indeed recommended for a decoration of the highest order for the actions of the past seven days. Along with Percy Gratwick, his citation appeared in *The London Gazette* dated 28 January 1943.

His VC was presented to his widow, Mabel, by the Governor-General, Lord Gowrie VC, on 27 November 1943. Money was raised by public appeal to buy a house for Kibby's family at Helmsdale. Later, Mabel donated his VC medal group to the Australian Memorial.

The attempts by the Sappers to clear the minefields in time for the armour to drive through and support the infantry had been delayed due to the sheer density of the Devil's Gardens. General Montgomery still insisted that the 10th Corps armour should attack as planned less the assault stall. General Herbert Lumsden, the 10th Corps commander, had a heated argument with Montgomery saying that it was impossible to send his armour into uncharted minefields and he wanted to pull his tanks back until they were cleared. Montgomery modified his order from six armoured regiments to one; the Staffordshire Yeomanry. Lumsden's argument was vindicated as the Staffords lost all but fifteen of its tanks.

Lumsden's confrontation rankled with his commander, which ended with Montgomery sacking him. In 1945, Lumsden was appointed

British liaison officer to Admiral Nimitz and was killed by a kamikaze attack on the USS *New Mexico*.

The assault by the infantry did make gains in the north and one of the outstanding North African Victoria Crosses was won by the commanding officer whose regiment was surrounded and fought off a massed enemy armoured attack. It was the turning point of the El Alamein battle.

Victor Turner VC

Victor (Vic) Buller Turner was born at Thatcham House, Thatcham, Berkshire, on 17 January 1900 into a military family. His father, Major Charles Turner, served in the Berkshire Regiment and played for Gloucestershire County Cricket Club, while his mother, Jane, was the daughter of Admiral Sir Alexander Buller. Vic's eldest brother, Alexander, served with the Royal Berkshire Regiment at the Battle of Loos and, on 28 September 1915, he was awarded a posthumous Victoria Cross. Vic was also related to General Sir Redvers Buller VC, which may have decided on him joining the Rifle Brigade.

Vic Turner was educated at Parkside School in Surrey before boarding at Wellington College. He entered RMC Sandhurst and was commissioned into the Rifle Brigade in 1918. He was soon on campaign with the regiment when it was sent to quell the Iraq Revolt of 1919–20. Following this he served with the 1st Battalion in India, with whom he was adjutant from 1931–34. He served in the same capacity from 1934–38 in the London Rifle Brigade. Described as a short, stocky man with an avuncular moustache, he was deceptively mild mannered and well liked. With the start of the Second World War, he was serving as major and second-in-command of the Rifle Depot at Winchester before rejoining the 1st Battalion Rifle Brigade (1/RB), which had lost so many officers at Calais in 1940.

The 1/RB had been converted to a motorised battalion in 1937 and was armed with Bren-gun carriers and anti-tank guns. In November 1940, Turner arrived with his regiment in North Africa and underwent a period of desert training before becoming assigned to the 2nd Armoured Brigade. He was part of the Eighth Army that followed up Operation *Crusader* and chased Rommel to El Agheila, but was in turn chased back to Gazala. In what became described as the 'Benghazi Handicap', the swinging fortunes of the British and Axis armies saw the northern part of Libya change hands several times.

During the fighting Rommel's superior Panzer tanks outclassed those of the 2nd Armoured Division, which were all but destroyed between 31 March and 2 April 1941.

One of the victims was Turner, whose plight was described in *The Rifle Brigade in the Second World War*:

> No one had a more exciting experience than Vic Turner, whose vehicle had been knocked out in the early stages of operations. He, together with (Captain) Geoffrey Fletcher and several riflemen, set out to walk back across that endless desert (to Gazala). To anyone who knows the desert the idea of walking it is quite fantastic. But they set out, lying up by day and walking at night. After six nights, during each of which they walked for ten hours, torrential rain added to their discomfort and they decided they must somehow secure a vehicle. They laid an ambush, featuring the apparently bloodstained body of a rifleman, and waited. For two days nothing came. On the third day a German staff car appeared and stopped to investigate. They set on the crew; seized the car and drove off across the desert, leaving the astonished Germans still standing with their hands above their head. Their troubles were not over, although the car was full of petrol and carried a reserve. When they were almost within their lines, the car broke down and the little party had to start off again on foot. They re-joined the Battalion after a memorable trek, avoiding capture by refusing to accept the apparently inevitable. They must have covered a hundred sandy miles on foot!

Turner had another close escape on 27 May behind the Gazala Line. The 7th Motor Brigade was on a surveillance mission in the south when it ran into the full force of Rommel's armour, which was executing a surprise flanking attack around the British line. An armour-piercing shell hit his command vehicle, killing one occupant and seriously wounding the driver but leaving Turner unscratched.

In July 1942, he took command of the 2nd Battalion Rifle Brigade (2/RB) as Montgomery and the Eighth Army prepared for a last-ditch battle against the Axis. The battalion's first task was to escort the sappers into the minefields and mark the narrow clear routes with backward-facing lanterns. From 23 October and for three exhausting days they catnapped when they could. Benzedrine, which could have been administered, had been forbidden by the Battalion's medical officer, who decided that it affected their marksmanship, something they were about to rely on.

Following an opening barrage on the night of 26–27 October, Lieutenant Colonel Turner led his motorised battalion pulling the new 6-pounder anti-tank guns about 3,000 yards west of the northern minefield. The 7th Motorised Brigade had orders to seize and hold positions at Kidney Ridge, which was not a ridge but a depression with raised edges. These were named 'Woodstock' and 'Snipe', and were not easy to locate in a uniformly featureless region. The 2nd Battalion King's Royal Rifle Corps (KRRC) was tasked with occupying 'Woodstock', while 2 miles south 2/RB would do the same at 'Snipe'.

Turner located a shallow, oval-shaped depression measuring about 800 yards by 400. Due to faulty interpretation of the map, 2/RB found itself about half a mile from where it was supposed to be, but Turner found the position suitable for defence and began to consolidate the area. He had thirteen 6-pounder anti-tank guns, plus another six belonging to 239 Battery of the Anti-Tank Regiment, Royal Artillery. They dug-in round the perimeter, which was little more than 3 or 4ft high. Around the rim grew camel thorn and tamarisk bushes, which added to their concealment. A patrol was sent out to locate the enemy and soon discovered that the battalion had ended up between two Axis tank leaguers. Turner's reaction to this news was, 'Here we are and here we damned well stay.'

The carrier platoon that made the reconnaissance could not resist the target they beheld. Lieutenant Dick Fowler described the scene:

> It became quite clear that these German tanks were in the process of being replenished and they had a number of lorries there. Quite clearly they were filling up with petrol and being replenished with food and water and ammunition. So we decided this was a super target in view of the fact that we could see about 200 or 300 yards.
>
> We started firing with our Bren-guns at these replenishment lorries. Being soft-skinned with no armour round them, a number of them very soon caught fire, which was very satisfying. As a result of this, of course, the German tanks started to open up. They weren't quite sure where we were or who we were but they managed to locate us and start firing mainly high explosive shells at us but also machine-gun fire from the gun turrets.

Fowler's patrol hastily retired, having captured fourteen prisoners on the way. Their weapons were not the regulation Bren-gun but a mixed arsenal they had picked up during their two years' campaigning. The riflemen had acquired unauthorised enemy Spandau and Breda machine guns, as well as the Vickers Mk V that gave them a greater firepower.

Soon after the patrol returned, Turner heard the sound of approaching tanks and saw their silhouettes against the rising moon. There were about twenty tanks from 15 Panzer Division and the Italian Divisione Littorio, including the formidable Panzer Mark IV with its long 75mm gun, an Italian Semovente self-propelled gun, a 75mm howitzer mounted on an M13 tank chassis and assorted Panzers and M14 tanks. Whether they had blundered on to the 'Snipe' position or were in pursuit of Fowler's patrol was unclear.

The leading Mark IV rattled towards one of the 6-pounders, unaware that it was waiting until it could fire over open sights. When it was just 30 yards away, it was hit in the turret and ground to a halt. Quickly loading another shell, the tank burst into flames, lighting up the other enemy vehicles. One of the Semoventes was destroyed and the rest of the tanks retired.

Just before dawn, the 2/RB discovered that it had inserted itself in the enemy leaguer. 'It was like a massive car park,' said one rifleman. There were many targets to choose from and the gunners had a chance to try their new 6-pounders, which proved to be very effective. Within a short time they had hit and disabled fourteen tanks and destroyed two Semovente self-propelled guns, several trucks, an 88mm gun and a staff car.

By now Turner's 300 riflemen were isolated from the main British force standing about a mile away. The map-reading problem was still an issue and the arrival of the Sherman tanks of 24th Armoured Brigade at Kidney Ridge resulted in a bombardment of 'friendly fire'. Eventually word was got to them and they moved off to chase the enemy tanks. Turner's men also managed to score a few additional hits. The 24th's Shermans came under fire from the deadly German 88mm anti-tank guns and soon seven were ablaze. Some of the riflemen risked their lives to rescue the crews and the Shermans withdrew to the east of Kidney Ridge.

The withdrawal of the 24th Armoured meant that the men of the 2/RB were once more on their own with no armoured support. All during the day, the Axis mounted armoured attacks and were beaten back. They managed to knock out several 6-pounders, killing or wounding the crews. The depression outside 'Snipe' was filled with the blackened carcases of knocked out tanks, which were used by the enemy snipers to fire at the riflemen. Some of the defenders took their rifles among the wrecks and began to pick off the enemy, who were below them and had to expose themselves to shoot.

Brigadier Lucas Phillips, who commanded a regiment at El Alamein, described what the men at 'Snipe' had to endure:

> The desert was quivering with heat. The gun detachments and the platoons squatted in their pits and trenches, the sweat running in rivers down their dust-caked faces. There was a terrible stench. The flies swarmed in black clouds upon the dead bodies and excreta and tormented the wounded. The place was strewn with burning tanks and carriers, wrecked guns and vehicles and all over drifted the smoke and the dust from bursting high explosives and from the blasts of guns.

By now it was becoming clear that ammunition was running low. Sergeant Joe Swann, whose gun had been knocked out, looked for another:

> When I got to the gun, I found there was no available ammunition so I scouted around and found a box with three or four rounds in it. I then took one of these rounds out, put it up the gun – at the same time noticing that the German tank was searching for me. He'd seen me go down somewhere and I thought I'll have a go and move the gun quick before he can get one out at me. I swivelled the gun round and let him have one over open sights. It hit the tank and jammed his turret. I then put another round up the breach and put this into him, causing casualties because two or three chaps jumped out leaving one man in there badly wounded who was screaming for help.

Turner had been moving around the perimeter helping short-handed crews and tending the wounded. He came upon Sergeant Charles Calistan and the platoon's commander, Lieutenant Jack Toms, and joined them. A number of Italian tanks were about 600 yards away and Turner ordered Calistan to hold fire until he was certain to make a kill. On they came until Calistan opened fire, hitting six of the lightly armoured M14s.

Now down to the last three shells, Lieutenant Toms ran 100 yards under machine gun fire to a jeep, which had four boxes of ammunition. He managed to drive the jeep back to within 10 yards of the gun when it was hit by incendiary rounds and burst into flame. Turner ran to it and helped drag off the ammunition and bring it to the gun.

Despite losing so many tanks, three Italians closed in, spraying the perimeter with machine gun fire. A Semovente self-propelled gun tried to find the anti-tank crews and one of the shells landed near Turner. A splinter sliced through his helmet and embedded itself in his skull, blood pouring over his eyes. Unable to carry on, Turner was lain down behind a thorn bush. Calistan then performed a remarkable feat of shooting; with three rounds he destroyed three M14s. Turner was heard to exclaim, 'Hat trick!'

The rest of the tanks withdrew and Calistan put a dixie of water on the bonnet of the smouldering jeep and brewed some tea. Turner was taken a mug, which he described; 'As good a cup of tea as I've ever had.'

In the late afternoon they again came under 'friendly fire', this time from 2nd Armoured Brigade's new 105mm Priest self-propelled guns, which caused more casualties.

The wound to his head caused Turner to suffer from hallucinations and after nightfall he was sent off in a jeep and treated at a New Zealand dressing station. The 2/RB was withdrawn having beaten off repeated armoured attacks. It was estimated that twenty-two German and ten Italian tanks plus other weaponry had been destroyed, with another twenty disabled. Of the 300 men who defended 'Snipe', seventy-two were killed or wounded, and out of nineteen anti-tank guns only one was recovered.

Montgomery was delighted by the stubborn defence by Turner's men. They had frustrated Rommel's efforts to destroy 1st Armoured Division and had inflicted losses that he could ill afford.

In less than four weeks, *The London Gazette* of 20 November 1942 published Colonel Vic Turner's citation. He was invested his Cross on 27 July 1943 by the King at Buckingham Palace. He always maintained that he accepted the honour on behalf of the men who fought with him at 'Snipe'. His VC made him one of four instances of brothers who had won the award.

When he had recovered from his wound, he spent most of the remaining years of the war commanding training appointments. In 1949, he retired from the Army. He was a member of the Bodyguard of the Yeoman of the Guard from 1950 to 1967 and was made Commander of the Royal Victorian Order (CVO).

Turner never married, nor did his two surviving brothers. They all lived together in a cottage at Ditchingham in Suffolk, where he died on 7 August 1972. His VC group is held at the Royal Green Jackets Museum, Winchester.

The fighting around Tell al-Aqaqir and Kidney Ridge inflicted such heavy losses on Rommel that he was forced to quit Egypt and make a fighting retreat back to Libya. General Montgomery knew that a major landing called Operation *Torch* would occur in Vichy French-held Morocco and Algeria in November and kept Rommel's attention fully eastwards. Rommel had taken the bait and concentrated his forces opposite the El Alamein line to the extent of sowing a double line of 5-mile deep minefields with all his armour waiting behind his well dug-in infantry.

On receipt of the Anglo–American landings thousands of miles to the west, he realised that his army would have to fight on two fronts and, with probable defeat at El Alamein, he began his long retreat west to confront the new menace in his rear.

Chapter 12

Operation Torch

The Soviet Union had pressed America and Britain to start operations on mainland Europe to relieve the pressure it was under from the German invasion. Churchill and his military commanders felt they were not yet ready and persuaded President Roosevelt that they should first help clear the Axis from Africa, from where they could invade southern Europe in 1943. This would relieve the pressure on the British in their defence of Egypt and the vital Suez Canal as well as releasing thousands of troops to fight in Europe.

Operation *Torch* gave the green US troops campaign experience against a less formidable enemy in the Vichy French. The landings were to be made in three groups. In the west, the Americans would land on the Atlantic side of Morocco centred on Casablanca and in the east at the city of Algeria. The Central Task Force would capture the important port of Oran, from where Allies could ship men and equipment to fight Rommel.

The Central Task Force under the command of General Lloyd Frendall, regarded as one of the worst American commanders of the Second World War, was beset with problems from the start. The landings were split between three beaches; two in the west and one in the east. Some delay and confusion was caused by the appearance of a French convoy, which interrupted Allied minesweepers clearing a path to the beaches. Also, it was found that the landing ships were damaged by the shallowness and sandbars as no reconnaissance parties had been landed. This was something later amphibious assaults put into practice.

The US 1st Ranger Battalion quickly captured the shore battery at Arzew, to the east of Oran. A further bold operation was to land other Rangers at the harbour to prevent the French destroying the port facilities or scuppering their vessels. It was during this part of the operation that one of the least-known VCs was earned.

Frederick Peters VC

Frederick (Fritz) Thornton Peters was born into an affluent family on 17 September 1889 at Sidmount House, Charlottetown, Prince Edward Island. He was the second of five children born to Frederick, a lawyer and politician, and Bertha (nee Gray) Peters. Fritz's great-grandfather was Sir Samuel Cunard, the founder of the transatlantic steamship fleet. The family moved to Victoria on Vancouver Island in 1898, at the time of the Yukon gold rush. In the hopes of expanding the family's coffers, Fritz's father lost money in the brief gold rush and the family declined into genteel poverty.

Fritz, as he was always known, was educated at Bolton School, before being sent to England to be educated briefly at Bedford School. After a year, he left to study at Cordwalles Boys School at Maidenhead, where pupils prepared for a career as naval officers. In January 1905 he joined the Royal Navy as a cadet on HMS *Britannia*. Successfully passing his exams, he qualified as a midshipman on HMS *Vengeance* under Admiral Arthur Wilson, the Sudan VC. Peters was a Victorian Age romantic who fervently believed in the British Empire. This was coupled with a great disdain for Americans, who he saw as brash and expansionist, particularly trying to nibble away at Canadian territory. Although he spent little of his adult life in Canada, he is honoured in that country as the highest-awarded Canadian of the Second World War.

Peters was serving as a sub-lieutenant on the pre-Dreadnought battleship HMS *Duncan* in 1908 when she was transferred to the Mediterranean Fleet at Malta. A few weeks after she arrived, a devastating earthquake measuring 7.5 magnitude struck the Straits of Messina between Sicily and Italy. The ports of Messina in Sicily and Reggio in Calabria were levelled and a tsunami completed the destruction. Some 75,000 in Messina lost their lives, with 25,000 dead in Reggio. The disaster made headlines around the world and rescue and relief efforts were launched. HMS *Duncan*, along with other Royal Navy vessels, joined those of the Russian fleet and other nations in the relief effort. In gratitude a medal was struck and Peters received his first award which was pinned to his breast by the Italian king, Victor Emmanuel.

Peters was then promoted to lieutenant in March 1912 and given his first command; the destroyer *Otter* on the China Station. This was cut short, for in the summer of 1913 Peters resigned from the Royal Navy, giving as his reason the need to help boost his family's finances. He took a job as third officer with the Canadian Pacific Railway in British Columbia, where the company had a fleet of lake cargo and passenger ships that connected its rail-lines. This interlude was brief as Fritz heard of the coming war and caught a tramp steamer back to England to re-join the Royal Navy. On 22 August 1914, he was appointed first lieutenant on the recently launched destroyer, HMS *Meteor*, commanded by Captain Meade. Fritz did not have to wait long before he saw his first action.

In December 1914, the German High Seas Fleet had been shelling towns on the east coast of England hoping to draw out and engage the Royal Navy. Intercepting and decoding German wireless transmissions, the Grand Fleet was aware of the next raid.

On 24 January 1915 in the Dogger Bank area, the German Admiral Hipper spotted smoke from Admiral Beatty's large approaching force and turned for his home port. Beatty's flagship, HMS *Lion*, sighted the German fleet and opened fire at a range of 20,000 yards (11 miles). No warship had engaged at such a long range before and although accurate gunnery was a challenge, the old armoured cruiser *Blücher* was hit. A further seventy hits and seven torpedoes completely disabled the German ship.

In the running battle, the rest of the German squadron left *Blücher* to her fate. The *Seydlitz* was hit by the *Lion*, causing an ammunition fire that knocked out the two rear turrets for the loss of 165 men. The prompt flooding of the magazines saved the battleship and the ship limped back to port. A German shell hit *Lion* and reduced her speed. Believing he had seen a submarine's periscope, Beatty ordered an end to the engagement and the German fleet escaped back to Cuxhaven.

The crippled *Blücher*, however, produced a sting in her tail. Captain Meade manoeuvred *Meteor* so she could fire a torpedo at the crippled ship when she was hit by the last round from the sinking cruiser. An 8in shell penetrated *Meteor*'s engine room, causing pipes to spew scalding steam and threatening an explosion of the boilers. With the danger of spreading fire, Peters dashed into the mayhem of the engine room and managed to halt the spread of the fire. He then rescued two engine room ratings that were badly injured. Also during that action, he pushed a live shell overboard.

For these acts of gallantry, twenty-five year old Fritz Peters was the first Canadian, and one of the youngest, to receive the Distinguished Service Order. Initially he was mentioned in despatches but this was upgraded. His award was also the highest honour bestowed to any participant in the aftermath of the Dogger Bank battle. In March 1915, he received his medal from the King at Buckingham Palace. His pride in being awarded the DSO was tempered by the news he received that his brother, Jack, had disappeared during the Second Battle of Ypres on 22 April. It was not for another two years that it came to light that he had been blown to smithereens by a shell. Peters also lost another brother killed at Vimy Ridge in 1917. (In Volume II of The VC and DSO 1886–1915 Book it erroneously records that Fritz Peters died of wounds on 7 December 1916).

After the serious damage inflicted on *Meteor*, she was towed back to port to be repaired. Peters was further rewarded in November 1915 when he was given command of HMS *Greyhound*, a rather aging destroyer. On 24 March 1916, *Greyhound* rescued survivors from the ferry boat SS *Sussex*, torpedoed between England and northern France. Fifty passengers and crew were killed and, although there were no Americans on board, the incident outraged public opinion in the States.

In 1917, he was pleased to take command of HMS *Christopher*, a new 35-knot destroyer. Writing home he declared, 'that it was great thing to have a decent craft again after a perishing thirty knotter. Another winter in the *Greyhound* would have driven me to drink or suicide.'

On 8 August 1917, Fritz and his new ship were involved in the two-day rescue of the crew of the famous Q-ship *Dunraven* skippered by Captain Gordon Campbell VC. *Dunraven* had stalked a U-boat in the hope that it would surface close enough for its guns to show themselves and sink the submarine. Instead, they had to endure a torpedoing and bombardment from the U-boat's deck gun. Having run out of torpedoes, the submarine sailed away leaving the badly damaged Q-ship.

The radio message was picked up and the destroyers HMS *Attack* and HMS *Christopher* arrived and sent their medical teams to board the *Dunraven* to treat the wounded. All the fires were extinguished and *Christopher* took her in tow. After a day, and barely making one knot, the *Dunraven* was slowly sinking. Finally, it was decided to take off the remaining crew. However, the seas had become rough and the *Christopher*'s whaler could take only four men at a time, and it was unlikely they could make more than one trip.

Peters decided on a hazardous manoeuvre. He carefully drew alongside and bumped against the sinking ship. The waves drove a gap between them and Gordon Campbell called out the name of one man to jump in the darkness and land on the destroyer. By repeating this dangerous tactic, all the *Dunraven*'s crew was saved. Still the stricken ship refused to sink so it was left to one of *Christopher*'s depth charges to finally end her death throes.

For his service in hunting U-boats and the rescue of the *Dunraven*'s crew, Peters received the Distinguished Service Cross from the King on March 1918, for 'showing exceptional initiative, ability and zeal in submarine hunting operations and complete disregard of danger, exceptional coolness and ingenuity in his attacks on enemy submarines.' Although he had by Royal Navy standards, an active war, he complained of the long periods of boredom.

With the ending of the war in November 1918, there was a radical downsizing of service personnel. One man the Royal Navy wanted to retain was Peters. He was promoted to lieutenant commander and invited to take a place at Staff College, but in 1920, he decided to retire as the prospect of peacetime service did not appeal to him. Also, he hoped that he would make more money as a civilian to overcome his insolvency problems.

One of his naval friends, who now worked as the managing director of the Gold Coast Political Service, gave him an introduction. He was hired by an unnamed company and from there moved on to growing cocoa. This is a period shrouded in mystery for farming seemed an unlikely occupation for a man of action. His friend, Sydney Saxton, told a London columnist in 1943 that there were at least three attempts on his life at this time. Saxton encouraged Peters to become a lawyer like his father, but this did not appeal. Instead, he would go to the Gold Coast (Ghana) for two or three years to make money and return to London for enjoyable reunions with his Navy friends. One of these, Cromwell Varley, had invented the midget submarine and got Peters to run a small company designing and making the specialised pumps for the craft. As he was not an engineer, this added to the mystery. There is some speculation that he was being employed by the Secret Service in some capacity.

With war against Germany in prospect, Peters returned to England and for the third time re-joined the Royal Navy as a commander. In October 1939, he took command of a group of anti-submarine trawlers; first with HMS *Lord Stanhope* and then HMS *Thirlmere*. During this time, he managed to sink two U-boats and was awarded a bar to his Distinguished Service Cross. He also took his trawler group to the brief campaign in Norway, during which a fellow armed trawler captain on HMS *Arab*, Richard Stannard, received the Victoria Cross.

In June 1940, he was seconded to Department D of the British Secret Intelligence Service (SIS) and was put in command of a former manor house at Brickendonbury, Hertfordshire, which was a spy and saboteur training centre for Station XVII (D for destruction). Here they trained expatriates who returned to their native countries in Occupied Europe to carry the fight to the Nazis. At this time neither America nor Russia had joined the fight against the Germans so Churchill looked for some way of fighting back. Among Peters's colleagues were Guy Burgess and Kim Philby, two of the infamous Cambridge Spy Ring.

The school had been set up by Burgess and the deputy head of D Section, Monty Chidson. Philby joined from being a war correspondent for *The Times* and worked as a propagandist. One of his ideas was to spread rumours that French women with venereal diseases were intentionally luring German soldiers to infect them.

Despite their political differences, both Burgess and Philby liked their commandant, Peters, and they dined several times together in London. The overlapping of the different agencies and subsequent infighting finally drove Fritz to tender his resignation and return to the Royal Navy. In his book *My Silent War*, Philby paid tribute to Peters and the awarding of a posthumous Victoria Cross:

> … for what was probably unnecessarily gallant behaviour in Oran harbour. When I heard of the award, I felt a pang that he would never have known about it. He was the type of strong sentimentalist who would have wept at such honour. Our trainees came to adore him.

Peters moved to anti-submarine warfare in Naval Intelligence and in April 1941 was appointed Staff Officer (Operation) to Admiral Sir William James, the Commander in Chief, Portsmouth. As a child, Admiral James sat for his grandfather, the painter John Millais, and was the subject of one his most famous paintings – *Bubbles*; an image that dogged him for the rest of his life.

In August 1941, Peters was promoted to acting captain and given command of HMS *Tynwald*, an auxiliary anti-aircraft cruiser. After a year on convoy escort duties around Britain she was assigned to take part in Operation *Torch* and was involved in the attack on Algiers on 8 November and on the 12th the occupation of Bougie harbour, 100 miles to the east. Unfortunately she was torpedoed and sunk by an Italian submarine.

By August 1942, Peters had left *Tynwald* to take part in the planning for Operation *Torch*. Admiral Sir Andrew Cunningham, Commander in Chief Mediterranean, appointed him as special operations and naval planner working under Admiral Bertram Ramsey. The command of the Central Task Force for American and British forces to capture Oran was given to the fractious and inexperienced Major General Lloyd Fredendall, a confirmed Anglophobe. His incompetence and cowardice was later revealed in the early fighting in Tunisia and he was replaced. Incredibly, he returned a hero to America, where he was promoted to lieutenant general.

This first Anglo–American operation ran into difficulties from the start. The British wanted to land as far east as possible so as to occupy Tunisia before the Germans. The Americans feared that the Vichy French and fascist Spain would close the Strait of Gibraltar and they would be trapped. There were more disagreements and disputes and Peters became exasperated by the American reluctance to accept the Royal Navy's advice on anti-submarine warfare. Decisions for the Oran harbour attack were made hastily, developing into an antagonistic atmosphere of mutual disrespect between British and American planners and leaders. As commander of the mission, Peters was in the thick of the hostile back and forth arguing.

There was also the reaction of the French in Algeria to the participation of the Royal Navy, who in 1940 had bombarded and destroyed the French Mediterranean Fleet in the port of Mers-el-Kebir near to Oran. With a predominantly British naval force in the waters of Oran Bay, the French Navy was understandably affronted and prepared to oppose any sort of assault.

The lead ship, HMS *Walney*, was an aging former US Coast Guard cutter of distinctly American appearance. The reason for picking her was that she was built with a strong hull to smash through the Oran defensive boom. She could raise no more than 15 knots, was not particularly manoeuvrable and was regarded as expendable. Her captain was Lieutenant Commander Peter Meyrick RN, with Peters's role of group commander. She was accompanied by her sister ship, HMS *Hartland*, and two motor launches for laying a smokescreen. Both cutters were reinforced by armoured plating and additional jagged blades were fitted to the bows to severe the chains linking the mixture of logs and coal barges that made up the Oran boom. While these additions were being fitted, Fritz and the landing group of US soldiers from the 3rd Battalion, 6th Armoured Infantry Regiment, went to a secret training establishment in Scotland to practise boarding enemy ships with grappling hooks and lines in the dark. Peters was also personally briefed on the mission by Winston Churchill and General Eisenhower.

Both cutters left Greenock on 23 October and made a great loop out into the North Atlantic to disguise their destination. On board *Walney* was an American war correspondent, Leo Disher from United Press International, who was reporting on the first Americans fighting in the European theatre. In the two weeks he was with him, Disher made some interesting observations of Peters and recalls some of his comments. One he said under his breath was: 'I hope I can see this through, but the chances of coming out alive are slim.'

Disher wrote:

> His courage was massive, like his shoulders. In appearance he was strikingly calm, almost annoyingly so, and the years had given him a deliberateness which made his speech as ponderous as his body. Physically, he was well-timbered, perhaps more full-bodied than portly. A deliberate man, he wore black battle dress with epaulettes on his shoulders. He had about him a sort of stubborn pride that caused him, on land or sea, in fair weather or foul, to razor his cheeks and jowls so closely that they had a blood sheen. He was a bachelor, snugly and smugly so.
>
> The mist, like rain, darkness and secrecy, followed him. And he would have one or the other, or all three, with him to the very last.

The *Walney* was overloaded with men and munitions, causing her to pitch and roll on the long voyage to Gibraltar. The unfortunate Leo Disher had a bad fall that broke his ankle. Although he could have legitimately disembarked at Gibraltar, he hobbled around on crutches determined to see his assignment through.

General Fredendall's troops were to come ashore along a 50-mile stretch of coastline at three different beaches to the west and east of Oran. Named Operation *Reservist*, the plan was for Peters's cutters to enter Oran harbour to secure the port facilities and prevent the eight French destroyers being scuttled, so saving the port for use by the Allies. As with so many plans, the outcome was terrifyingly different.

The beach landings were made with little opposition and Fredendall radioed a confusing message ending with the words: 'Don't start a fight unless you have to.' Another message that was not received said 'expect resistance'. Peters concluded that the mission was still on and ordered the attack. Flying the Stars and Stripes, *Walney* and *Hartland* entered Oran Harbour with 400 American troops and a small party of Royal Marines, who would be rowing themselves ashore to secure the mole.

Oran harbour was separated by a west-to-east, 3,000-yard breakwater that ran parallel to the harbour front. Within the harbour were four main basins separated by quays that extended towards the breakwater, leaving a narrow passage of water that extended the length of the harbour. The port was protected by coastal guns, eight naval destroyers and two submarines. As the small flotilla approached the harbour entrance, they were caught in the searchlights from shore. Lieutenant Paul Duncan RN, dressed in an American helmet and combat gear and holding a Tommy gun under each arm, announced in a heavily American-accented French over the ship's loudspeaker, 'Don't shoot. We are your friends. We are American.' This was met by gun-fire, so Duncan repeated the message, until he was struck down and killed.

One of the eyewitnesses to the attack was Lieutenant Wallace Mosley RN:

> We completed the circle, increased our speed to 15 knots and made for the southern end of the boom. Shells and bullets crashed into us, and almost as the Walney shuddered with the impact she snapped the boom. We were through. It had been as easy as that.

Leo Disher recalled that Peters took Duncan's place at the loudspeaker and spoke French with an American accent: 'Cease firing. We are your friends. We are American, cease firing.'

Once inside the harbour, Moseley said:

> While lowering the canoes (for the Royal Marine Special Boat Squadron) in the Avant Port, we were subjected to heavy but inaccurate fire from guns mounted on the jetties and mole. We were also hit several times aft from pom-pom fire which probably came from Ravin Blanc. All telephonic communication aft was cut and the S.R.E put out of action.

As the SBS canoes set off, a French destroyer sailed out of the darkness.

> We attempted to ram and sink her, but the cutters being slow and unhandy craft, we failed and she passed on our port side but did not appear to open fire.

Although under almost continuous fire, *Walney* did not return fire and had suffered little damage and few casualties. Illuminated by gun flashes and raked by machine gun fire, the order was given to take positions for boarding in Quai Centrale As she approached the destroyer *L'Epervier*, the boarding parties comprising of a Royal Naval officer and six ratings, together with seven members of the US 6th Armoured Infantry, prepared to launch two whalers on the port side. Before this could be put into action, another destroyer attacked her at almost point-blank range with two broadsides that caused heavy damage.

Disher wrote:

> It seemed to me that all hell broke loose around us. We were hit time and again at almost muzzle-range. The bridge was raked and raked again.

Moseley recalled:

> The following action is fuzzy and because we had our faces and hands blacked and wearing American and British helmets no one could identify one another. All grenade throwers were killed and all but two officers and three men from the combined boarding parties. They lay in a bloody heap on the bow.

Two enemy shells burst in the engine room and put the boilers out of action. Now without power, *Walney* drifted towards its target landing site. Another close-range barrage shot away the armour-encased bridge killing seventeen, including every officer except Peters, Disher and Moseley, who were each wounded. The medical staff in the wardroom were all killed and the steering compartment destroyed.

Barely afloat, *Walney* had managed to travel to the end of breakwater with the Quai Centrale as her target. Despite a serious eye and head wound, Peters was seen to scramble from one end of the ship to the other to prepare to tie the helpless vessel to the jetty.

Moseley again:

> Our remaining gun was silenced and the ship was on fire forward and amidships. We had lost over half of our ship's company and the carnage among the troops on the mess-decks was indescribable.
>
> I therefore gave the order to unprime the five-charge pattern of depth charges still primed, followed by an order to abandon ship.

The *Hartland* was suffering a similar fate and was torn apart by an explosion and sank beside Mole Ravin. The harbour was full of floating debris as the survivors abandoned the stricken ship. Moseley recalled:

> I swam off and some of the others were killed swimming but probably not by the enemy. I was hauled aboard L'Epervier.

Disher was in a desperate state with his broken ankle. As he went into the water he found that his life jacket had been punctured by shrapnel and he thought he would drown. Somehow he managed to reach the jetty and haul himself out of the water, only for a bullet to hit him in his crippled ankle. Unable to walk, he pulled himself along the jetty until a spent bullet hit him on the temple and he passed out until he was picked up and taken to hospital.

Partially blinded from the blood in his head wound, Peters swam to an inflated raft and reached the shore, where he, along with the other survivors, was taken prisoner. Lieutenant Moseley recalled two grim days spent in the barracks of the Second Zouve Regiment:

> The supply of food for extra mouths was non-existent and the sanitary arrangements – French.

During the course of the action, three French destroyers left the harbour but ran into the British naval force outside. In a brief exchange of fire, *Tramontane* was sunk and *Tornade* beached. The following day, two more French destroyers attempted to escape. One was set ablaze and was beached while the other returned to port and was scuttled at the entrance.

The prisoners had to endure a march through crowds of spitting, jeering Frenchmen, but two days later, after they surrendered, the prisoners were greeted as liberators. Peters was even carried shoulder-high through the crowds as he was accompanied by the US soldiers through the streets of Oran. He now wore an eyepatch over his injured eye and prepared to return to England for medical treatment and to report to Churchill on the gallant failure of Operation *Reservist*.

Climbing aboard a Sunderland flying boat at Gibraltar for the day-long flight back to England, Peters prepared for a bumpy ride as the weather forecast was poor. After twelve hours' flying, the Sunderland ran into thick fog and with only fifteen minutes of fuel left, attempted to land at the entrance to Plymouth Naval Dockyard. The pilot noted that the altimeter showed they were at 600ft, just as the flying boat hit the sea, causing the aircraft to flip over and split apart. Miraculously, all eleven crew survived but their passengers were all dead, apart from an unconscious Peters. Without a life raft, the pilot took hold of him and kept him afloat for an hour until he realised that Peters was dead. Despite a search, his body was not found and Peters has no known grave. The Portsmouth Naval Memorial is the only place where his name is recorded.

Some American officers, predominately Fredendall, blamed Peters for the high rate of casualties in Oran harbour. They said he could have aborted the attack or surrendered, something not in his psyche. Not so General Eisenhower, who recommended Peters for the American Distinguished Service Cross. Eisenhower also took full responsibility for the mistake in the timing of Operation *Reservist* as he misjudged the French attitude to any Allied encroachments on their territory.

Lieutenant Moseley concluded his report with the observation:

> In is my opinion that the naval side of the operation might have been successful if carried out by two modern Fleet destroyers and that even the cutters could have accomplished it if they had entered the harbour two hours earlier.

Acting Captain Fritz Peters's citation appeared in *The London Gazette* on 18 May 1943 and is a masterpiece in brevity. The reason was undoubtedly that now the French were back on the side of the Allies, any 'unpleasantness' was to be downplayed and is the reason that this outstanding and interesting recipient has been almost entirely overlooked. Of the 182 VCs in the Second World War, fifty-three year old Peters was the oldest. His exceptional Victoria Cross group is displayed at the Lord Ashcroft Gallery in London's Imperial War Museum.

Chapter 13

Tebourba

Alan Moorhead questioned in his book *The Desert War*, that:

> Had not Montgomery's offensive and Eisenhower's North African landing been staged in exactly the wrong order? Had we gone to Tunisia first, Rommel would have fought his desert campaign knowing that he had no base on which to retreat, and that would have been very bad indeed for German morale and German supply lines from Italy.

A good question, for the Vichy French in Tunisia had a lightly armed defence force and could have been overwhelmed as comfortably as their compatriots in Morocco and Algeria. The British planners of the Anglo–American Operation *Torch* were all for immediately driving east and occupying Tunisia. Their partners were more cautious and wished to consolidate their position before embarking on another mission. In the event it was the Germans who reacted swiftly, sending troops and armour from Sicily on 9 November, the day after Operation *Torch* began. Their lines of supply were much shorter and their aircraft could operate from closer airbases and spend longer in the air, something that would restrict the Allied fighters. Another result of the collapse of the Vichy French in North Africa was that Hitler took control of the remainder of France, so bringing to an end the shameful puppet government.

For the Germans, control of Tunisia was vital to prevent Rommel being trapped between the Eighth Army in the east and the First Army in the west. Unlike the other parts of the North African littoral, Tunisia was mountainous and ideal for defence. The poor road and rail communications prevented the Allies moving more than a small division-sized force (78th Division) into northern Tunisia, starting the 'race to Tunis'. An officer of a county regiment that was part of this advance performed an act of gallantry that was prematurely awarded a posthumous VC, but he was later found alive in the hands of the enemy.

Herbert Le Patourel VC

Herbert Wallace Le Patourel was born on 20 June 1916 at Villa Magnol, Fosse Andre, St Peter Port, Guernsey, the youngest of three children of Herbert Augustus Le Patourel, a lawyer who became attorney general for the Island, and his wife, Mary Elizabeth (née Daw), who came from a Devon farming family. His older brother, John, became an eminent Medievalist and university lecturer. Both brothers were educated at Elizabeth College, Guernsey, which could boast four Victoria Cross recipients: Duncan Home, John McCrea, Lewis Halliday and Herbert Le Patourel.

Wallace, as he was known to his family and friends, represented the school at shooting and hockey and showed an interest in the military. During the last year of his schooling, his father died and he was persuaded by his family to remain on the island and look after his mother. At the age of eighteen, he became a bank clerk at the National Provincial Bank but satisfied his military interest by joining the Royal Guernsey Militia as a second lieutenant.

He received a legacy of £500, enabling him to prepare for the Army entrance examination, which he succeeded in passing. On 16 June 1937, he was commissioned as a second lieutenant in the 2nd Battalion, Hampshire Regiment, stationed at Aldershot.

With the outbreak of the war, the 2nd Battalion was the first British battalion to be sent to Belgium as part of the British Expeditionary Force (BEF). No only was it the first to arrive but it was among the last to get away from Dunkirk on 2 June 1940 with its equipment complete. During the retreat, Le Patourel was both wounded and mentioned in despatches. By 1941, he had risen to captain before being appointed in August 1942 as temporary major in command of Z Company.

His mother and sister, Edith, has been evacuated from Guernsey before the German occupation and settled for the duration of the war at the village of Huntington, near York. Le Patourel visited them just before he and his regiment were sent abroad. On 11 November 1942, 2/Hampshires sailed for North Africa, arriving in Algiers on the 21st. They were immediately sent east to join the 78th Division of the First

Army as it advanced into Tunisia. Initially things went well and the 11th Brigade of 78th Division captured Medjez el Bab and Tebourba, just 20 miles west of Tunis. When the 2/Hampshires caught up with the advance on 29 November, they were sent to relieve the 6/Northamptons east of Tebourba. At this point the Germans had reinforced their front, bringing in, among others, the 10th Panzer Division, hardened veterans of the Eastern Front.

The Allied advance came to a grinding halt as the Germans brought up armour and their feared 88mm guns, making the most of the highly defensive terrain. Colonel Lee, the Hampshires' commander, decided to withdraw and consolidate his men at Tebourba, thus precipitating one of the great battles of the North African Campaign. The following five months of desperate fighting in Tunisia saw the awarding of twelve Victoria Crosses.

The 2/Hampshires dug in on the night of 29–30 November in a not-ideal position as they were overlooked to the left and in front by an enemy that had command of the high ground. In a desperate and heroic fight, the battle for Tebourba lasted for four days, during which the Germans outnumbered the 689 Hampshire soldiers by four to one. During that time two officers won the DSO and five the MC. It was on 3 December that an eighth officer performed an act that resulted in the awarding of the Victoria Cross.

At first light on the 3rd, the enemy began a very heavy artillery and mortar attack along the whole front. This lasted until 10.00 hours, when the Germans launched a massive attack concentrating on the battalion's left flank, defended by Z Company. An hour later, Major Le Patourel reported that the enemy had gained possession of some high ground called Point 186 to their left, which the Germans had captured from units of the East Surreys.

The Germans reinforced this position with heavy machine guns and mortars, which pinned down the men of Z Company. Le Patourel ordered an assault to take back Point 186, which they managed to do but were unable to hold it due to heavy enemy fire from the from the hills to their left. The rest of the morning was one of confusion with the Hampshires desperately holding their position but unable to dictate the action.

In an attempt to recapture Point 189, Major Le Patourel requested permission to make one last effort to dislodge the enemy and protect his exposed flank. Calling for volunteers to go with him to brave the heavy fire and neutralise the machine gun nests, Lieutenant Lister, Sergeant

Wells, and Privates Winkworth and Cotterell agreed to go with him. Moving forward quickly, they managed to silence three enemy strong points with grenades and bayonet while moving up the slope of Point 186. By then his small group were either dead or wounded. Le Patourel made a final charge alone with pistol and grenades and in the confusion of the fight he was presumed to have been killed.

By the following day the 2/Hampshires were outflanked on both sides and Colonel Lee had little option but to pull his surviving troops back through the Tebourba 'Gap' to prevent them being caught in the Germans' pincer movement. Ordering everyone to arm themselves with as many automatic weapons, rifles and grenades as they could carry, fixing bayonets, they charged and fought their way out of the trap back to Tebourba. By the close of the battle, the 2/Hampshires had lost 495 men, around 72 per cent of their initial strength, but in doing so they enabled the 78th Division to hold its line at Longstop Hill.

In the aftermath, Colonel Lee made his recommendations for gallantry awards, including two Distinguished Service Orders, five Military Crosses, four Miltary Medals and many mentioned in despatches. Above all, the posthumous Victoria Cross was recommended for Wallace Le Patourel. His citation appeared on 9 March 1943 in *The London Gazette*. It was discovered soon after that Le Patourel had been badly wounded but survived.

Le Patourel had managed to almost reach the top of Point 186 when he collapsed due to wounds he had received earlier in the attack. There he lay until nightfall. One of the German soldiers spotted movement among the dead soldiers in the area and crawled forward to investigate. Finding Le Patourel, he gave him some water and called on some stretcher bearers to collect him. This humane gesture was somewhat marred when Wallace's benefactor stole his wristwatch.

Le Patourel was patched up at a field hospital before being flown to Italy, where he was treated by an English doctor who was a prisoner of war. On 31 January 1943, the Red Cross informed his mother that he was severely wounded but alive. When he had recovered sufficiently he was sent to Castra hospital near Naples, which was attached to a POW camp. The War Office sent a greetings telegram to Wallace informing him that he had been awarded the Victoria Cross.

In a letter held by the Royal Hampshire Regiment Museum, Le Patourel's name is mentioned as a fellow patient of a wounded officer. Although both appear to be recovering from their wounds, Le Patourel confessed:

The real trick was not to be sent from hospital to camp and as a result he and Dick had planned to continue indefinitely in rather poor shape.

Camp life was more regimented and as they felt they got on so well together in their little group in hospital, playing bridge and learning Italian, they played up the severity of their wounds. Finally, Le Patourel was exchanged on 2 June 1943 for 435 Axis prisoners of war and flown to Cairo. He was present on 14 June when 5,000 troops, tanks and armoured cars paraded through the city. General Henry Maitland Wilson, the Commander in Chief of the Middle East, took the salute and presented Victoria Cross ribbons to two officers – Brigadier Lorne MacLain Campbell and Major Wallace Le Patourel.

Following this, Le Patourel returned to England for months of convalescing but recovered enough to attend his investiture to receive his Victoria Cross on 21 October 1943 from the King at Buckingham Palace. He returned to his mother's home in Huntingdon, where he was greeted by the town and took the salute of the local Home Guard.

Recovered from his treatment, Le Patourel returned to military service but not did not immediately go back to active duty. However, in June 1944 he landed on Gold Beach on D-Day plus four as a brigade major in the Brigade HQ of the 53rd (Welsh) Infantry Division, and served with the unit until October 1945, when it reached Vienna.

On 9 May 1945, he was invited for an official visit to Guernsey for its liberation parade. With the end of the war, Le Patourel was promoted to lieutenant colonel and in November 1945 was appointed instructor at the Indian Staff College in Quetta. In 1948 he was appointed an instructor at Warminster School of Infantry and on 26 October 1949 married Babette Theresa Beattie in St Peter Port Town Church, Guernsey.

In the same year he trained as a parachutist and was appointed second in command of the 2nd Parachute Regiment. With his new regiment, he served at the Suez Canal and Cyprus, where his first child was born. In 1953 he served on the staff as deputy assistant adjutant general at the War Office. In 1956 he returned to regimental duties with the 14th Battalion Parachute Regiment.

He served as general staff officer 1 (GSO) with the British Joint Services Mission to Washington from 1958 to 1960. From there he was promoted to brigadier and became deputy commander of the newly formed Ghana Army 1960–61. This was a brief appointment as he suffered a heart attack.

His final posting was as deputy commander of 43 Division in 1961–62, before retiring from the Army. His first three years as a civilian were spent as manager of the Fowey–Bodinnick Ferry in Cornwall. In 1966 he became a director of Showerings Vine Products in Somerset, where he settled in Bishop Sutton. On 12 November 1974, he was appointed Deputy Lord Lieutenant of the County of Avon.

He planned to spend the remaining years of his retirement raising Jacob sheep on a small farm in Chewton Mendip but sadly before he realised his dream, on 4 September 1979 he died of another heart attack at the early age of sixty-three. His ashes were scattered on his new farm at Chewton Mendip.

He was further honoured in 2002 when a series of six stamps was issued by Guernsey Post depicting his service life. His medal group is displayed by the Royal Hampshire Regimental Museum, Winchester.

Hugh Malcolm VC

Hugh Gordon Malcolm was born on 2 May 1917 at Broughty Ferry, near Dundee, to Kenneth Sinclair Malcolm and his wife, Marjorie. His early education was at Craigflower Preparatory School, Dunfermline, before attending Glenalmond College, Perthshire, from 1931 to 1935. By that time he had decided that he would make the Royal Air Force his career and, on 9 January 1936, he entered RAF Cranwell as a cadet.

In December 1937, he graduated as a commissioned pilot and was posted to 26 Squadron, which had just been equipped with the new Westland Lysander aircraft.

The roll of the Lysander was reconnaissance, aerial photography and to cooperate with the Army in artillery spotting. Despite its clumsy appearance, it was aerodynamically advanced and had a very low stalling speed of 65mph. It may have been this that contributed to Malcolm's near fatal accident just months before the outbreak of the Second World War. He and his observer were practising for the Empire Air Day at Manchester on 20 May 1939, when he crashed. As he cheerfully wrote in his log book, 'It just fell out'er me hands!' He suffered severe injuries, including a fractured skull that left him with an indentation on his forehead.

He spent four months in the Princess Mary Hospital at Halton and was told that he would never fly again. The upside was that he met, fell in love and married Helen, one of his nurses. His recovery was swift and he was passed fit for flying again on 26 September 1939, returning to 26 Squadron. In the summer of 1940 he had two postings in quick succession, ending with another Lysander-equipped unit, 225 Squadron. He was also promoted to flight lieutenant and 'B' flight commander at Thruxton.

In December 1941, Malcolm was elevated to squadron leader and joined 18 Squadron, which were equipped with Blenheim Mk IV bombers. They flew mainly night intruder sorties against Luftwaffe night-fighter airfields, based mainly in the Low Countries; these were in support of the high-altitude raids on the Ruhr. Malcolm and his crew of Pilot Officer Robb (navigator), and, Flight Sergeant Grant (observer/gunner) were commended for helping the rescue of a downed crew who had taken to a dinghy off the Dutch coast. They managed to locate the dinghy and stayed circling above for four hours until a rescue launch picked them up.

The Blenheim Mk IV was rapidly approaching obsolescence and in need of a replacement. In its wisdom, the Air Ministry had ordered the Blenheim Mk V, briefly named the Bisley, better known to the aircrews as the 'Grisly Bisley'. This lumbering 'improvement' was underpowered and 20 per cent heavier than the already obsolete Blenheim. It was difficult to fly and described by crewmen as 'wallowing'. Instead of being an improvement, it was inferior in performance and reliability to its precursor. Those that flew in them wondered why they did not receive the superior American light bombers, the Boston or Mitchell.

With little say in the matter, 18 Squadron stood down, re-equipped with its new aeroplane and prepared for overseas service along with the other Bisley units; 13, 114 and 614 Squadrons, which together formed 326 (Light Bomber) Wing. The newly promoted Wing Commander Malcolm was now in charge of his squadron. In support of the Anglo–American occupation of Vichy French Algeria, 326 Wing landed on 11 November 1942 at Blida airfield near the Tunisian border.

No.326 Wing found itself relentlessly flying day and night raids, largely without the protection of a fighter screen. This was due mainly to the limited range of the Spitfire escorts and winter weather rendering the forward airstrips unusable. The unsuitability of the Bisley was soon exposed in 18 Squadron's first sortie on 17 November. It was ordered to take advantage of low cloud to mount an attack on the airfield at the port of Bizerte. The attack was to be aborted if the cloud cover was not sufficient but, 20 miles from the target, the sky was clear despite the poor weather. Being so near the target, Malcolm decided to carry out the mission.

Approaching in a line with two abreast, the twelve aircraft managed to drop their bombs and shoot up the dispersed planes. Unfortunately, two of the Bisleys collided with each other as they approached and were lost. Another was hit by anti-aircraft fire and crash-landed. Then, as they departed, a fourth was shot down by an escort of Messerschmitt Bf 109s covering a Junkers transport. To lose four out of twelve aircraft did not auger well.

During the height of the battle for Tebourba, Wing Commander Malcolm won the only VC awarded to a member of the RAF in North Africa. On 4 December, eleven Bisleys of 18 Squadron moved forward to Souk-el-Arba ready for operations over the front. Six had flown off in search of suitable targets and came upon an enemy satellite fighter airfield about 6 miles east of Mateur. Flying low over the airfield, they dropped their bombs and sprayed the parked aircraft before returning safely to Canrobert to refuel and rearm. They then flew back to re-join by the rest of the squadron at Souk-el-Arba.

In the afternoon they received orders from the Army Command to return and bomb their morning target again, despite the fact the Germans would be on full alert. At this point there were no fighters available for protective escort. As most of these were known to be over the general target area involved in dogfights and sweeps, it was felt safe to despatch the vulnerable bombers without such a comforting presence. Fully understanding the danger of returning to an area bristling with alerted enemy fighters, Malcolm ordered the rearming of his squadron and two extra aircraft from 614 Squadron.

At 15.15 hours, eleven Bisleys took off. Almost immediately their number was reduced when one of the aircraft suffered a burst tailwheel and could not leave the ground. Twenty minutes later another Bisley dropped out with engine failure and returned to crash-land near Souk-el-Arba. The remaining nine bombers continued flying at an altitude of only 1,000ft. As they approached the target the crews could see numbers of Spitfires above locked in combat with Messerschmitt Bf 109s and Focke-Wulf Fw 190s.

As Malcolm searched for the target, the Bisleys were set upon by a large mixed group of enemy fighters, an estimate of fifty to sixty was too high, and they were chased to and from the target. Despite his diminished force, Malcolm pressed home his attack and headed back for Allied lines. A Luftwaffe fighter pilot, Oberleutnant Julius Meimberg, reported:

In the afternoon we heard that 12 Bostons (sic) were on the way to the Mateur. We sighted them and chased them: the bombers were flying at a low level. All the Bf.109s attacked at once and one of the Bostons (sic) was on the ground in flames already before I had a chance to open fire. I attacked one and it started to burn at once, losing height and crashing.

I then attacked one on the left; as I was flying in a curve I could see five already shot down. Several Bf.109s at this time were in quite a crowd behind the Yankees (sic). I then shot down a third which went down burning and crashed. I could only fire a little at a fourth I attacked, as all my ammunition was gone. It was only as I returned to base that I saw one of the Spitfires which had kept away during the fight. The battle lasted about five minutes.

There was one participant who recalled the action in his book, *Carrier Observer*. Sub-Lieutenant Gordon Wallace of the Fleet Air Arm had been seconded to 326 Wing in anticipation of attacking enemy shipping. Instead he acted as observer/gunner in one of the Bisleys that was shot down during the raid:

Reaching the Sidi N'sir junction we turned east, following the road through the valley to Chouigui. We must have crossed the front line about 15.45 with no sign of the violent struggle going on in the hills below … I flicked the bomb master switch and buttoned up my face mask … We were some ten miles east of the target and after turning to a westerly heading for Hill 394 we began a shallow dive. I was concentrating on the lead aircraft, ready to release bombs but when we reached the hill we began a wide left hand circle. It seems likely that Malcolm was unable to locate the target. I never saw it, believing it to be some three miles further west. Catching a quick glimpse of a Bf.109 flashing low across us from ahead, I yelled in the intercom and almost immediately Henry called out that we were under attack from a swarm of 109s from all directions. I saw Malcolm's section dropping their bombs and hurriedly released ours although I could still see no target and we were in a shallow dive over the hills.

(Squadron Leader) Eyton-Bill's aircraft started dropping down and passed close below my aiming panel with its starboard engine on fire and streaming a plume of dense black smoke. There was an almost continuous rattle from the rear turret guns overlaid by a terse command from Henry to break to the right.

We banked away from the formation and now so low that I could see a line of cannon shells stitching the ground in front of us. Mesmerised by the sights and sounds, I was slow to react and only then began to struggle into a position to fire my own guns. As we banked left under a full boost in an attempt to re-join the formation, I felt shocks as we received the first hits on the starboard wing. All I could see through my periscope was a blurred view of the ground as we continued violent evasive action.

We were hit again in the starboard engine which went on fire. The intercom went off and Henry was no longer able to give Ted (Pilot Officer Edward Holloway) any help in evading the continuing attacks. I could feel the aircraft shudder as we continued to be hit. That distinctive orange glow of flaming petrol lit up the cockpit as the fire spread along the wing to the starboard inner fuel tank and began to come into the cabin alongside of me. I began struggling back aft.

Although having the utmost difficulty in controlling the aircraft, Ted managed to belly land it on the side of a rocky hill some six miles south of Mateur. The rumbling and tearing of metal was followed by a surge of flame with the heat penetrating my throat but I was free of the narrow passage and rapidly pulled open the top hatch and dropped down onto the ground. Ted followed almost immediately and helped Henry to climb out of his rear hatch, his leg covered in blood where a cannon shell splinter had entered his calf.

Our aircraft was now an inferno of flames from which oily black smoke boiled up. A single Bf.109 roared low overhead and Ted shouted to us to hit the deck but it did not open fire. Ammunition in the aircraft began to explode and we stumbled as fast as we could go up the hill and sat down. There was a large explosion – it was four 40 lb bombs which once again I had forgotten to release – it was only a miracle that they didn't go off when we hit the ground …

A Bren-gun carrier emerged manned by two soldiers (ours fortunately). I noticed that it appeared to be following a line of white tapes to our hillock. It was just as well we had not moved around much as it transpired that the whole area was mined.

It was believed that Malcolm's aircraft was the last to be downed. It was seen about 15 miles from the target within Allied lines, where it crashed and erupted into flames. Three soldiers arrived within minutes and attempted to save the crew but only succeeded in pulling the lifeless body of Pilot Officer Robb from the inferno. All three crew were buried in the Beja War Cemetery. In the space of a few minutes, 18 Squadron had lost almost its entire aircrew.

Malcolm was recommended for the Victoria Cross by Group Captain Laurence Sinclair, the commander of 326 Wing. This was followed by a 'for and against' debate by the Royal Air Force Awards Committee until a compromise was reached. The award was for 'sustained gallantry', taking in other operations led by Malcolm over a prolonged period. This opened the way for similar 'sustained gallantry' VC awards to Squadron Leader Robert Palmer and Wing Commander Leonard Cheshire.

On 27 April 1943, Malcolm was awarded the posthumous Victoria Cross for his courage and determination in leading an almost suicidal mission. A survivor of the raid paid tribute to his popular commander:

> ... we would have gladly followed Malcolm anywhere. He was superb. Malcolm radiated a joy of living and fighting which was irresistible.

His VC was presented by the King to Malcolm's widow, Helen, and is now on display at Lord Ashcroft's Gallery, the Imperial War Museum.

With the ending of the battle of Tebourba, the Germans under the command of Generaloberst Hans-Jürgen von Arnim, succeeded in counter-attacking and driving the First Army back 20 miles in one week. The onset of winter rain and glutinous mud brought mechanised operations to a halt. It was not until February 1943 that the Germans sought to eject the Allies from Tunisia or at least keep them from threatening their supply ports at Bizerte and Tunis.

Chapter 14

The Mareth Line

During the 1930s, the French built a strong defensive barrier called the Mareth Line to repel any incursion by Mussolini from Libya. With the defeat of France and its Vichy absorption into the Axis sphere, the Mareth Line lost its importance and was abandoned. With the defeat of Rommel's Panzerarmee Afrika at El Alamein, they staged a fighting retreat across Libya to recently Axis-occupied Tunisia. Now the Mareth Line took on a vital role in halting the relentless advance of Montgomery's Eighth Army.

Axis engineers refurbished the series of blockhouses that resembled the Maginot Line in Alsace–Lorraine. Extensive minefields were sown, more than 62 miles of barbed wire lain and reinforced concrete bunkers constructed to house anti-tank, heavy machine guns and mortars. It was fronted by a formidable barrier called the Wadi Zigzaou, which ran from the sea inland for 22 miles to the Matmara Hills. This dried riverbed with its steep 70ft-high banks served as an effective anti-tank barrier as well as a daunting area to cross by infantry. West of the Matmara Hills was inhospitable desert, making the coastal route the only easily negotiated way into northern Tunisia.

On 19 March 1943, the Eighth Army began Operation *Pugilist* with a concentrated artillery barrage followed by a frontal assault. It was during this operation that a Victoria Cross was won by the battalion commander of a Yorkshire regiment.

Derek Seagrim VC

Derek Anthony Seagrim was born in Bournemouth, Dorset, on 24 September 1903, the third of five sons born to the Reverend Charles Seagrim, rector of Whissonsett in Norfolk. Derek's mother, Annabel

166

Emma (née Halstead), is unique in being invited twice to Buckingham Palace to receive the two highest awards for gallantry, the Victoria Cross and the George Cross, posthumously awarded to Derek and his younger brother, Hugh.

Derek and Hugh were educated at Norwich School and both chose a career in the Army, the former in the British and the latter in the Indian. In 1923, Derek was commissioned in the Green Howards and during the period between the wars, served in Jamaica and China before a three-year secondment to the King's African Rifles in East Africa.

In 1939 he returned to the 1st Battalion Green Howards in Palestine as intelligence officer and at the outbreak of the Second World War, returned to East Africa as air liaison officer. He was then appointed as a staff officer during the Greek Campaign before being promoted to temporary lieutenant colonel of the 7th Battalion Green Howards in 1942.

The 7/Green Howards had fought at Gazala and been involved in the retreat back to the El Alamein line as part of 69 Brigade of 50th Division. These hardened veterans of desert warfare were initially suspicious of Seagrim, who had spent much of his Army service behind a desk. He quickly won them over with his easy and relaxed manner.

The Eighth Army began its four-month fighting pursuit of the Germans after the Battle of El Alamein, during which Colonel Seagrim proved an inspirational leader. When the battalion reached the Mareth Line, it was given the task of assaulting the 'Bastion', the strongest point on the Axis defences.

At 10.15 pm on 20 March, the battalion moved up to the 'start-line' some 500 yards from the deep anti-tank ditch. At zero hour it followed the tape laid by Royal Engineers until it came to the edge of the ditch. The enemy started laying down a heavy fire aimed at the ditch. Undeterred, Seagrim calmly walked along the top of the tank ditch directing the operations. B Company was the first to cross the ditch, climb the ladders laid against the earthworks and disappear into the maze of trenches leading to the Bastion.

C Company followed, only to be met with a hail of machine gun fire that halted them. Seagrim went forward, calmed the men and scaled one of the ladders with a cry, 'Come on Green Howards, we can't let the New Zealanders down!' He charged ahead of his men and destroyed a machine gun nest with grenades and pistol. Followed by his men, he tackled a second machine gun post, where he killed the crew and captured twenty enemy prisoners. Finally, the Bastion was captured but the rest of the night was spent fending off fierce counter-attacks and the enemy got within 20 yards of his position. However, inspired by Seagrim's example, the Green Howards drove them off. At some point during the fighting he sustained wounds but would not be moved until the Bastion was firmly secured.

Seagrim's calm conduct during the battle led directly to the capture of an important objective. He was recommended for the Victoria Cross but tragically died of his wounds two weeks later on 6 April in the military hospital at Sfaz. He was buried at the Sfaz War Cemetery and his posthumous VC citation appeared in *The London Gazette* on 13 May 1943. His medal was presented to his mother on 23 February 1944 by the King at Buckingham Palace.

Derek's brother Hugh's George Cross citation appeared in *The London Gazette* on 12 September 1946:

> Major Seagrim was the leader of a party which included two other British and one Karen officer working in the Karen Hills of Burma. By the end of 1943 the Japanese had learned of this party who then commenced a campaign of arrests and torture to determine their whereabouts. In February 1944 the other two British officers were ambushed and killed but Major Seagrim and the Karen officer escaped. The Japanese then arrested 270 Karens and tortured and killed many of them but still they continued to support Major Seagrim. To end further suffering to the Karens, Major Seagrim surrendered himself to the Japanese on 15 March 1944. He was taken to Rangoon and together with eight others he was sentenced to death. He pleaded that the others were following his orders and as such they should be spared, but they were determined to die with him and all were executed.

Both brother's exceptional medal groups are on display at the Lord Ashcroft Gallery, Imperial War Museum.

In a reconnaissance, the Long Range Desert Group found that the Mareth Line could be penetrated by attacking from the west through the Matmata Hills at the Tebaga Gap, so bypassing the coastal plain behind the Mareth Line. General Montgomery sent the 2nd New Zealand Division on the 200-mile detour dubbed as the 'left hook'.

It was during this phase in the fighting that a posthumous Victoria Cross was awarded to a young Maori officer.

Moananui-A-Kiwa Ngarimu VC

Moananui-A-Kiwa Ngarimu was born on 7 April 1918 in Kokai Pa on Kokai Hill near Ruatoria in the East Coast region, the son of Hamuera

Meketu Ngarimu and his wife, Maraea. After an education that ended in his fourth form year, he worked as a shepherd on his father's sheep farm.

On 11 February 1940, Ngarimu joined the New Zealand Army and was assigned to the newly raised 28th (Maori) Battalion, which embarked with the Second Echelon of the 2nd New Zealand Expeditionary Force destined for the Middle East. Instead it was diverted to England to help defend the country against an expected German invasion. When the threat lessened, the Second Echelon then proceeded to Egypt, where it joined the 2nd New Zealand Division.

The 28th (Maori) Battalion, more commonly known just as the Maori Battalion, had been formed due to pressure on the New Zealand Government for a full Maori unit to be raised. It fought in Greece and Crete, and the subsequent North African and Italian campaigns; by the end of the war it was the most decorated New Zealand battalion.

The Maori Battalion fought in the retreat from Gazala, at El Alamein and in the advance across Libya until it reached the Mareth Line. Ngarimu had been chosen for intelligence duties and, in April 1942, was promoted to second lieutenant. In March 1943, he resumed his infantry role as platoon commander in C Company.

The troops of the 'left hook' attack left on 19 March and arrived at the Tebaga Gap two days later. The Gap was some 6 miles wide and set in mountainous terrain. General Freyberg waited until he had enough support with the arrival of 8 Armoured Brigade, a force of Free French under General Leclerc, Royal Artillery and later the 1st British Armoured Division. The New Zealanders were to lead the infantry assault with close support from the Desert Air Force.

Initially, all went smoothly and the gap was easily forced with several Italian positions captured. It was not until the attackers came to the Panzer Grenadiers dug in on Point 209 that they met serious opposition.

To attack this strong point, the Maori Battalion had to capture the high ground 1,000 yards to the front of Point 209. There was some confusion due to the unusual topography and poor map reading, which was to have an adverse effect on the assault. On 26 March, C Company was sent to capture this high ground, which was thought to be Point 209 and became known to the Maoris as Hikurangi, after a mountain in their tribal lands. This feature was heavily defended by mortar and machine gun posts supported by fire from Point 209.

Second Lieutenant Ngarimu moved his platoon by section rushes to reach the base of Hikurangi. With No 15 Platoon pinned down by fire coming from Point 209, Ngarimu led his men straight up the steep rocky slope into the face of machinegun fire. During the advance, Ngarimu destroyed two machine gun nests by himself and soon the crest was captured.

Consolidating his position, the men of 13 Platoon joined him. The two platoon commanders realised that they had not captured Point 209, which overlooked them. An attempt was made to advance further but the heavy fire from Point 209 convinced them to dig in. During the night, the Germans made several determined counter-attacks, which were fought off by the defenders, who were either killed or wounded. The Germans then resorted to a heavy mortar barrage, which on the rocky terrain had a devastating effect. The Germans followed this with a bayonet attack, which was thrown back by the Maoris. During this attack, Ngarimu was shot in the shoulder.

The next counter-attack succeeded in penetrating the perimeter. Ngarimu grabbed a sub-machine gun and rushed into the threatened area, spraying the enemy until they fled. Unable to find a grenade, Ngarimu resorted to throwing rocks, which hastened the enemy's departure.

In another attack, the Germans took the crest but only to have it taken away by Ngarimu rallying his men and forcing the Germans back. In the process, Ngarimu was wounded in the leg. Colonel Bennett arrived to access the situation and ordered Ngarimu to report to the medics, but he pleaded to stay. When dawn broke on 27 March, No 14 Platoon was still in procession of the crest but their numbers had been reduced to thirteen men, of which only two were not wounded.

Reinforcements arrived in time for another German onslaught. Colonel Bennett could clearly see Ngarimu lead another charge firing his machine gun from the hip. Silhouetted against the ridgeline, he was seen to be hit. Fresh waves of Germans arrived only to be thrown back to Point 209, where they remained.

Brigadier Kippenberger visited the Maori Battalion and quickly saw that it was not on Point 209 as it had reported. He quickly ordered a heavy artillery barrage on the German positions, which lasted the rest of the morning, after which the Germans surrendered. In the aftermath, the Maori Battalion counted twenty-two killed and seventy-seven wounded.

Second Lieutenant Moananui-A-Kiwa Ngarimu was recommended for the Victoria Cross. His commander, Colonel Bennett wrote:

> Displaying courage and leadership of the highest order, he was himself first on the hill crest, personally annihilating at least two enemy machine gun posts.
>
> He was killed on his feet defiantly facing the enemy with his tommy-gun at his hip. As he fell, he came to rest almost on top of those of the enemy who had fallen, the number of whom testified to his outstanding courage.

Ngarimu's citation appeared in *The London Gazette* dated 4 June 1943 and his Cross was presented to his parents at a *hui* (gathering) at Ruatoria on 6 October 1943 by the Governor-General. In attendance were government leaders, diplomatic representatives and 7,000 Maoris.

The attack through the Tebaga Gap succeeded and, combined with a fresh frontal attack, made the Mareth Line untenable. Many of the Axis forces escaped encirclement and retreated to Wadi Akrit, about 37 miles further north. It now seemed that the enemy was on the point of collapse but there was still stiff resistance to overcome.

Chapter 15

Wadi Akarit

The position at Wadi Akarit, or the Gabès Gap, was one that Rommel had long favoured as an excellent defensive line with no chance of any flanking movement by the Allies. He also had the advantage of a shorter supply line from Sicily, something the First and Eighth Armies did not enjoy. He could resist Montgomery's advance from the south and attack the First Army coming from Algeria. He had seen the inexperienced Americans defeated at Kasserine Pass in February and was confident he could inflict a telling defeat on the First Army.

Before he could put his plans into operation, he handed over command of the Army Group Africa to General von Arnim. He returned to Germany on 6 March 1943 to persuade Hitler about the hopelessness of the situation. He was by this time physically sick and a shadow of his past glory. Instead he was awarded the Knight's Cross with Oak leaves and ordered to take sick leave.

His hopes of prolonging the North African campaign were about to be dealt a blow in what turned out to be a two-day battle. The Gabès Gap was the last readily defensive position before the Eighth Army reached Sfax and formed a continuous front with the First Army.

Wadi Akarit lay on a short east–west line from the Mediterranean Sea and the impassable Chott el Djerid salt lake to the west. Rommel's defence line followed the Wadi Akarit, with its water-filled bottom, for 5 miles. It then widened into a dry *wadi* that also acted as a tank-trap, backed by a long hill called the Djebel er Roumana, which was the last high ground before the eastern end of Chott el Djerb.

In this brief battle three Victoria Crosses were awarded to men who opened the door of this seemingly formidable barrier and hastened the end of the North African conflict.

Lalbahadur Thapa VC

Lalbahadur was a Thapa (surname) of the Magar tribe and was born in February 1906 in the village of Somsa in Western Nepal. He enlisted in the 1st Battalion 2nd King Edward's Own Gurkha Rifles in 1925 and served in 1936–7 on India's North West Frontier. In 1937, he was commissioned as a Gurkha officer with the rank of *jemedar* (lieutenant).

In 1942, the battalion joined the 7th Indian Infantry Brigade of the 4th Indian Division in the Middle East in time to take part in the Second Battle of El Alamein. It then crossed Libya in pursuit of the Axis forces until it reached Tunisia, where the 4th Indian Division was amalgamated with the British 50th Infantry Division.

Having advanced through the Mareth Line, the Eighth Army was confronted with the Wadi Akarit Line, which was reached on 30 March. With no option but to launch a frontal attack, the assault was given the code name Operation *Scipio*. Three divisions were chosen for the initial assault: 51st (Highland) Infantry Division of the right, 50th (Northumbrian) Infantry Division in the centre and the 4th Indian Infantry Division on the left. The plan was for the latter to take the Fatnassa heights on the Rass-ez-Zouai feature in a silent night assault to enable the Eighth Army to wheel round behind the Axis forces. While the Allies prepared themselves, the enemy positions were pounded around the clock for a week by Allied bombers.

Major General Francis Tuker, the commander of the 4th Indian Division, ordered the 1/2nd Gurkha Rifles and the 1/9th Gurkha Rifles, skilled in mountain warfare, to capture the 800ft hill. This was defended by the Italian 80th Infantry Division *La Spezia*, 101st Motorised Division *Trieste*, and the German 164th *Leichte Afrika* Division. The description of the action is graphically illustrated in Subada (Captain) Lalbahadur Thapa's citation that appeared in *The London Gazette* of 15 June 1943:

> On the night of 5/6 April 1943, during a silent attack on the Rass-ez-Zouai feature, Subadar Lalbahadur Thapa was second in command of 'D' Company. The commander of No.16 Platoon was detached with one Section to secure an isolated feature on the left of the Company's objective. Subadar Thapa took command of the remaining two Sections and led them forward towards the main feature on the outer ridge to break through and secure the one and only passage by which the vital commanding feature could be seized to cover the penetration of the Division into the hills. On the capture of these hills the whole success of the Corps plan depended.

First contact with the enemy was made at the foot of a pathway winding up a narrow cleft. This steep climb was thickly studded with a series of enemy posts, the inner of which contained an anti-tank gun and the remainder medium machine-guns. After passing through a narrow cleft, one emerges into a small arena with very steep sides, some 200 feet in height, and in places sheer cliff. Into this arena and down the sides numbers of automatic weapons were trained and mortar fire directed.

The garrison of the outer posts were all killed by Subadar Lalbahadur Thapa and his men by kukri or bayonet in the first rush and the enemy then opened very heavy fire straight down the narrow enclosed pathway and steep arena sides. Subadar Lalbahadur Thapa led his men on and fought his way up a narrow gully straight through the enemy's fire, with little room to manoeuvre, in the face of intense and sustained machine-gun concentrations and the liberal use of grenades by the enemy.

The next machine-gun posts were dealt with, Subadar Thapa personally killing two men with his kukri and two more with his revolver. This Gurkha officer continued to fight his way up the narrow bullet-swept approaches to the crest. He and two Riflemen managed to reach the crest, where Subadar Thapa killed another two men with his kukri, the Riflemen killed two more and the rest fled. Subadar Thapa then secured the whole feature and covered his Company's advance up the defile.

The pathway was found to be the only practicable route up the precipitous ridge, and by securing it the Company was able to deploy and mop up all enemy opposition on their objective. This objective was an essential feature covering the further advance of the Brigade and of the Division, as well as the bridgehead over the anti-tank ditch.

There is no doubt that the capture of this objective was entirely due to this act of unsurpassed bravery by Subadar Lalbahadur Thapa and his small party in forcing their way up the steep gully, and up the cliffs of the arena under withering fire. The outstanding leadership, gallantry and complete disregard for his own safety shown by Subadar Lalbahadur Thapa was an example to the whole Company, and the ruthless determination of this Gurkha officer to reach his objective and kill his enemy had a decisive effect on the success of the whole operation.

The Fatanassa Hill was captured, which enabled the 4/6th Rajputana Rifles to advance as far as the plain 5 miles behind the hills and take

2,000 prisoners. Unfortunately this breakthrough could not be exploited as the British X Corps had been held up by German counter-attacks, but there were breakthroughs elsewhere on the front.

Lalabahudur Thapa stayed with the battalion for the remainder of the Tunisian Campaign and part of the advance up Italy. Initially Thapa had been recommended for the Military Cross by his commanding officer, Lieutenant Colonel Showers but this was changed to the Victoria Cross by General Alexander.

He travelled to London to be invested with his well-deserved Victoria Cross on 26 September 1943 by the King. In 1944, he returned to India and was appointed Subadar Major of 5/2nd Gurkha Rifles.

He retired in 1948 after his regiment moved to Malaya to become part of the British Army in the aftermath of Indian independence. He received the Order of British India (1st Class) and the Star of Nepal (4th Class). He died at the early age of sixty-two in the college town of Paklihawa, Nepal, on 20 October 1968.

Lorne Maclaine Campbell VC

Lorne MacLaine was born on 22 July 1902 at Airds, Argyll, the eldest of three sons of Colonel Ian Maxwell Campbell and Hilda Mary (née Wade). He was boarded at Dulwich College in south London, where his uncle, Vice Admiral Gordon Campbell VC, had attended. In 1921, he passed into Merton College, Oxford, and graduated with a degree in Greats (*Literae Humaniores*). In the same year he was commissioned as a Territorial officer in the Argyll and Sutherland Highlanders. In December 1935, he married Amy Muriel (née Jordan) and together they produced two sons.

As a Territorial battalion, the 8th was one of the first to be sent as part of the BEF (British Expeditionary Force) to Belgium and France in August 1939. During the retreat to the French coast in May–June 1940, Lieutenant Colonel Campbell managed to extricate his battalion from the 51st (Highland) Division's entrapment at Saint-Valery-en-Caux west of Dieppe and was awarded the DSO (Distinguished Service Order). Coincidentally, it was the 51st (Highland) Division that liberated the town on 11 September 1944.

At the Second Battle of El Alamein, Campbell received a Bar to his DSO for the success in capturing several important objectives. In 1942, he took command of the 7th Battalion, Argyll and Sutherland Highlanders and it was with this unit that he was awarded the Victoria Cross.

On 6 April 1943, the 51st (Highland) Infantry Division was one of the three divisions attacking the line at Wadi Akarit. The 7th Battalion was tasked with the job of crossing the anti-tank ditch to the east of the Roumana ridge to form a bridgehead for the 152 Brigade of the 51st to advance.

The 7th Battalion made its advance in darkness and had to cross the *wadi* under heavy machine gun and mortar fire. Having successfully reached the far bank, the men had to negotiate a deep minefield, which the enemy had not been successful in concealing. By now it was daylight and the Germans launched several counter-attacks that were beaten off, although there were several casualties. Colonel Campbell rallied his men and pressed on towards the northern end of Roumana Ridge.

About 13.00 hours, eighteen British bombers made a welcome appearance but unfortunately dropped their bombs on A Company. This, together with the enemy shelling, caused further casualties but Campbell displayed a composure that calmed his men. They were helped by the supporting artillery, who made their presence felt when they broke up a concentration of enemy infantry and tanks.

About 16.30 hours the enemy put in a determined counter-attack and Colonel Campbell displayed a disregard for his safety as he inspired his men by moving to those parts where the attack was the strongest. The 7th Battalion stood firm as darkness fell and it was not until the battle died down that the men realised that Campbell had been painfully wounded in the neck by a shell fragment. Even then he refused to be evacuated but did allow his wound to be dressed.

The 7th Battalion had been under fire for the whole day but managed to hold its position. The gallant manner in which Campbell conducted his battalion was noted and on 8 June 1943 his citation appeared in *The London Gazette*, but it was not until 10 October 1944 that he was able to attend his VC investiture at Buckingham Palace.

Following the Battle of Wadi Akarit, Campbell was temporary command of 153 Infantry Brigade 51st (Highland Infantry Division). A month later he was given command of 13th Infantry Brigade serving in Syria, Egypt, Sicily and Italy until April 1944. Then, for just eight days, he was acting General Officer Commanding, 5th Infantry Division, at the time of the Anzio beachhead. By the end of the war, Campbell was serving in Washington as a brigadier with the British Army Staff.

He died on 25 May 1991 at the age of eighty-two in Edinburgh and was buried at Warriston Cemetery. His medal group is displayed at the Argyll and Sutherland Highlanders Museum, Stirling Castle.

Eric Anderson VC

Eric Anderson was born on 15 September 1915 in Fagley, Bradford, West Yorkshire, the only son of George and Mary Anderson. He was educated at Blakehill Primary School and sang in the choir at Eccleshill Parish Church. After he left school he became a driver for a building contractor in Idle, West Yorkshire, until he was called up in 1942. He joined the 5th Battalion East Yorkshire Regiment and was sent to North Africa. Whether or not he requested a non-fighting role due to his religion is not clear, but he joined the medical section of the regiment as a stretcher bearer.

The 5th Battalion was part of 69th Infantry Brigade, 50th (Northumbrian) Division that was ordered to attack the centre of the Wadi Akarit line. On 6 April 1943, A Company of the 5th led the attack on a strong enemy position and made good progress until it met intense machine gun fire from some Italian positions just 200 to 300 yards away. The advance stalled and the company pulled back, leaving a few wounded men behind on the forward slope of the hill.

Eric Anderson could see that these men were totally exposed to enemy's machine guns and unable to crawl to safety. Ignoring the heavy fire, Anderson descended the slope and heaved the first wounded man into a fireman's lift and carried him to safety. He went back found another wounded man and using the fireman's lift carried him back to the medical officer. He went forward again and brought a third wounded man to safety.

Without hesitating, he went out a fourth time and found a wounded man. As he was giving some medical aid, he was shot and mortally wounded. His four trips had been seen by most of A Company and he was unhesitatingly recommended for the Victoria Cross, which was presented on 28 October 1943 to his widow by the King in a private audience. His medical officer, Captain Robert Clark, wrote to Mrs Anderson about her husband's gallantry:

> It was on one of these occasions that Private Anderson was mortally wounded and was buried on the ridge, which saw so much of his fine work, beneath the sands of the desert we know so well. I have nothing but admiration for the way in which he conducted himself both in and out of battle.
>
> I came to know him well and I found him to be a man of outstanding character, with lofty ideals which he gave his life to uphold. Our small squad (medical section) has lost a friend we could

ill afford to lose, whose dauntless courage and untiring devotion to duty was out of the realms of men to fathom. His memory will always be hallowed in our ranks.

Eric Anderson's body was later reinterred in the Sfax War Cemetery in Tunisia. His VC group is on display at the Prince of Wales Own Regiment of Yorkshire Museum, York.

With the Eighth Army breaching the Wadi Akarit line, the Axis pulled back on 7 April, pursued by the 2nd New Zealand Division and the 1st Armoured Division. In the fight for Wadi Akarit, the Eighth Army had 1,289 casualties. The Axis had suffered considerably, losing men, weapons and vehicles with more than 7,000 prisoners taken.

Chapter 16

Battle of Tunisian Djebels

By 18 April the pressure exerted by Eighth Army from the south and the flanking attack by the Allies from the west had pushed the Axis into a diminishing perimeter line on the north-east coast of Tunis. The supply line from Sicily that had seemed so strong a few weeks ago had been mauled by the Allied air force and the Royal Navy.

Despite a lack of fuel, the Axis still had plenty of ammunition with which to stall the Allied advance. The use of the chain of rugged *djebels* (hills), each one a fortress, delayed the inevitable Allied victory. It was during this endgame that four VCs were awarded.

Chhelu Ram VC

Chhelu Ram was born on either the 4th or 10th May 1905 in Dhenod Village in Haryana State, India. His father was Chaudhary Jairam, a Jat from the Garhwal *gotra* (clan). He enlisted on 10 May 1926 and was assigned to the 4th Battalion 6th Rajputana Rifles, the most senior regiment in the Indian Army.

With the outbreak of war, the regiment was sent to Egypt in October 1939 as part of the 5th Indian Infantry Brigade. It took part in the Battle of Keren in 1941 and was involved in the lengthy campaigns in North Africa before fighting on the Mareth and Wadi Akarit lines.

On 19 April, the battle for Djebel Garci or Garcio started. This was a large mountain and one of the toughest obstacles faced by the 4th Indian Division, now reduced to two weak brigades. After three days of hard fighting, the Djebel was partly taken. The enemy strength and those of the surrounding hills had been greatly underestimated and on 22 April operations were abandoned in favour of attacking the enemy in the Enfidaville area. This was particularly galling for the 4/6 Rajputana Rifles, who had fought so hard to gain vital ground and in the process lost their Havilda Major, Chhelu Ram.

For his outstanding gallantry he was awarded a posthumous Victoria Cross and his citation was published on 27 July 1943 in *The London Gazette*.

> He was with one of the two leading Companies, and during the advance to the Battalion's second objective, the forward troops were held up by an enemy machine-gun position on some high ground. Company Havildar-Major Chhelu Ram armed with a Tommy gun immediately rushed forward through the intense machine-gun and mortar fire and single-handedly silenced the post, killing its three or four occupants and thus enabling the advance to continue.
>
> When the leading Companies were approaching their third objective the enemy brought down intense machine-gun and mortar fire on them which mortally wounded the Company Commander. Chhelu Ram went to the officer's assistance in a completely exposed position and attended to him, during which he himself was seriously wounded.
>
> He then took command of his own Company and elements of the other leading Company and quickly reorganised them. Almost immediately the enemy put in a heavy counter-attack and our troops began to run short of ammunition. During the fierce hand-to-hand fighting which followed, this NCO's bravery and determination were beyond praise. Rushing from point to point, wherever the fighting was heaviest, he rallied the men and drove back the enemy with the cry of 'Jats and Mohammedons, there must be no withdrawal! We will advance! Advance!' He then advanced ahead of the two Companies. Inspired by his fine example, the counter-attack on this vital ground was driven back by bayonets, stones and rocks.
>
> During this fighting Chhelu Ram was again wounded, this time mortally. He refused to be carried back and continued to command and inspire his men until finally losing consciousness. A few minutes later he died from the effects of his wounds.

He was buried in the Sfax War Cemetery and his posthumous Victoria Cross presented to his widow on 5 January 1944 by the Viceroy Lord Wavell at the Red Fort, Delhi.

John Thompson McKellar Anderson VC

John Thompson McKellar Anderson (known as Jock to his friends) was born on 12 January 1918 in Hampstead, London, to John and Mary MacNicol McKellar Anderson. He was educated at Stowe School in the same house as Leonard Cheshire, where they became close friends. He left school for Trinity College Cambridge and gained a Bachelor of Arts degree.

Leaving university, he joined the 8th Battalion (Territorial) Argyll and Sutherland Highlanders and married Moira, who lived in Chessington, and the couple settled in nearby Bagshot. When the war started, the regiment was sent to France as part of the BEF. Anderson was under the command of Colonel Lorne Campbell, later a fellow Tunisian VC, who managed to lead 200 of his men out of an enemy encirclement at St Valèry-en-Caux near Dieppe. They managed to find a boat at Le Havre and sail back to England, where Anderson was given an emergency commission in the 8th Battalion.

Although he was a lieutenant he was soon made up to temporary captain and later acting major. When brought up to strength, the battalion was sent to North Africa and was part of the First Army that advanced from Algeria into Tunisia. Anderson was awarded the DSO and his citation appeared on 18 May 1943 in *The London Gazette;* 'in recognition of gallant and distinguished services in North Africa'. Even in his mid-twenties, Anderson was obviously a born leader and a natural soldier.

The 8th Argylls took part in the fierce fighting as the First Army pushed towards Tunis and attempted a link-up with the Eighth Army approaching from the south. An attempt to carry the heights of Djebel el Ahmera and Djebel Rhar, known collectively as Longstop Hill, in late December 1942 had been unresolved. With the start of mid-winter weather conditions, a further attack was delayed until the spring.

The Second Battle of Longstop Hill began on the night of 21–22 April 1943. The feature, sometimes referred to as a massif, was an 800ft high hill known as Djebel el Ahmera linked to a Djebel Rhar by a 2-mile long hog's back ridge. It commanded the Medjerda Valley and, until it was captured, nothing could move to begin the final assault on Tunis.

The 8th Argylls, together with their fellow 78th Division battalions, 1st Surreys, 5th Buffs and 6th Royal West Kents, dug in as best they could in the open ground at the foot of Djebel el Ahmera. At 20.00 hours the artillery opened up with 400 guns aimed at the summit of Longstop Hill. It is doubtful if the sheltering soldiers managed to sleep during a barrage that lasted until the following morning.

At 11.30 hours, the Argylls and the Surreys led the advance, slowly climbing through the spring corn into the face of heavy machine gun fire. Casualties quickly reduced the four battalions and the commanding officers of the Argylls, the Buffs and the West Kents were all killed. Major Jock Anderson took command of the Argylls, who had lost cohesion and, despite being wounded, led the remaining forty officers and men on to Longstop's summit. They were soon among the defenders and started to neutralise the ring of machine gun positions. Anderson was subsequently recommended for the Victoria Cross and his citation published on 29 June accurately describes the action:

> Over a period of five hours Major Anderson led the attack through intense enemy machine-gun and mortar fire. As leading Company Commander he led the assault on the Battalion's first objective, in daylight, over a long expanse of open sloping hillside and most of the time without the effective cover of smoke. Enemy infantry opposition was most determined and very heavy casualties were sustained, including all other rifle Company Commanders, before even the first objective was reached.
>
> On the first objective and still under continual enemy fire, Major Anderson re-organised the Battalion and rallied men whose Commander, in most cases had been either killed or wounded. The Commanding Officers having been killed, he took command of the Battalion and led the assault on the second objective.
>
> During this assault he received a leg wound, but in spite of this he carried on and finally captured Longstop Hill with a total force of only four officers and forty other ranks. Fire had been so intense during this stage of the attack that the remainder of the Battalion were pinned down and unable to advance until Major Anderson successfully occupied the hill.
>
> During the assault, he personally led attacks on at least three enemy machine-gun positions and in every case was the first man into the enemy pits; he also led a successful attack on the enemy mortar position of four mortars, defended by over thirty of the enemy. Major Anderson's force on the hill captured about 200 prisoners and killed many more during the attack.
>
> It is largely due to this officer's bravery and daring that Longstop Hill was captured, and it was the inspiration of his example which encouraged leaderless men to continue the advance.

By nightfall the Argylls, reinforced by the Surreys, had managed to occupy Djebel el Ahmera. It is significant that the attack was supported by the Churchill tanks of the North Irish Horse, who surprised the German defenders with their ability to climb the hill's 1:3 gradient; something no other tank was able to do.

By 7 May, Tunis was in British hands and the North African campaign was at an end. For Major Jock Anderson there was still much fighting to be done, this time with Montgomery's Eighth Army in Italy. Once the Allies had landed in Italy, the British were tasked with advancing up the Adriatic Coast during the onset of the 1943 winter. As part of attack on the Volturno Line, Operation *Devon* was the code word given for the amphibious landing made by British Commandos at the important port of Termoli. This was carried out on 3 October and later reinforced by the battalions of the 78th Infantry Division, which included Major Anderson's 8th Argylls. The attack was successful and the Germans were taken by surprise.

On the 5th, the Germans counter-attacked in pouring rain and during the heavy fighting, Jock Anderson was killed and laid to rest at the Sango River War Cemetery. His VC/DSO group of medals is now displayed at the Argyll and Sutherland Highlanders Museum, Stirling Castle.

Congreve Alexander Willward Sandys-Clarke VC

Born at Southport, Lancashire, on 8 June 1919, Congreve Alexander Willward Sandys-Clarke was the son of William Edward Clarke and Edith Isobel Congreve (née Sandys). It would seem that his mother was largely responsible for the array of forenames with which he had been foisted. His aunt declared that she would always call him Peter and fortunately the family acquiesced.

His birthplace was not his home, which was Egerton, a suburb of Bolton, but where his parents had gone for a holiday and were taken aback by their son's early arrival. The family business was the cotton mill founded by his grandfather, T.E. Clarke, at Turton near Bolton. Peter was sent to Moorland House Preparatory School on the Wirral before joining Uppingham School at the age of fourteen in September 1933.

When he left in 1938, he worked at the family's cotton mill but his real interest was with the Army and he joined the 5th Battalion (Territorial) Loyal North Lancashire Regiment. By late 1938, he was commissioned under the surname Clarke as the Army thought Sandys was a forename. From being christened with a string of forenames he had ended up as plain Peter Clarke.

When the Second World War began, the 5th Loyals found themselves on home defence duties in Kent. In September 1940, Clarke was involved in a road accident that left him with a serious head injury, a severely damaged left eye and numbness on the left side of his face. Thanks to several operations and months of medical treatment, he retained his sight, although he did later wear a monocle in his left eye. He was still being treated when he learned that his regiment was being sent to Singapore. Anxious to join them, he appeared before two Army medical boards, who informed him that he was unfit for military service. The news was devastating but it also spared him the anguish of incarceration by the Japanese for within days of arriving in Singapore, his battalion comrades were sent to POW camps in Korea.

Unwilling to take no for an answer, Clarke again appeared before the board and managed to convince them that he was fit to serve. In 1941, he married Irene Deakin, the sister of a fellow Loyal officer. On 1 March 1943 he was posted to the 1st Battalion Loyal North Lancashire Regiment and sailed from Liverpool to join the First Army in Algiers. On arrival on 9 March, the Loyals formed part of the 1st Division and by the end of the month had contacted the Germans in the area of Banana Ridge and the Medjez Plain.

On 22 April, the Loyals had to defend and counter-attack German Panzers at Djebel Kesskiss to the west of Tunis and the following day suffered heavy casualties in a hard-fought battle for the heavily fortified Gueriat el Atach ridge. They were on the flank of the 8th Argylls and in an action similar to that of Major Jock Anderson, Clarke turned a critical situation into victory. His posthumous citation dated 29 June 1943 describes his exploit:

> By dawn on that date (23 April 1943), during the attack on the Gueriat el Atach feature, Lieutenant Clarke's Battalion had been fully committed. 'B' Company gained their objective but were counter-attacked and almost wiped out. The sole remaining officer was Lieutenant Clarke who, already wounded in the head, gathered a composite platoon together and volunteered to attack the position again.
>
> As the platoon closed on to the objective, it was met by heavy fire from a machine-gun post. Lieutenant Clarke manoeuvred his

platoon into position to give covering fire and then tackled the post single-handed, killing or capturing the crew and knocking out the gun. Almost at once the platoon came under fire from two more machine-gun posts. Lieutenant Clarke again manoeuvred his platoon into position and went forward alone, killed the crews or compelled them to surrender and put the guns out of action.

The officer then led his platoon on to the objective and ordered it to consolidate. During consolidation, the platoon came under fire from two sniper posts. Without hesitating, Lieutenant Clarke advanced single-handed to clear the opposition but was killed outright within a few feet of the enemy.

This officer's quick grasp of the situation and his brilliant leadership undoubtedly restored the situation whilst his outstanding personal bravery and tenacious devotion to duty were an inspiration to his Company and were beyond praise.

Peter Clarke was buried in the Massicault War Cemetery, south-west of Tunis. His Victoria Cross was presented to his widow on 14 June 1944 by the King at Buckingham Palace.

Charles Anthony Lyell VC

Charles Anthony Lyell was born on 14 June 1913 at Cadogan Gardens, Kensington, London, to the Honorable Charles Henry Lyell and his wife Rosalind (née Watney). The young Charles was destined to assume the title of the 2nd Baron Kinnordy on the death of his grandfather, Lord Leonard Lyell, in 1926.

Charles, or Lord Lyell, was first educated at Durnford School, Langton Matravers, Dorset, before being sent to Eton. From there he studied at Christ College, Oxford, and, in 1936, attained a Bachelor of Science degree. On 4 July 1938, he married Sophie Mary Trafford and the following year they had a son, also named Charles, who became the 3rd Baron Kinnordy.

With the outbreak of the war, Lyell joined the 1st Battalion Scots Guards and in 1940 moved his wife and son from 37 Eaton Square to the ancestral seat at Kinnordy House, Kirriemuir in Angus. The house had not been a home since 1928 and lacked central heating and an effective electrical supply, which was not installed for another ten years.

In March 1943, the 1st Battalion arrived in North Africa as part of the 24th Guards Brigade and took part in the heavy fighting at Medjez Plain and Djebel Bou Aoukaz. Temporary Captain Lyell performed a series of gallant acts culminating in a suicidal attack that resulted in his death.

His company had been put under the command of a battalion of Grenadier Guards and during the five days from 22nd to 27th April he accomplished each engagement with great dash and energy. On the 22nd, he led his men down a slope under heavy mortar fire to repel a German counter-attack, which he repeated the following day when he captured a high point and defended it. He was also able to use the radio to direct the artillery on to the enemy's tanks and infantry positions. His cheerful disposition had a marked effect on his men, which lifted morale.

In the late afternoon of 27th April, his company was taking part in the battalion's attack on Djebel Bou Aoukaz but found itself held up by heavy fire on the left from an 88mm gun and a heavy machine gun in separate pits. As his company was the nearest, Lyell asked for volunteers from the men not pinned down to attack and neutralise this troublesome post. Lance Sergeant Robinson, Lance Corporal Lawrie and two guardsmen answered his call and they began a flanking movement to take the two posts from the side.

As they descended a small slope, Robinson was hit and killed, as was one of the guardsmen. The other, Guardsman Chisholm, was wounded but Corporal Lawrie managed to get to a position to give some covering fire. In the meantime, Lyell was well in advance of his men and lobbed a grenade into the machine gun nest that killed the entire crew.

With Lawrie's covering fire, Lyell dashed into the 88mm's sandbagged pit armed only with a service revolver and his Scottish dirk. Firing and slashing, he managed to kill or wound five of the enemy until he was overwhelmed and clubbed to death. Still under fire from Lawrie, the remaining crew abandoned the gun and retreated back to their lines. The way was now open for the battalion to advance.

Lyell's body was found and buried next to the enemy's strong point until it was reinterred in Massicault Commonwealth War Graves Cemetery. He was awarded a posthumous Victoria Cross for a near-suicidal assault on a well-defended enemy position but his self-sacrifice opened the way to Tunis. For their part in the attack, Lance Corporal Lawrie and Guardsman Chisholm received Military Medals. Lady Lyell received her husband's VC in February 1944 in a private audience with the King at Buckingham Palace.

On 26 April, Djebel Rhar was captured and by the 27th, Longstop Hill was in British hands, so opening the advance down the Medjerda Valley.

The Eighth Army was being held at Enfidaville with the strongly held and difficult terrain to its north. General Alexander and Montgomery agreed that they would hold the Eighth Army's position and transfer the 7th Armoured Division, the 4th Indian Infantry Division and the 201st Guards Motor Brigade to the First Army as they were the most likely to deliver the final defeat on the Axis army.

John Kenneally VC

The most intriguing story of all the recipients of the Victoria Cross must be that of John Kenneally, the last VC of the Africa Campaign. It is a plot that would do justice to a Catherine Cookson novel.

He was born Leslie Jackson on 15 March 1921, the illegitimate son of eighteen year old Gertrude Noel Robertson, the daughter of a Blackpool pharmacist, and he was given Gertrude's new surname of Jackson. In those days, a pregnant unmarried daughter of a respectable middle class family was a social pariah, so Gertrude was sent off to a family friend in Birmingham and told never to darken their door again.

The other half of this liaison was Neville Leslie Blond, the Jewish son of a wool manufacturer, who had served as an officer in the Royal Horse Guards during the First World War and been awarded the Croix de Guerre. He later married the daughter of Simon Marks of Marks & Spencer Ltd.

Jackson's mother made her living as a dance hall hostess and a fairly high-class prostitute. There was enough money for him to receive a private preparatory education at Calthorpe College until it closed due to the public suicide of the headmistress. There followed a toughening process courtesy of the Tindall Street Junior Council School, which gave him the resilience that bore him in good stead in later life.

Gertrude managed to obtain a maintenance order against Neville and she started a ladies' hairdressing business. In 1932, Jackson gained a scholarship place at King Edward's Grammar School in Kings Heath, Birmingham, where he was an average scholar but did exceed in sports and represented the school in athletics and swimming. He also enjoyed the Army cadets and later joined the Boy Scouts.

Life was still unsettled at home and money tight. Gertrude's business failed and she took a series of poorly paid jobs. In 1938, Jackson matriculated and left school, then spending a short and mutually unhappy spell in the office of an engineering firm. There followed a job in a garage, which was to be his introduction to the motor trade.

In early 1939, he and a friend joined the Territorial Army and took the advice of an old soldier:

> Don't join the bloody infantry, all that muck and mud and you march everywhere. Join the Royal Artillery and you will ride.

By the time war was declared, Jackson had received a thorough training and, on 3 September 1939, graduated to being a regular soldier. He became increasing disillusioned with the Royal Artillery, particularly when he was posted to the Honourable Artillery Company in London instead of going with his battery to France. In a rebellious mood, he extended a five days leave to nine and was court-martialled. This rather harsh step was taken to set an example to the large intake of young soldiers and that absence without leave would not be tolerated.

Because of his previous good record, he was sentenced to just one month's detention at Wellington Barracks, near Buckingham Palace, the home of the Brigade of Guards. The regiment occupying the barracks at that time was the Irish Guards and it made an immediate impact on Jackson to the extent that, when his sentence was completed and he returned to the HAC, he put in a transfer request to join the unit. This was turned down flat. Instead, he was posted to a light anti-aircraft battery defending an RAF aerodrome at Waltham Abbey. During the Battle of Britain, he and his crew fired at the German aircraft that came in low to strafe the airfield.

Overlooked for promotion because of his blemished record, Jackson put in for another transfer to the Irish Guards, which was again refused. This time he was assigned to the Motor Transport Section, which entailed him driving around London and making deliveries to the scattered gun sites. This made him a free agent and led to the biggest change of his life.

In one of the cafés he frequented during his rounds he met and befriended a group of Southern Irishmen, who had come over to do manual work such as demolition, clearing bomb debris and blacking out factories. They were each issued with an identity card that expired after six months. Under wartime regulations they were then eligible for call-up.

As the gang were going to Glasgow to work, Kenneally was invited to a farewell drink. Towards the end of the evening a fight broke out between servicemen and civilians; a not uncommon occurrence. It was broken up by the local and military police and Kenneally and his friends narrowly evaded arrest. In the cold light of the following morning, Kenneally saw that the bruises and ripped uniform would lead to further punishment when he returned to HQ. Also, in the fight he had lost his cap showing his name and number.

It did not take a lot of persuasion to accept the offer of joining the Irish gang and go to Glasgow under a fresh identity; John Patrick Kenneally. This was the name of a worker who had returned prematurely to Ireland and didn't need his ID card.

After four weeks working in Glasgow, his Irish friends returned to Ireland and Jackson travelled to Manchester as John Kenneally to enlist in the Irish Guards. In a way he never dreamed possible, he had at last joined the regiment of his choice.

He took easily to his new life and was very proud to become a Guardsman. After intense training, initially at Caterham Barracks, then at tough training areas around the country, the newly renamed Kenneally was appointed to No.1 Company, 1st Battalion Irish Guards and he felt he could go no higher.

In February 1943, the regiment embarked on the P&O troopship *Strathmore* bound for North Africa as part of the 24th Guards Brigade. During his embarkation leave, he married Elizabeth Francis by special licence. He was not alone, for many men in the regiment married their sweethearts during embarkation leave. The *Strathmore* survived a German air attack, including torpedoes, off the coast of Tunis before arriving at Bône on 13 March.

The first action involving the Irish Guards was a disaster. No.2 Company of 103 men was ordered to make a probing attack on a well-defended ridge. After a fifteen-minute heavy exchange of firing, the entire company, save five wounded guardsmen, were wiped out. When the Germans were forced to retreat, they occupied a line of hills that barred the way to the plain beyond and so on to Tunis. The steep and rocky terrain meant that tanks could not operate effectively and that the job of clearing the way was left to the infantry.

The initial advance successfully pushed the Germans off the first ridge line. On the way, the Irish passed remnants of a company of Scots Guards who had been involved in fighting on their left flank. Their company commander, Lord Lyell, had been killed and later received a posthumous Victoria Cross.

The main German position was on the massive rock-strewn feature called the Djebel Bou Azoukaz, simply referred to as 'the Bou', which dominated the approaches to the plain. It was essential to the final thrust on Tunis that this feature should be captured and held. On the afternoon of 27 April, the Irish Guards began their advance. Instead of setting off under cover of darkness, orders had been changed at the last minute and the Guards had to cross a mile of cornfield in the heat of the sun and in full view of the enemy. Greeted with sustained artillery and mortar fire, they suffered heavy casualties. Instructions had been given to mark the spot of the fallen with their rifle and bayonet so they would not be crushed by the following tanks.

Kenneally wrote of this terrifying advance:

> It seemed that all the artillery in the German army was having a go. As we entered the cornfield, the fire seemed to intensify. We plodded on grimly, our eyes fixed on Captain Chesterton and Lieutenant Eugster, who were leading. I was dazed and shocked; the noise was devastating, the hot blasts from explosions scorching my face, patches of corn were burning fiercely, stones and earth thrown up by shell bursts were rattling down on my steel helmet, machine gun bursts were scything down the corn like a reaper and down with the corn went officers and men alike. It was a bloody massacre.

Taking shelter in an olive grove, Kenneally's company commander, Captain Chesterton, gathered together the remnants of No.1 Company and No.4 Company, who had lost all their officers and senior NCOs. Just as they were about to continue their advance to take Points 212 and 214, Lieutenant Eugster was killed. As dusk was falling, Captain Chesterton led the depleted force to their target and forced the Germans to retreat.

The high ridge of the Bou stretched some 1,500 yards between Points 212 and 214. It consisted mainly of solid rock for about 25 yards each side of the slope. It then tapered down into barren scrub. Only 173 men had survived to reach the summit and their situation was about to get worse.

Lance Corporal Kenneally was appointed second-in-command to Sergeant Fanning and, taking half a dozen men, he went in search of supplies that were supposed to have been dumped by carriers at the bottom of the Bou. They did not find any dumps but found instead a carrier that had hit a mine. Taking sacks of bread, tins of bully beef and .303 ammunition, Kenneally also decided to include a couple of land mines. Because of the high slopes, it had not been possible to bring up the heavy mortars and machine guns nor the cumbersome No.19 radio set. This meant that Points 212 and 214 were both isolated and out of touch with Brigade HQ. To add to their problems, the Germans had moved to virtually surround them.

At noon, the Germans began a three-hour long heavy barrage followed by an attack on 214. A runner was sent to 212 to ask for reinforcements, so Kenneally took nine men and ran over to 214. About 100 Germans were sheltering among the rocks 50 yards away, firing semi-automatics and throwing stick grenades. Setting his Bren on single shot, Kenneally accounted for enough of the enemy to make them fall back and retreat through the cornfield. He then returned to his own company at 212.

As the day wore on, so thirst and the heat of the African sun became a real hardship. Towards dusk, the enemy shelling increased and the Germans once again put in an attack on 214. This time, despite fierce resistance, they overran the position and headed along the ridge towards 212. Fortunately, a 3in mortar and just twenty bombs had just arrived and, firing off all rounds, the Germans turned and ran, with the remnants of the men on 212 harrying them.

By the morning of 29 April, there were just fourteen men left of No.1 Company. Kenneally moved to a position on the forward slope from which he could see trucks and armoured vehicles disgorging infantry at the bottom of the lower slope. An increase in the shelling kept his head down. When the firing eased, he again looked but had lost track of the enemy reinforcements. What happened next is told in his words:

> I could not see them but I could hear them. There were two large boulders about ten yards in front of me so I ran to them and took cover. A German voice was very clear now. I left the Bren behind the boulders and crawled through the scrub. The ground fell away into a deep gully and there they were. Most of them were squatting round a German officer. He was holding an 'O' group and was pointing here and there. Some were lying down taking a breather and they were bunched like a herd of cattle. What an opportunity!
>
> I crawled back to the boulders and quickly took off all my equipment – speed was to be of the essence in this operation. I put a new magazine on the Bren and one in each pocket. 'Here goes', I said to myself. I took a deep breath and belted forward, firing from the hip. I achieved complete surprise. I hose-piped them from the top of the gully. They were bowled over like ninepins and were diving in all directions. I had time to flip on another magazine and

gave them that too. Enough was enough, and I fled back to the boulders and safety.

This was not the only action Kenneally saw that day. Later that morning, he was sent down the hill with three men to find if any supplies had been dumped during the night. Halfway down, he met Company Quartermaster Sergeant Mercer, who had left a carrier packed with supplies further down. The three men were sent down to collect everything they could carry while Mercer and Kenneally walked back to 214.

On the way, they walked slap bang into four Germans setting up a machine gun position. Kenneally gave them a quick burst with his Bren, hitting two of them. The other two began to lob stick grenades, making life very uncomfortable. While Kenneally kept them occupied with his Bren, CQSM Mercer worked his way above the Germans and took them out with his Sten gun.

In the afternoon, the Germans began another attack on 212, this time supported by three tanks in single file. With no anti-tank guns and all 3in mortar ammunition expended, there looked no way to repel this attack. Through an inspired piece of ingenuity, the two mines that Kenneally had rescued from the wrecked carrier were improvised into anti-tank shells.

Tying a hand grenade with a seven-second fuse to each mine, they were hurled into the path of the leading tank. The two huge explosions did no damage but it was enough to deter the tanks, who thought that the British had anti-tank guns.

The following morning, 30 April, was relatively quiet and they were able to take stock of the situation. There were now only ten, including Kenneally and Sgt Fanning left of No.1 Company. In all, just eighty men held the Bou.

At about 11 am, the Germans commenced a fierce barrage as the prelude to the last attempt to retake the Bou. Kenneally was in the same OP as the previous day with a Sergeant Salt of the Reconnaissance Corps. As the enemy disappeared into the gully below, Kenneally told Salt of his success there. Then, together, they dashed forward, Kenneally firing his Bren and Salt his Sten. They each emptied a magazine, spraying bullets all around.

The Germans rallied and returned fire, climbing out of the gully. As they ran back, Salt was shot dead and Kenneally hit in the leg. Meanwhile No.1 Company had advanced and put the Germans to flight.

While this was going on, Point 214 was being overrun, so all available men crossed the ridge to help. The wounded Kenneally, with the aid of another Guardsman, hopped over with his Bren. It was touch and go, with much close combat. Suddenly, the enemy were no longer around. They had started to break and were finally chased off the hill by the surviving Irish Guards.

More than 700 Germans lay dead on the slopes of the Bou and just eighty of the 1st Battalion Irish Guards remained. Kenneally was flown to the General Hospital at Algiers, where the bullet was removed from his calf. After a short convalescence, he re-joined his unit by hitching a ride in a Royal Artillery truck. As luck would have it, he was recognised by one of the crew from his days in the RA and had to explain that he had transferred to the Guards.

The battalion was at only company strength and it would be several months before it had four rifle companies. Awards were given for the recent campaign, including an MC for Captain Chesterton. Kenneally was slightly miffed at being overlooked but did receive promotion to lance sergeant and was sent away for a month's course at the Allied School of Infantry in Constantine, Algeria.

It was mid-August and the last week of the course when, as Kenneally was cleaning his weapon after the day's training, the Allied Forces network news came over the radio. The final news item was that His Majesty King George VI had awarded the Victoria Cross to Lance Corporal John Patrick Kenneally!

Large packages of mail kept arriving offering congratulation from all over the world, including one from his father. A special parade was held on 27 August, at which General Alexander presented Kenneally with the VC ribbon. The battalion was formed up on three sides of a square under a very hot sun. After General Alexander had inspected the parade, Kenneally was marched through the battalion by RSM McLoughlin to be presented with his VC ribbon. He then joined the general at the saluting base as the battalion marched past.

A few days later, Kenneally presented himself to General Alexander's HQ to sit for his portrait painted by the war artist, Captain Henry Carr. For the next twelve days he sat for two or three hours until it was completed. Although Kenneally was not particularly fond of it, the painting is now displayed in the Imperial War Museum.

On 7 December 1943, the 1st Battalion landed at Taranto in southern Italy. Seven weeks later, on 22 January 1944, they were part of the Guards Brigade that landed unopposed at Anzio. Days of inaction by the American commander, Major General Lucas, allowed the Germans to rush reinforcements to the area and put the Allies under siege. Constant shelling in miserable wet and cold conditions led to heavy casualties. Kenneally was now in the HQ Company so was spared the initial onslaught but he did have a close encounter with the enemy.

The battalion had been depleted after three to four days of heavy fighting so Kenneally was detailed to drive down to the beachhead to pick up any reinforcements if they had arrived. He found one guardsman and drove back up into the hills. As he rounded a bend there was a loud crack and the newcomer slumped across him, shot through the neck and stone dead.

Kenneally swerved and halted by a ditch. As he laid the dead soldier on the ground, there was another sharp crack as a bullet ploughed into the dead man's leg. Kenneally dived for cover under the truck and tried to work out from where the firing came. It appeared that the only likely place was a clump of pine trees about 250 yards above and to the left. Cautiously, Kenneally managed to remove his Bren gun from the cab and sprinted 10 yards to a deep irrigation gully.

From there, he crawled about 100 yards and then worked his way through the undergrowth until he was about 70 yards from the trees. Watching for what seemed like an age for a sign of the sniper, he was rewarded by the slightest of gleams from the end of a telescopic sight. He eased the butt of the Bren into his shoulder and blasted the whole magazine off into the trees. In the silence that followed, he waited and then heard a loud rustling in the trees as the dead sniper fell through the foliage and landed in a crumpled heap in the long grass.

Kenneally debated whether or not to return to HQ or go to the beachhead. He decided on the latter but soon ran into an enemy barrage concentrated on a transport convoy. He pulled up behind an RAMC ambulance, dashed across the road to a cemetery and took shelter in a substantial-looking lodge. Here he found an RAMC corporal, who asked him to help him move the four people he had in his ambulance. Besides two wounded British soldiers, there was a heavily pregnant girl accompanied by an elderly woman. During a lull in the shelling, they managed to move them all into the lodge.

The shelling began again and some exploded in the cemetery, which terrified the women. It had the effect of sending the girl into labour and the corporal delivered a baby boy. After the horrors of the day, it was something that lifted everyone's spirits.

To celebrate the birth, Kenneally suggested a drink and made his way back to his truck, which was lying on its side. Fortunately, the bottle of cognac inside was intact but, as he made his way back though the cemetery, another shell landed among the graves and a chunk of marble embedded itself in his wrist.

This was the end of the Italian campaign for Kenneally, for he was evacuated to the main hospital in Naples. He recovered to join his battalion as they sailed for England and Chelsea Barracks. On 24 May 1944, he went to Buckingham Palace to receive his Victoria Cross.

He received praise from Winston Churchill in a rather ironic way. While denouncing Éamon de Valera, the Irish premier, for 'frolicking' with the Germans, Churchill said that all bitterness for the Irish race 'dies in my heart' when he thought of Irish heroes like Kenneally!

After the surrender, Kenneally considered leaving the Army and joining the police force, especially as he was now a family man with a son. Instead, much to his wife's dismay, he signed on for a further five years and trained as a parachutist in the 1st Guards Parachute Regiment. In April 1947, he was sent to Palestine during that turbulent period that led up to the establishment of the state of Israel.

The British troops were tasked with keeping the Arabs and Jews apart and became targets for both sides in the process. Kenneally, being half Jewish, was delighted to be given the job of organising the defence of a kibbutz in northern Galilee. Thanks to his efforts and tactical skills, the kibbutz survived a major Arab night attack. As a result, he was tempted by an offer to remain in Israel and join their army, but with thoughts of his family, which had increased with the birth of another son, he declined.

At the conclusion of this particularly unpleasant tour of duty, he was persuaded by his wife to purchase his discharge (£120) and marched out of Pirbright Camp on 22 July 1948 as a civilian.

Moving back to the Midlands, he used his pre-war interest in motors to open a car showroom in Solihull. When his first marriage to Elsie, with whom he had Michael and Shane, ended in 1955, he married Elizabeth Evelyn, a divorcée with a child of her own, Timothy. They settled in the village of Lapworth near Birmingham and together produced four more children, Martin, Joanne, John and James. Tragically, Martin was killed in a road accident in 1981.

During a period when the car business failed, he was employed by Unigate as a security advisor. When he retired from this post, he again started selling cars until he finally retired. He lived out his life in Lower Rochford, Tenbury Wells, Worcestershire.

He kept in touch with his old regiment and, in 1987, he went with a party of Irish Guards veterans to visit the Tunisian battlefields and to see the scene of his VC exploit. On St Patrick's Day 1998, Kenneally was given the singular honour of distributing shamrocks to the regiment at a ceremony at Wellington Barracks.

He died on 27 September 2000 and was buried in St Michael's and All Angels churchyard, Rochford. His medals are displayed at the Guards Museum, Wellington Barracks, London.

The First Army's final assault was at 3.30 am on 6 May led by IX Corps; a fierce artillery barrage, followed by a surge forward by the British armour and infantry. Thousands of demoralised Germans and Italians were captured, all surprised at the speed of the advance from all sides. The following day, 7 May, British tanks rumbled through the streets of Tunis. After 2,000 miles and six months of hard fighting from El Alamein to Tunis, the Allies succeeded in reaching their goal. In the process, they inflicted a massive defeat on the Axis. Just under 250,000 prisoners were taken and the loss of equipment was staggering. Despite the superiority of the German soldier and his weaponry, the enemy lost some 33,530 killed and 30,000 wounded. For the Allies, the Desert and Tunisian campaigns cost an estimated 20,500 dead.

Compared with other theatres such as Russia and Burma, the North African campaign was a cleanly fought war with no atrocities committed by either side. Rommel described the Desert Campaign as a 'War without Hate'. This would change once the Allies crossed to nearby Sicily and Italy.

Bibliography

Alamein by C.E. Lucas Phillips, 1962.

Ball of Fire: The 5th Indian Division in the Second World War by Anthony Brett-James, 1951.

Calculated Risk – The Memoirs of a Great Commanding General in WW2 by General Mark Clark, 1950.

Carrier Observer by Gordon Wallace, 1993.

Churchill's School for Saboteurs – Station 17 by Bernard O'Connor, 2013.

The Desert War – The North African Campaign 1940–43 by Alan Moorhead, 1944.

Eastern Epic Vol.1. by Compton Mackenzie, 1951.

El Alamein – The Battle that Turned the Tide by Bryn Hammond, 2012.

Evolution of the Victoria Cross by M.J. Crook, 1975.

Focus on Courage by Christopher Wallis and Ron Cassidy, 2006.

Forgotten Voices of the Desert Victory by Julian Thompson, 2011.

Forgotten Voices of the Victoria Cross by Roderick Bailey, 2010.

For Valour – The History of South Africa's Victoria Cross Heroes by Ian S. Uys, 1973.

Gamp VC – The Wartime Story of Maverick Submarine Commander Anthony Miers by Brian Izzard, 2009.

Geoffrey Keyes VC by Elizabeth Keyes, 1956.

Heart of a Dragon by W. Alister Williams, 2008.

Hero of the Upholder – The Story of Lt. Commander M.D. Wanklyn VC, DSO by Jim Allaway, 1991.

A History of the Mediterranean Air War 1940–45. Vol.3 by Christopher Shores & Giovanni Massimello, 2012.

The Honour and the Shame by J.P. Kenneally, 1991.

In the Face of the Enemy by Glyn Harper and Colin Richardson, 2006.

Journal of the Victoria Cross Society 2002–2016. Edited by Brian Best.

Mark of the Lion; the Story of Capt. Charles Upham VC & Bar by K. Sandford, 1962.

My Silent War by Kim Philby, 1967.

Nine Valiant Academicals by Alasdair Macintyre, 2007.

Official History of New Zealand in the Second World War 1939–45 by Kippenberger and Fairbrother, 1949.

One Man's Desert by Rex Woods, 1986.

The Bravest Canadian: Fritz Peters, The Making Of A VC in Two World Wars by Sam McBride, 2012.

The Rifle Brigade in the Second World War by Major R.H.W.S Hastings, 1950.

The Sapper VCs by Gerald Napier, 1998.

The Seven VCs of Stonyhurst College by H.L. Kirby and R.R. Walsh, 1987.

Submariners VC by William Jameson, 1962.

Valour and Gallantry by Chris Kempton, 2001.

VC Battles of WW2 by C.E. Lucas Phillips, 1973.

Victoria Cross – Australia's Finest and the Battles They Fought by Anthony Staunton, 2005.

The Victoria Cross at Sea by John Winton, 1978.

The Victoria Cross Wars by Brian Best, 2016.

With Utmost Spirit: Allied Naval Operation in the Mediterranean by Barbara Brooks Tomblin, 2004.

Index